Stepping to the Dance

THE TRAINING OF A FAMILY THERAPIST

Carolyn Cressy Wells
Marquette University

Brooks/Cole Publishing Company
ITP® An International Thompson Publishing Company

*Pacific Grove • Albany • Belmont • Bonn • Boston • Cincinnati • Detroit • Johannesburg • London
Madrid • Melbourne • Mexico City • New York • Paris • Singapore • Tokyo • Toronto • Washington*

Sponsoring Editor: *Lisa Gebo*
Marketing Team: *Jean Thompson, Margaret Parks*
Marketing Representative: *Jean Thompson*
Editorial Assistant: *Shelley T. Bouhaja, Terry Thomas*
Production Editor: *Kirk Bomont*
Manuscript Editor: *Barbara Kimmel*
Design Editor: *E. Kelly Shoemaker*
Interior Design: *Hallie Warshaw*
Cover Design: *Terry Wright*
Cover Illustration: *Katherine Arion, FIS*
Typesetting: *Publications Development Company of Texas*
Cover Printing: *Phoenix Color Corporation*
Printing and Binding: *Maple-Vail Book Mfg. Group Inc.*

For more information, contact:

BROOKS/COLE PUBLISHING COMPANY
511 Forest Lodge Road
Pacific Grove, CA 93950
USA

International Thomson Editores
Seneca 53
Col. Polanco
11560 México, D. F., México

International Thomson Publishing Europe
Berkshire House 168-173
High Holborn
London WC1V 7AA
England

International Thomson Publishing GmbH
Königswinterer Strasse 418
53227 Bonn
Germany

Thomas Nelson Australia
102 Dodds Street
South Melbourne, 3205
Victoria, Australia

International Thomson Publishing Asia
221 Henderson Road
#05-10 Henderson Building
Singapore 0315

Nelson Canada
1120 Birchmount Road
Scarborough, Ontario
Canada M1K 5G4

International Thomson Publishing Japan
Hirakawacho Kyowa Building, 3F
2-2-1 Hirakawacho
Chiyoda-ku, Tokyo 102
Japan

Printed in the United States of America

10 9 8 7 6 5 4 3 2 1

Library of Congress Cataloging-in-Publication Data

Wells, Carolyn Cressy.
Stepping to the dance : the training of a family therapist / Carolyn Cressy Wells.
p. cm.
Includes bibliographical references.
ISBN 0-534-34950-1
1. Family social work—United States. 2. Family counseling—United States. 3. Family therapists—Training of—United States. 4. Social work education—United States. I. Title.
HV699.W45 1998
362.82'86'071073—dc21

97-22912
CIP

❀

To my husband, Dennis Loeffler,
who postponed many joint adventures
so that I could complete this book.

❀

About the Author

Carolyn Cressy Wells is a professor of social work at Marquette University in Milwaukee, Wisconsin, where she developed the social work program during the mid-1970s. She has served as program director from 1978 until the present, except for the years 1990–1993. She is an active member of the Council on Social Work Education, the National Association of Social Workers, the Association of Baccalaureate Program Directors, and the Academy of Certified Social Workers, and she has participated in a number of CSWE site visits, most recently as chair. She is author of two other social work texts, *Social Work Day-to-Day: The Experience of Generalist Social Work Practice,* and *Social Work Ethics Day-to-Day: Guidelines for Professional Practice,* both published by Longman. She is co-author with Mary Ann Suppes of *The Social Work Experience: An Introduction to the Profession and Its Relationship to Social Welfare Policy,* published by McGraw-Hill. She maintained a part-time private practice in marriage and family therapy for many years. She received an undergraduate degree in anthropology from the University of California at Berkeley, and an MSW and Ph.D. in child development and family relationships from the University of Wisconsin at Madison. She is a Wisconsin-certified marriage and family therapist and independent clinical social worker.

❀

Contents

❀

Preface

Many fascinating books have been written about family therapy. What is unique about this one is that it allows the reader to identify with both therapist and client. *Stepping to the Dance* introduces JoEllen Madsen, a professional social worker at a time of crisis in her life. Despite her deepest desires and two stints of marriage counseling, JoEllen's marriage fails.

The book then introduces the Peterson family. Molly and Henry Peterson's marriage is also in trouble, and their son and daughter are having serious problems at school. On recommendation of the school psychologist and social worker, the Petersons engage in family therapy for the sake of the children. The therapist they encounter is none other than JoEllen Madsen, now a student in a postgraduate training program accredited by the American Association for Marriage and Family Therapy.

Issues in JoEllen's own life that closely parallel many of the Petersons' constantly interweave throughout the narrative. How the trainee rises to this challenge, with the assistance of her instructors and fellow trainees who are organized into consultation teams, is explored in depth in this book. Ideally, of course, a therapist should be free of personal problems before ever taking on a client. However, in the real world, such an ideal is rarely, if ever, achieved. Probably most therapists are dealing with the same issues encountered by everybody else, at least some of the time. This book illustrates how ongoing consultation, supervision, and personal work by the therapist are necessary to achieve creditable results in this profession.

Chapters on systems theory, family therapy in systems perspective, and reframing as a therapeutic tool have been included in the text, although these chapters are not intended to be definitive. They are included only to help explain many of the skills and techniques JoEllen Madsen learns and practices in her training program. The reader is encouraged to read the many fine theory-oriented books that are available on these topics.

Stepping to the Dance is written primarily for students of family counseling and therapy who are enrolled in professional programs such as social work, psychology, educational psychology, counseling, pastoral counseling, the ministry, nursing, and related fields. Because it is written in an informal, novel-like style, the book will serve well as an introduction to the field for undergraduate students. However, because the narrative presents and integrates a wealth of information, the book is also appropriate for graduate and postgraduate students. It will serve best as a supplement to more standard texts, providing in-depth case materials pertaining to both therapist and client that help humanize theory. The appendix section outlines questions for each chapter that are intended to stimulate further thinking and discussion.

All the characters described in this book are "composites," not "real" people. Characterizations have been extracted and synthesized over time from a variety of therapists-in-training, supervisors, hardworking clients, and many others. Names, ages, and other characteristics have been changed to protect the privacy of any individuals involved.

Stepping to the Dance is intentionally written to engage the reader both emotionally and intellectually. In this way, the potential family therapist can learn vicariously what family therapy is about, to better make an informed decision as to whether to pursue it as a career. However, the book is also aimed toward the lay reader who has a special interest in family counseling and therapy. It will make provocative reading for many.

Acknowledgments

My first words of thanks go to a man I have never met, Dr. Augustus Napier. I thrilled to the narrative of Napier's *The Family Crucible* many years ago, marveling that a text intended to teach family therapy concepts could be such a pleasure to read. While Napier's exquisite prose sets a standard I can never meet, my desire to write a book telling a story for the purpose of teaching began with his example. To augment rather than duplicate his efforts, *Stepping to the Dance* focuses on a different dimension of the family therapy process, the training of the therapist.

I next want to thank the many instructors who have assisted me in the ongoing process of learning family therapy. These include Ms. Ramona Hietpas, Dr. Beth Sirles, Dr. Thomas Edward Smith, Ms. Cecelia Vallejo, Ms. Myra Mae Van Uxem, and Ms. Karol Wendt. In addition, I owe a large debt to the many other teachers and the many clients who have worked with me over time.

Although the desire to write a book about family therapy was my own, the timely encouragement of Ms. Eileen Murphy, at the time, a representative with Wadsworth/Brooks-Cole publishing company, was instrumental in making the project a reality. Eileen was enthusiastic from the first about the idea of a novel-like book on family therapy. She introduced me to her colleague, Peggy Adams, who endorsed the project. Claire Verduin took over as my editor at Brooks/Cole Publishing Company, and her patience allowed me to continue my writing despite initial slow progress. When Claire Verduin retired, Lisa Gebo became my editor. Lisa's enthusiasm, encouragement, and support have lent a special joy to the final development of this book. I wish to give special thanks to Lisa, and her editorial assistants Terry Thomas and Shelley Bouhaja, for their ongoing assistance and encouragement. In addition, I want to give special thanks to the production team for this book, Kirk Bomont and E. Kelly Shoemaker, and to my excellent, eloquent copyeditor, Barbara Kimmel.

Finally, I want to thank the reviewers of the manuscript, who offered many useful suggestions that have significantly strengthened the final version: Jeremiah Donigian, SUNY–Brockport; Martin Fiebert, California State University–Long Beach; Bruce Friedman, Wayne State University; Beth Sirles, University of Alaska, Anchorage.

Carolyn Cressy Wells

CHAPTER 1

The Therapist Trainee

JoEllen Madsen didn't want to eat supper alone that evening. She wasn't sure why; she had eaten alone many times since her husband, Chip, began attending technical school some 40 miles away. She didn't usually mind eating by herself. In fact, she had encouraged Chip to return to school. Her husband was an energetic young man in his early thirties, and JoEllen believed he needed a new challenge. Their unfinished home, laboriously built by the two of them over the past several years under Chip's inspiration and direction, was now livable, and Chip seemed to have become bored with the project. The factory jobs he took occasionally to earn money didn't provide him with much satisfaction. JoEllen felt anxious. Her worst fear, rarely acknowledged even to herself, was that Chip was becoming bored with her as well.

JoEllen was a few years older than her husband. She hadn't married until her late twenties. Finding a mate at last whom she loved and who seemed to love her had given her great happiness, so she was willing to make sacrifices for the marriage. Her sacrifices included bearing the pressures of providing most of the family income while Chip fulfilled his dream of building a house. JoEllen was fortunate to have developed a viable and fairly long-term career that provided enough income to support the two of them and, to a moderate degree, their home construction project (the house was still far from finished).

Prior to her marriage, JoEllen had earned a master's degree in social work. Now she possessed several years' experience in a variety of settings. She had worked with adults with disabilities, children in foster care, elderly people in nursing homes, and, most recently, children in the public school system. A conscientious young woman, she devoted long hours to her work, usually with good results. Sometimes, however, especially in the past few weeks, JoEllen couldn't help but feel that being a professional social worker was a personal burden. Social workers should have their own lives in order, she firmly believed. They should *provide* help, not require it themselves. But lately her life was beginning to fall apart, and a part of her knew it.

For example, Chip was very late coming home the night before; he had been late the night before that as well. He had called to explain both times, his voice sounding dutiful over the telephone. A classmate, whom he described as a "very nice young woman," was helping him learn some difficult new material, and there was going to be a quiz soon. It seemed to make perfect sense. But tonight Chip was late again, and he hadn't called. It was well past supper time. Where was he? What if he were in an accident on the highway? What if he were hurt? What if he needed help? What if he were having an affair? The last "what if" seemed the worst possibility of all, so JoEllen tried not to let herself think about it.

At about 8:00 in the evening, the telephone rang at last. JoEllen was startled out of a deep reverie. She still hadn't eaten any supper. Thankfully, it was Chip.

"Hello," her husband said cheerfully across the wires. "Don't worry, Honey. I'll be late again but I'm fine. I'm studying over at Faye's again this evening. She's made me a very nice supper, and we're going to work on our math homework now. I'll be back a little after midnight. Don't bother to wait up for me. Bye."

It was the last "what if" scenario—or maybe it was—spoken with nonchalance by the man JoEllen had cherished for over a decade. She tried hard not to feel anything, especially not to panic. She knew it was important for Chip to make new friends, and he really was having difficulty with some of his classes. He had been out of the school setting for many years, and his study skills did require assistance. Certainly, they needed assistance.

But . . . just who was this young woman named Faye, and why had Chip chosen to study with her alone for the past few evenings? JoEllen sat still in her chair, her mind swirling in crazy loops. Her cheeks acquired fiery spots, and her long dark hair became unruly as she tugged at it with anxious fingers.

Perhaps nothing was "going on" after all. Perhaps Chip *was* just studying with Faye. But what if he wasn't? It shouldn't matter, it shouldn't matter at all, JoEllen reminded herself fiercely. She had agreed to an "open marriage." Ten years ago, in her fervent desire to marry Chip, no price had seemed too high, and that was what it had taken to get the man she loved to the altar. Besides, she reminded herself again and again, there should be much more to marriage than sex. Of course there *was* much more to marriage than sex. A fling here and there shouldn't be any problem, then, as she and Chip had discussed so rationally time and time again.

Except for jealousy. JoEllen frequently experienced jealousy in her relationship with her husband. Chip was a very attractive man, tall, sandy-haired, and well built. He loved to flirt, and he developed a real expertise in that vocation. Many women flirted back enthusiastically. On the one hand, JoEllen sometimes enjoyed basking in a kind of reflected glory; she was the woman who went with that handsome young man other women so obviously admired! On the other hand, sometimes a gnawing pain attacked her, miserable and unwelcome. It was jealousy, in full form.

JoEllen viewed jealousy as *her* problem, a major personal weakness, a matter of insecurity. Chip did also. Gallantly, he offered to solve JoEllen's problem by not telling her when he was having affairs. That became their compromise, a way to make their marriage work, and the two were rather proud of it. At the time they reached this agreement, the concept of "open marriage" was almost fashionable, so JoEllen didn't question its merit. Moreover, her own parents were monogamous, and their marriage didn't seem very happy to her. She thought there must be a better way. She would try something more daring, yet protected from her jealousy and insecurity by Chip's discretion. It all made perfect sense.

Several years passed. JoEllen managed to believe that her marriage was monogamous despite the open marriage agreement. She experienced flashes of jealousy over Chip's frequent and open flirtation, but she didn't let herself think her husband was doing more than flirting. She closed her eyes. She worked hard to control her feelings. She even boasted to friends that she had the "best of all possible worlds," an open marriage agreement with a husband who never felt the desire to stray. This fiction was shattered in the seventh year, on information from a woman friend who thought it was time for JoEllen to "get real."

When she first learned of that affair, JoEllen experienced violent feelings of jealousy and anger—red hot, powerful, uncontrollable at first. The anger protected her from pain for the better part of a day. Then came confusion: after all, JoEllen had no right to be angry. She had agreed to precisely what had happened. Chip was behaving exactly according to their marital bargain. It wasn't his fault that a friend had revealed to JoEllen what he was doing.

Next came depression and pain. Absolutely unreasonable, the woman whispered to herself as she struggled alone through the first days of her unwanted discovery. After all, Chip was keeping his part of their agreement. He was doing his best to maintain secrecy, as he had promised. JoEllen counseled herself to carry out her part of the bargain, too. She worked hard to control her jealousy, anger, depression, pain. These feelings were, after all, weaknesses.

So JoEllen said nothing to Chip about her new knowledge at first. But the effort was great, and she began to act distracted and strained at home. Chip knew his wife well enough to recognize there was a change, and he finally asked her what was wrong. JoEllen broke down and told him, through floods of tears and apologies for her poor control and her emotional weakness. Chip was genuinely sorry—not that he was having affairs, but that he had been careless enough for JoEllen to find out. Chip said he had never intended to hurt his wife. He offered to give up his current liaison, since JoEllen now knew about it. After all, the man said sincerely, JoEllen was the one with whom he wanted to spend the rest of his life.

JoEllen felt a rush of relief and forgiveness, and she eagerly accepted Chip's offer to end the affair. She almost dissolved in tears of gratitude, in fact. She admitted she was being unreasonable, that she ought to be stronger. But this affair was particularly hard to live with, she explained, since she knew the woman involved. How should she act when she met her again, perhaps at the home of a mutual friend? Chip admitted things could be awkward. He ended his liaison.

The agreement on open marriage in general, however, was so important to Chip that he would not consider changing it, even when JoEllen timidly brought up the subject a few weeks later. After all, he pointed out—and JoEllen couldn't help but agree—no one person can meet another's every need. Chip promised to do a better job on the secrecy issue, and he kept his word. If there were other affairs after that, JoEllen didn't know about them. Several months passed.

Now, as she lay on her bed alone, JoEllen found herself unable to sleep. She wondered about every evening her husband had been late in the last few months. What had he been doing? Every noise of the night disturbed her now, except for the one she wanted to hear: the sound of tires on the long gravel drive. The hours passed slowly, the clock ticked interminably, and eventually JoEllen drifted into a sort of "twilight zone." She may have slept a little. Morning came.

JoEllen arose feeling exhausted and scared. Chip still wasn't home. She took her morning shower and dressed. Her mind felt almost blank, simply waiting, not wanting to take in the meaning of what was happening. She couldn't concentrate. She wandered over to the refrigerator, remembering that she hadn't eaten anything since lunch the day before, but she still wasn't hungry. She drank some orange juice. She looked out the window again. No one was coming down the drive and it was time for her to leave for work. JoEllen numbly put on her coat and began fumbling for her briefcase. Suddenly, she heard the sound of a familiar motor and tires moving along loose gravel. She froze. She waited. Chip walked in, smiling.

"Sorry I'm late!" The handsome young man boomed cheerfully. "I thought it would be safer to drive home in the daylight after I had some rest. I didn't call you when I finally decided to stay at school because I figured you'd already be asleep."

That was reasonable; it made perfect sense. JoEllen usually fell asleep well before midnight, and of course she wanted her husband safe. But what she said next wasn't reasonable. In a voice that shocked her she rasped out five short words, totally unexpected even to herself.

"Did you sleep with her?"

Chip flinched, and looked away. He was a very honest man, however. His face gained color as he turned back to look at the woman to whom he was married. "Yes," he said simply.

The air between the two persons in the room suddenly seemed devoid of oxygen. Without warning, JoEllen turned and bolted out the door. She ran to her car, leaped inside, backed it out of the garage, and drove right past Chip, who had followed her several yards behind. JoEllen gunned the vehicle down the driveway as fast as she could maneuver the ruts. She wasn't thinking; she was hardly aware of what she was doing.

She didn't get to work that morning. She stopped along the way and wandered along the trails of a wooded area, unable to think clearly, tears streaming down her face. She didn't want anyone to see her like that. Finally, she headed off to school in the early afternoon, informing the secretary that she'd been sick when she arrived. No one questioned her, but they noticed her disheveled dark brown hair, the streaks on her gaunt face, the muddy shoes. Kindly, they left her alone.

JoEllen didn't earn her salary that day. She barely had the presence of mind to cancel her appointments. When she emerged from the school building in the late afternoon, her eyes still streaked and hair twisted into knots, Chip's car was waiting in the parking lot, with Chip sitting inside. JoEllen saw him and ran right past in unthinking alarm. She leaped into her own vehicle, drove off much too fast, and smashed against the gate post at the right side of the entrance of the parking lot. She dented her fender badly. The sound of the crunch was alarming and embarrassing, to say nothing of the appearance of the car.

Shocked, JoEllen kept on driving. At the first opportunity, she steered away from home and headed down a different road, not knowing where she was going. Finally, she saw a telephone booth next to a small gas station. She stopped to call her best friend, Sonia. She needed help deciding what to do. She looked at her car then and burst into tears just as Sonia picked up the telephone.

The young social worker stayed at Sonia's home for one very long week. Chip, worried about losing his wife entirely, agreed to marriage counseling. At that point, JoEllen went back home. She asked around and was given the name of a counselor who had helped some people she knew. The counsellor was willing to work with the couple even though Chip admitted to maintaining an active outside affair. Chip refused to give up this affair, as he was too powerfully attracted to his new friend, Faye.

The counselor helped husband and wife clarify that they wanted different things from their marriage. JoEllen finally admitted she wanted a monogamous relationship, even though she was ashamed of her inability to handle jealousy. Chip wanted his freedom *and* his marriage. The two were unable to agree on a compromise. After a few weeks, Chip left home to stay with a male friend for a while. He didn't go to live with Faye because he wasn't ready to leave his marriage entirely. He cared for JoEllen very much, even if he wasn't sure he loved her any more; and, in addition, a divorce would be financially difficult for him. He thought that if he left his wife by herself for a while, her loneliness would drive her to do anything to get him back—even agree to the affair. After all, that was the understanding with which the two had married.

JoEllen, however, felt somewhere deep inside that her marriage was over. She knew from what Chip had said in counseling that she came second to Faye in his heart. That was too much for her to bear. Just as she was beginning to cope somewhat satisfactorily alone, however, Chip came back. He said he wanted to try to work things out. He agreed to go to a different counselor, since the first one hadn't been able to help them reach a workable compromise. Emotionally exhausted but still wanting to save her marriage, JoEllen asked a professional colleague for the name of a different counselor. She was referred to a therapist who specialized in marital work.

The new therapist insisted that Chip give up his outside relationship, not just the sexual part but the whole thing, at least for the duration of counseling. The counselor said he didn't believe a marriage could be put back together with an intimate third party actively involved. Chip initially agreed to do so, although with great reluctance. For a while, JoEllen felt strong hope for a new life together with the man she loved. However, after a few weeks, Chip told a sobbing JoEllen, in the new therapist's office, that since he had to make a choice, he was choosing Faye. That was truly the end of the marriage.

JoEllen survived, as most women do in similar circumstances. There were days when she considered driving into bridge abutments as she drove to work along the highway, and days when she considered jumping out of the highest windows of tall buildings. Oddly, there were also days of mild euphoria. However, JoEllen had enough presence of mind to realize she was barely surviving emotionally, even on the euphoric days. Worst was her crisis of faith in herself, in her own ability to choose a mate. How could she ever trust herself again if she had made such a bad mistake in marriage? And how could she continue to do her work if her mind was constantly embroiled in "why's" and "what if's"?

JoEllen wanted to heal her emotional wounds, not only for personal but for professional reasons. She knew that her confusion and pain could only negatively affect her work. Many of the children who were referred to her at school, for example, suffered as a result of marital problems between their parents. JoEllen wanted to be able to assist these children and their families in a professional, objective manner without misusing leftover baggage from her own failure in marriage.

Shortly after her second separation from Chip but before the divorce was final, JoEllen decided to engage in individual counseling. She made a wise decision. The experience was positive for her, providing both badly needed emotional support and a clearer understanding of her role in the failed marriage. By the time she left counseling, the young woman felt much more hopeful again. She continued to heal through the merciful passage of time and through good friendships with both women and men.

Two years after the divorce was final (nearly four years after the initial separation), JoEllen learned that a social service agency near her home was developing a training program in family counseling. The program was designed to meet accreditation standards of the American Association for Marriage and Family Therapy (AAMFT), a national organization dedicated to the advancement of education and training in family therapy.

The developing program achieved accreditation shortly thereafter, and the newly established Family Therapy Training Institute sent out a call for applications. People with graduate degrees in social work, psychology, educational psychology, nursing, psychiatry, pastoral counseling, the ministry, and related fields were preferred. In some cases, students still currently enrolled in master's programs in these fields were eligible. JoEllen felt ready for a new challenge. Because of her master's degree in social work and her many years of professional experience, she felt she was qualified. She applied, noting on her application that she was divorced and had been in therapy herself, both individual and marital.

At her personal interview with the Institute director, Dr. Kurt Knaak, JoEllen learned to her relief that her status as a divorcee would not hinder her application. And although it is an unfortunate truth that for some positions, participation in personal therapy would be viewed negatively, JoEllen's experience was considered a "plus" by the institute. Dr. Knaak said he regarded JoEllen's experience in counseling as a valuable part of her training. Moreover, he noted, considerable time for healing had elapsed since the divorce. Shortly after the interview, JoEllen was accepted into the program.

JoEllen smiled somewhat ruefully as she read her acceptance letter from the Family Therapy Training Institute. She knew that her interest in family therapy stemmed from personal as well as professional considerations. Despite the insights she had gained through her own individual therapy, she still experienced periods of deep questioning regarding the demise of her marriage. She still missed Chip a great deal, and many aspects of their life together. She knew she would be working on unfinished personal business as she studied to learn a skill that hopefully would help others avoid her fate. JoEllen recognized that she embodied the classic "wounded healer," the therapist or other health care provider who chooses her profession to assist in resolving a personal problem or need.

Some clients might be reluctant to work with JoEllen if they learned she had failed in marriage. Others might respect her because of her determination to understand and mend her own life. She would have to deal with this reality step by step, client by client.

As a student therapist at the Family Therapy Training Institute, among the many clients JoEllen worked with was the Peterson family.

CHAPTER 2

❀

The Peterson Family

Long before JoEllen Madsen enrolled in the Family Therapy Training Institute, Molly, Henry, George, Charlotte, and Josh Peterson were experiencing difficulties as a family. That wasn't *their* perception of the situation, of course. Like most people, each Peterson felt that some other Peterson was the problem. For example, Molly and Henry, the parents, were often angry at Josh, their younger son. They did not perceive that their relationship as husband and wife affected their role as parents, which in turn affected their children's behavior. Nor did they perceive that their children's behavior often affected their own relationship as spouses.

On the very day that JoEllen filled out her application for family therapy training, Molly Peterson came home from work feeling particularly fatigued. She dropped her large stack of books on the low counter that ran along the side of her kitchen and then sighed heavily. She wished she didn't have to make dinner. She walked wearily over to the sink. As Molly was about to wash her hands, she saw a scribbled note lying next to the telephone: "Meyers called from school. Something about Josh. Wants you to call back. Henry."

Molly immediately felt a flash of anxiety and embarrassment. She knew Martin Meyers well. He was a psychologist who worked at the same school where she was employed as a physical education teacher. Martin's call probably meant trouble of some kind. Molly wondered if Josh, her youngest child, had gotten into more trouble at the junior high. The boy was supposed to go to detention that afternoon.

Molly was proud of her position at the school, and she worked long hours to make sure she did a good job there. Useful work and a secure income were both important to her, because the family in which she grew up had fallen into poverty during her childhood. Molly earned the college degree that permitted her professional employment only through determination and hard work. She valued education and she valued her career.

Physical education was not only Molly's job but her avocation, and she applied its principles in all aspects of her life. At 45, this mother of three had the slim, lithe body of an 18-year-old and the glowing, firm skin of a woman in her twenties. These facts were not lost on her students. Given Molly's petite, youthful appearance, cheerful disposition, and determined optimism, she was a favorite teacher at the school. Only the woman's unusually taut, upright, almost military posture gave any clue to the effort required to maintain her consistently positive demeanor.

Martin Meyers had called Molly about problems with the children before—alas, not Molly's students, but her own children. Only Charlotte, the middle child, 16 years old and in the 11th grade, helped Molly maintain her cheerful carriage at the school. Charlotte was a model student, well behaved, and a high achiever academically. By contrast, Molly's two sons were both sources of embarrassment.

George, Molly's oldest son, now 21, had flunked out of high school during his senior year. Molly's inner distress had been enormous at the time, but outwardly she had maintained a posture of control and an expression of calm serenity. George had eventually earned his diploma, but it had taken him a year longer than it should have.

During George's extra year in high school, Martin Meyers had sought permission from Molly to counsel with the boy. The mother had given it gratefully. She knew George wasn't achieving according to his ability and she hoped Mr. Meyers could fix the problem. She had been unable to get the boy to study even after he flunked most of his classes. Moreover, the boy's father, Henry, had recently kicked George out of the house in frustration, yelling that his son needed to learn responsibility. Nearby friends had taken George in, to Molly's great relief. The mother had surreptitiously slipped the boy money to pay for his room and board, and she had expressed enormous gratitude to the friends.

After meeting with George at school, Mr. Meyers had called Molly again to recommend family counseling. The psychologist had made his suggestion gently and carefully, but still Molly had felt a rush of alarm.

"Family counseling!" She had exclaimed in an incredulous tone. "It's George who is having a problem, Mr. Meyers! The rest of this family is fine!"

With an anxious heart she had awaited Mr. Meyers' reply. Like many parents, Molly felt that her children's behavior reflected her own worth. Although she told Martin Meyers she believed George was the only one having a problem, inside she feared she personally might be responsible for his school failure in some way. She dreaded hearing an authority at the school suggest that this might be so.

Martin Meyers had then told Molly frankly—perhaps more frankly than he might have told another parent, since she was his long-time colleague—that he felt George's problems might reflect difficulties at home. From what George was telling him in counseling, he related as tactfully as he could, the boy seemed to be experiencing a great deal of difficulty with his father. And, the man continued after a slight hesitation, it seemed as if there might be some marital distress affecting George as well.

As Mr. Meyers spoke his quiet, careful words to Molly, the woman had felt frightened. What if staff at the school should learn certain information about her private life with her husband? Molly had refused family counseling, firmly, and had never mentioned the call to Henry. When Mr. Meyers called to ask her to consider it once more, she answered him in a closed, cautious tone. She said she did not think family counseling was necessary. After all, only George had a problem, she said logically.

Molly did, however, hesitantly give permission for George to continue regular individual counseling sessions with Mr. Meyers. It frightened her to think what the two might talk about, but the special attention seemed crucial to keeping the boy in school. During the extra year it took George to graduate, she suspected that Mr. Meyers was the only reason the boy stayed on to earn his diploma. And to everyone's immense relief, George did earn his diploma. He then went out and found a job, all on his own.

But now Mr. Meyers was calling to talk about Josh—again, in fact. He had called about the child several times before. Josh, 13, was now in seventh grade. He didn't do his homework any better than his brother George had before him. Josh's teachers described him as a stubborn child and a dawdler. They said he usually sat in class staring out of the window and avoiding his classroom assignments. Josh was often late to school as well, which frustrated Molly because she drove him to school every morning and so knew he arrived on time.

Josh apparently deliberately hung out in the hallways until after the late bell rang. The teachers responded by giving the boy detention as punishment. Josh routinely skipped detention, only to be assigned extra days for that transgression as well. Today the boy was at school late for detention, or at least he was supposed to be. He owed several days more as well. The teachers had told Molly privately that Josh had told them he didn't care. They could give him as much detention as they liked, the boy had said to them defiantly, but they couldn't make him go.

Molly sighed again as she read her husband's note. Josh's behavior at school was highly awkward for a mother and teacher. She sometimes wished she could get a job elsewhere, where she would be less visible. However, in fact Molly had never tried to get a different job. She felt at some level that it was important that she work as close to the children as possible, to protect them as best she could. To protect them from what at school she wasn't quite sure. But she couldn't protect them very well at home; that she knew all too well. So being with them at school seemed like another chance, although at times the effort was exhausting.

Molly wanted to do what she could for her children at school because she felt they were shortchanged at home. Her husband wouldn't speak to them for days at a time, for example. Henry hadn't wanted children, though neither Molly nor Henry had known that in the beginning. Young and deeply in love, they had agreed to marry and to have children almost in the same breath. Henry was a handsome, delightful, spirited, and truly charming suitor. Molly had expected him to be a cheerful, doting husband and father, and perhaps Henry Peterson had expected himself to be that kind of partner as well.

Molly sighed a tired sigh as she let her mind wander back in time. She remembered the evening when she first met her husband. She could see herself dressed in her best at the Friday night dancing class for singles at the neighborhood church. Like all the other women in the class, she attended hoping that she would meet someone special. And she did. Henry was the dancing instructor, and a dashing one at that. He was a favorite with the ladies.

Molly was a young college graduate at the time. She had recently moved to the city because she had been offered a teaching job there.

The job had started out well enough, but Molly had felt very lonely. She knew almost no one. When she met Henry, she was more than ready for personal attention. And Henry was a bachelor of considerable charm—surrounded by a number of pretty, obviously adoring women that first evening.

Molly had been almost unable to believe her good fortune when Henry asked her to dance with him. A few days later Henry called to ask if she would assist him in teaching a class. Molly felt literally swept off her feet, especially as she knew that many other women in the class envied her. Even as she danced as Henry's partner, lovely ladies flirted to catch his eye and smile. Henry engaged them all in gallant repartee. Charmed and challenged, Molly fell in love.

When Henry proposed to Molly a few months later, the young woman was ecstatic. She could still remember the thrill of that enchanted time. She accepted the proposal with joy, and later, when she asked Henry if he wanted children (she had asked before, but she wanted to make sure), Henry had replied earnestly, in his most endearing way, "Don't you think any man would be proud to have children of his own?" He meant it, to the best of his own knowledge at the time.

Molly, who had grown up in the household of an alcoholic, unpredictable father, had felt very close to heaven as her wedding approached. Not only would she have a husband she could believe in, she exulted to herself, but their children would have the attentions of a steady, willing, dedicated father.

Henry and Molly had a festive marriage, attended mostly by Henry's friends—a number of whom were female and pining for him. On Molly's side, only her mother came, as her parents were divorced and not on speaking terms. Her only brother had died at a young age, while a junior in high school, of uncertain causes. Molly's father had refused to attend the wedding. Henry's parents were also divorced, but they both lived in the same city and they attended politely enough, maintaining a careful distance from one another. Henry's father brought his second wife to the ceremony, and his mother brought a sister, to whom she stayed as physically close as possible.

The young couple began their life together in great happiness, and about a year after the wedding, they agreed it was time to conceive their first child. George was born about a year later. By the time of the birth, however, the joy of parenthood was already fading, and both parents knew it.

When Molly was only five or six months pregnant, Henry began to realize what a nuisance a child could be. It wasn't that the man consciously wanted or meant to dislike George, or any of his children for that matter. But even before George arrived in the world, he began to interfere with his father's plans. Molly simply became less available to Henry as a recreational companion and as a sexual partner as her body grew larger in size.

Henry was a man who enjoyed not only the dancing he taught but many strenuous outdoor sports activities as well. He had chosen Molly as his wife, from among many other admiring and available hopefuls, in large part because she was one of the few women who could keep up with him. Molly was a small person, but her delicate frame hid unexpected strength. She was wiry, lithe, and virtually untiring, despite the strenuous pace Henry could set. The two enjoyed regular dancing, jogging, swimming, biking, and hiking together in the early days of their courtship and marriage.

But when Molly entered the final months of her pregnancy, things changed. She became unable to keep up her end of the unspoken bargain. Try as she might, she couldn't serve as Henry's fancy dancing partner or as his equal on a racing bicycle. Henry became extremely annoyed. Gradually he made his feelings known. After George was born, Henry told Molly he didn't want any more children. Molly, crushed at the time, attempted to comply. She loved her husband and didn't want to lose him. Nevertheless, two "little miracles" (as their mother called them later) came along in due time: Charlotte and Josh.

Henry Peterson treated George as a nuisance from the moment the child was born. Henry probably didn't intend to be cruel, but sometimes he wouldn't speak to the boy for days at a time. When George was very young, a good deal of the gap in communication occurred because his father wasn't home very much. Henry traveled in his work as a sales representative, and when he was home he liked to go out dancing in the evening. Sometimes he still taught classes, but after Molly was burdened with care of her children she could rarely accompany him.

Intentional silence on the part of the father toward the son occurred with increasing frequency as George grew older. The boy would want to spend time doing projects with his father. To be sure, Henry tried to oblige as he knew a father should. He did care about his son in his own way. But the man was a perfectionist, so the boy's accomplishments rarely pleased him. Then, as George grew older, he began to transgress in the ways so common for young boys. He would borrow his father's tools and leave them lying in the wrong place; or, he might mow the lawn, but not quite the way Henry wanted. Most of the feedback from father to son came in the form of criticism or critical silence.

Molly knew how difficult Henry Peterson's verbal criticism—and even more his critical silence—had been for George. The boy probably would have found his father's anger easier to bear if the criticism had been balanced with praise and positive attention, but it was not. When George was little, he asked his mother why Daddy was so mad at him all the time. Molly could only tell George to try not to mind, that it wasn't the boy's fault.

Molly had talked to her husband many times about how he treated George, hoping that Henry would give his son the positive attention all children crave. But instead, Henry seemed to double his complaints about George as the child grew older. For example, George's appetite became enormous as he entered his later teen years. George's impressive capacity for food was his mother's secret pride and joy, because he had been rather small for his age in junior high school, short and slight of stature. Suddenly, however, George grew noticeably and filled out in fine proportion. By the time he was a senior in high school, he had grown to be a solidly built six-footer, standing taller than his father. Molly was delighted and proud. By contrast, Henry seemed to become even more angry at his son. He continually criticized the boy for eating too much and implied that he was bankrupting the family. Ludicrous little things seemed to distress Henry, such as the amount of salad dressing, butter, or jelly his son consumed.

When Henry carried on about money in front of the children, especially with respect to the food they ate, Molly would sometimes become very angry. She remembered then that she was the one who brought home the steady income in the family. She did almost all of the shopping herself, and certainly all of the cooking. She paid for all of the food she purchased. So at a certain point in Henry's complaints, Molly would break down and have words with her husband. Arguments at the supper table became routine, usually with Molly and the children taking one side and Henry taking the other. Evening meals could be miserable events indeed, although the family continued to eat their dinners together as a proper middle-class family should.

When George flunked out of high school, Henry kicked his son out of the house. Molly was extremely upset at the time; she believed the boy ought to be allowed to live at home as long as he was willing to work toward his diploma. She was unable to change her husband's mind, however. It made her sad that Henry didn't even praise the boy when he finally earned his diploma. Henry said only something like, "It's about time," and then made it clear to his son that he was now fully on his own.

Lately, Henry seemed to be just as angry at Josh as he had been with George before him. As with George, Henry had been unhappy with Josh even before he was born. While Molly had secretly been overjoyed with each pregnancy, Henry had been angry. At first he had even accused Molly of deceiving him by getting pregnant on purpose. He stopped talking to his wife for days at a time when she told him she was pregnant. Eventually he began to communicate again, but instructed Molly that he expected her to keep the children out of his hair.

Despite continuing anger at his two sons, Henry had learned to appreciate his daughter, Charlotte. Charlotte was the pride of both her parents, in fact. She was now 16, and an exemplary youngster. Not only did she earn excellent grades at school, but she was popular and had many friends. She was a favorite among her teachers as well. And from her earliest years she seemed to have a sixth sense about how to deal with her father. She had a natural beauty and grace that were a source of great pride for her father. Charlotte's talents for music and dance resembled Henry's own. When the girl reached her teens, Henry sometimes took her with him in the evenings to help demonstrate dance steps in the classes he still taught part time.

But then there was Josh. Sullen at home now, doing poorly at school, he had few if any friends. Teachers considered him a problem, and he knew it. Molly was afraid the boy had a serious problem of some kind. As she examined the note from the school psychologist on her kitchen counter, she felt as if she were reliving her troubled years with George. She dreaded returning Mr. Meyers' call.

The tired mother tried to pull herself out of her ruminations. She had to decide what to do. Should she call back now? It was already 4:45 in the afternoon. Molly doubted that Mr. Meyers would still be at school. Yet if she waited until morning, she might have to speak with the man face to face. That might feel worse, and besides, if she waited she would have to worry all evening.

Where was Henry, Molly wondered. Why hadn't he taken a more detailed message? Usually he was home at this hour; often he was home all day. A sales representative for heavy industrial machinery, Henry worked on commission, and his hours were his own. In the past few years, he had worked less and less. He said he didn't enjoy making sales calls any more.

After a few moments, Molly realized she wouldn't have time to find Henry and still hope to reach Mr. Meyers at school that afternoon. Henry probably wouldn't have asked about the reason for the call anyway. He wouldn't have wanted to know. Molly knew that the school secretary went home at 5:00 and that the telephone system shut down when she left. The mother took a deep breath, squared her shoulders, picked up the phone and dialed.

The secretary put her call right through to Mr. Meyers. He seemed to be waiting for her.

"Good afternoon, Molly," the psychologist said in his resonant voice. "Or is it good evening by now?"

"Probably somewhere in between, Martin," Molly responded in a cheerful voice. "My husband left me a note that you called." Then, hesitantly, "Is anything wrong?"

"Wrong . . . well . . . nothing serious," the man replied. "But did you know that Josh skipped detention again this afternoon?"

"No, I'm afraid I didn't," the mother replied. "He isn't home, at least not yet."

"Well, I wanted you to know, so that you could talk with him about it when he does get home. Frankly, I'm worried about Josh, Molly."

"Worried?" the woman replied lightly in tone, while feeling a numbness settle into her stomach like a wave.

"Well, we both know he isn't working up to his capacity," Mr. Meyers replied.

"That's certainly true," Molly said. "Remember last year you suggested testing him for learning disabilities. I was almost hoping the tests would show he had a learning disability of some kind. That would explain why he does so poorly."

"Yes, and the tests showed he was normal in every way with respect to basic learning ability, and well above average in intelligence. Yet he's still practically failing in every subject."

Molly was grateful for the privacy of the telephone. She felt tears rising and she didn't want Mr. Meyers to know. After a short silence to regain her composure, Molly asked quietly, "Martin, is there anything else you can recommend?"

"Well, in fact there is something, Molly. One of the teachers has referred Josh to the special education program for evaluation for behavioral disturbances. I'm asking your permission to give it a go."

"Behavioral disturbances! Do you mean an E.D. evaluation—an evaluation for emotionally disturbed kids?! That's for the kids who bounce off the walls! Martin, Josh may not be working up to his capacity but he's not emotionally disturbed!"

"Well, I don't think so myself, Molly, but you know, his teachers say they think he is depressed. Some kids qualify for services as having behavioral or emotional disturbances not because they act out in school but because they withdraw. Josh may well fall into the latter category."

"But what could you do for him at school if that were the case? I would never want Josh in a classroom with disruptive kids—you know how the classroom for kids with behavioral disturbances can get, Martin!"

There was a short silence. Martin then replied gently, "I think we need to do something, Molly, though to tell you the truth I'm not sure what myself."

There was another short silence, and then the psychologist continued. "How about this. Let me make an appointment for you with the school social worker, Roger Steinberg. You know he does a careful job doing family assessments. Roger can talk with you at home about Josh—after all, you're the expert on your own child, and you're a professional yourself. Perhaps together you and Roger can come up with some ideas that might help us understand what is going on with the boy, and what might help him at school."

Molly was silent for a few moments. Then she sighed. "I guess it couldn't hurt to talk with Roger," she said finally.

"Good. Tell you what," Mr. Meyers responded. "I'll ask Roger to call you tomorrow to make an appointment so that the two of you, or the three of you if your husband wants to be involved, can decide on a mutually convenient time to meet together."

"All right, Martin."

"I'll need to send you a permission slip to sign, to authorize the evaluation. The E.D. teacher will want to observe Josh in the classroom. Is that OK with you?"

"I guess so, Martin. We may as well evaluate again."

"Thank you, Molly. I'll keep in touch. Good-bye."

Molly hung up the telephone, washed her hands wearily, and began making dinner for her family.

CHAPTER 3

An Interview with the Parents

Roger Steinberg arrived at the Peterson home at 4:00 in the afternoon, nearly three weeks after Molly's discussion with Martin Meyers. This was the earliest time the social worker and the parents were able to organize their various schedules to meet. Molly worked full time and was unable to leave school early without careful preplanning. Henry had decided he wanted to be present, but suddenly he seemed to have more sales calls to make than usual. Roger's schedule was filled in the late afternoons for several days in advance because so many families were in the same situation, with two parents working outside the home with little if any flexibility to meet during regular daytime hours.

Because both parents in many families are employed outside the home, Roger had worked a number of very long evenings, and even some Saturdays, when he first took on his job as a school social worker. He rapidly had become exhausted and frustrated. Time to meet his own family responsibilities had suffered. Finally, after a number of complaints from his wife and two young children, Roger knew he couldn't continue to work such long hours. He consulted with a more experienced colleague and concluded that he must protect his evenings and weekends. That would mean he wouldn't get his work done as quickly as he would like, but he would probably maintain better health, both physical and emotional. And he would have a happier family life. It was a trade-off, but a necessary one.

Roger knocked briskly on the Petersons' door. When Molly answered he greeted her warmly. She was a respected and longtime colleague. Molly introduced Roger to her husband, Henry. Then husband and wife escorted Roger into their comfortable living room and offered him a cup of coffee. Roger gratefully accepted. By late afternoon, after a long day at work, he was tired. He looked with appreciation out the huge plate glass windows surrounding him and enjoyed the country scenes they framed: woods to both sides, and a long sloping back yard with winter-bare trees not quite concealing a little pond at the bottom of the hill, sparkling in the setting sun. Unlike Roger's compact city house, built almost on top of its neighbors, this home had a wonderfully open, spacious feel, both inside and out.

"What a wonderful home you have here," he began naturally, "and what great views you have." Roger always began his conversations with parents with "small talk" that he hoped would engage them, help put them at ease, and begin to build rapport. Roger knew parents often anticipated his visits with alarm, and he wished to create as relaxed an atmosphere as possible. He himself had felt anxious about meeting Mr. Peterson, as Molly had never said a word about her husband at school. So Roger was surprised and pleased to meet the pleasant-looking man with thinning hair slightly flecked with gray, whose deep blue eyes were alert and welcoming. The social worker began to feel more at ease.

Roger's opening comments and cordial queries had the effect he'd hoped. The Petersons talked readily about their early adventures finding a house lot and building their home. They were justly proud of their accomplishments. Talking about the home began to build a comfortable connection among the three adults.

Social pleasantries continued for several minutes. Then Roger sensed the time had come to settle down to business.

"Molly," he began, "you and I have talked on the telephone about my purpose in visiting you today. But," he continued turning toward Henry, "we haven't had the chance to talk about it yet, Mr. Peterson. I'm wondering if you have any questions to start us off." Roger made a special point to include the father immediately, because he knew from experience that fathers often feel excluded from the planning for their children.

"Call me Henry," the man replied cordially. Roger noticed with pleasure the man's straightforward, open manner. Henry's voice registered sincerity and concern. His face had a pleasant, angular shape with high cheekbones and a prominent but well-formed nose. A strong chin gave him a look of confidence and steady resolve. Henry's body movements demonstrated a natural grace; he seemed almost to dance with his hands and shoulders as he leaned forward in an inquiring manner.

"Thank you, Henry," the social worker replied. "Please call me Roger. I'm here today specifically to talk about your son, Josh. Do you have any questions at this point?"

"Not really," Henry replied. "I hear from Molly, of course, that Josh has been misbehaving at school. Skipping detention among other things, I'm told. I'm not surprised, because that kid is nothing but trouble at home either."

"That's part of the reason I've come to talk with you," Roger continued. "It would help the school staff to know how Josh behaves when he's here at home—whether it's the same as at school or different."

Molly spoke up quickly. "Josh seems to have been a little better both here and at school for the last couple of weeks. I think he was scared when he heard you were coming. We really got after him for missing detention at school—he's made up most of his time by now, and he hasn't gotten assigned any more as far as I know. I've asked his teachers to keep me posted."

"You're right," Roger replied. "In fact, I checked at the front office myself just before I came here this afternoon. Josh has been going to detention regularly and has just about finished the time he owes."

"So do you think it's necessary to continue with a special education evaluation?" asked Molly.

Roger heard the anxiety in the mother's voice. He paused for a few moments before answering. When he spoke, his words were thoughtful.

"I think so, Molly. The E.D. teacher, Mrs. Henderson, observed Josh in class last week and told me that while your son is not disruptive, he doesn't do his classroom assignments and he stares out of the window most of the time. According to Mrs. Henderson's notes, Josh was 'on task' only six minutes during the hour she observed him."

"Only six minutes!"

"Yes, and that's enough information for the school to believe further evaluation might be helpful. My role here this afternoon is to learn how your son behaves at home. I'd also be interested in how he behaves when he isn't at home or at school. Have the neighbors ever complained, for instance? Does Josh obey your rules to come home when you expect? These kinds of things will help us determine whether the boy is simply having a problem with the school, or whether it's a more general problem."

"What do you mean, whether Josh is just having a problem with the school or a more general problem? What's the difference?" asked Henry Peterson. His voice took on a sharp edge and the features of his intelligent face seemed to draw together.

"Well," Roger replied, "some children who have difficulties at school are model children at home and in the neighborhood or community. Then we staff at school have to consider that we may be doing something wrong ourselves. We would tend to see the problem as ours rather than the child's. But if the child has problems outside of the school as well, then we would be more likely to determine that he or she has at least some degree of behavioral disturbance."

Roger chose his words carefully. He knew that many parents became upset when told that their child might be "disturbed." In his experience, the words "behavioral disturbance" seemed easier for parents to hear then "emotional disturbance," so he began there.

Henry spoke forcefully. "The kid is sure a nuisance at home," he said, "there's no doubt about that."

"In what ways is he a nuisance, Henry?"

"Well," the father replied, "Josh is 13, but you'd think he was 3 the way he does his chores. I tell him to mow the lawn, and he leaves strips of grass between the rows all up and down the yard. You just wouldn't believe how bad a job he does. Josh thinks he's finished when the lawn is still a mess. He doesn't clean the lawn mower afterward the way I tell him to, either. He leaves big lumps of grass and dirt on the blade. I tell you—I get so mad at that kid I'd like to belt him sometimes."

"I see," said Roger quietly. "And do you ever find it necessary to belt him, Henry?" His tone was careful, and he used Henry's own words. Roger didn't want to seem accusing, but he did want to find out if (and if so, how much) this father used corporal punishment. He experienced a sudden sinking sense in the pit of his stomach that perhaps this child was physically abused. Perhaps that was the reason Josh did so little and stared off into space at school.

"Of course not," Henry replied forcefully, thoroughly surprising his new audience. "I have never hit Josh. I don't believe in physical punishment for any of my children. My father would have become a priest if he hadn't met my mother—he was that kind of man, he was in the seminary for a while—and he didn't believe in hitting a soul. He never laid a hand on me when I was a boy. My mother did, but my father got after her about it. I sure do get angry at Josh—Molly says I criticize him too much—but I never hit any of my children."

The conviction in Henry's voice caused Roger to feel a good deal of respect for the man. He sighed, relieved.

"Well, I must say I'm glad to hear that, Henry," Roger replied. "You'd be amazed how many parents hit their kids, and in my experience it usually only makes matters worse. The kids get resentful and start to strike back. Let me congratulate you for your views on this matter."

Roger paused, and began again. "Now I'm going to ask you a different question. You said you were not pleased about how well Josh mows the lawn. How regular is Josh in doing his chores? Do you have to nag him a lot, for example?"

"Well, Josh mows the lawn when I tell him to. He just doesn't do it right."

"How do you try to correct him?"

"I tell him what I don't like—I yell at him sometimes—but it's no use. That kid never listens. When I get mad enough, I stay away from him."

"Josh tries so hard," Molly spoke up then. "I've seen him push that mower around the lawn until he's mowed the whole thing twice before you see it, Henry, hoping to please you. I don't think he could please you no matter what he did. George certainly couldn't. I think you are too much of a perfectionist. Roger, I want you to know that the neighbors all think Josh is just great—you can ask them yourself if you want to. Why, the Woodfords next door hired Josh to mow their lawn all last summer and they never complained one time about his work."

"Josh doesn't have any trouble at all with the neighbors?" Roger checked.

"That's right—nobody around here has ever had a problem with Josh that I know of," reported Molly.

"Yet you aren't satisfied with Josh's behavior, Henry."

"That's for sure," the father replied. "My standards for my lawn are higher than the Woodfords and they should be. Those people don't care if their lawn is a mess. I do."

"How often do you and Molly disagree on what to expect from Josh?" Roger asked.

"All the time," Henry responded. "Molly would let the kids run wild if I let her. Charlotte doesn't take advantage of her mother, so it's not a problem with her. Charlotte's always been a good kid and she does what she is told. But George and Josh wrap Molly around their little fingers and get away with murder."

"Henry, you are too hard on both the boys," Molly said sharply. "Sometimes when you're angry you won't speak to either of them for a week. It hurts them a lot. Somebody has to give them some love and attention."

"That's not true, Molly," said Henry.

"What's not true, Henry?" asked Roger.

"Molly says I won't talk to the kids for days," said Henry. "That's just plain not true. I'll speak to them anytime they'll admit they've done something wrong. They're just too stubborn. But I can wait them out."

"I see," said Roger. "You actually might not speak to them for days, but you feel they know you would, if they'd do things right, the way you want."

"You've got it, Roger," said Henry.

"What else does Josh do that makes you angry, Henry? For example, what specific kinds of things is he stubborn about?"

"Well," the man answered, "he's very inconsiderate about the amount he eats. I don't mind Josh having a decent supper, but he's getting just like his brother lately. George used to cost me a fortune eating expensive extras he didn't need, like butter and salad dressing—now Josh is doing exactly the same thing. And their mother encourages them both. I don't mind the kids eating a good meal, but the extras are expensive and enough is enough. Josh won't listen to me when I tell him to cut down, and a good part of that is his mother's fault. She doesn't back me up."

"Henry," Molly said, "I want the children to eat salad for dinner. You know how hard it is to get kids to eat a balanced meal nowadays. If I can get Josh to eat salad by buying him a dressing he likes, I'll do it, and I don't think you should get on the kid's back about how much of it he eats! Besides, I pay for it!"

"It's not how much he eats that I get on his back for, Molly," Henry replied. "It's that he doesn't obey me, and you don't help by sticking up for him all the time."

Molly glared at Henry. Henry glared at Molly. Silence reigned.

"So the two of you disagree on how to discipline Josh," Roger reflected, uncomfortable with the silence after a few moments.

"Yes," said Henry, "and you see, Molly, that's why Josh is having problems at school. You let him get away with so much here, he thinks he can do what he pleases there, too."

"That's not true," said Molly. "Josh does his chores regularly here at home, and in general he's a pretty good kid. He doesn't stay out late at night, and he gets home when he's told after school."

"Now, Molly, that's not true and you know it," retorted Henry. "You can't get him to do his homework here at night, or to get to his class on time in the morning even though you drive him to school yourself."

"That has to do with school, Henry," Molly replied. "Doing his homework and getting to school on time are problems for Josh, I agree. But here at home, he's not a bad child. He does do his chores when you tell him to, almost all of the time. And a lot of the time he does his chores before you tell him to, and he usually tries very hard to do them well. It's just that you are never satisfied."

"Well," Henry responded, "you may have a point there, Molly, but you have to admit the kid is sloppy with my tools and does a lousy job on the lawn."

"I don't think he's any worse than any other boy his age," Molly replied.

Roger Steinberg spoke then. "Let me summarize what I'm hearing," he said. "It sounds to me that what you are saying is that Josh obeys you both reasonably well here at home. He does his chores when Henry asks him to, sometimes even sooner, but not up to the standard Henry expects of him. Josh comes home when he's supposed to most of the time, and doesn't get into trouble in the neighborhood. Molly, you have some trouble getting Josh to do his homework and to get to school on time. Does that sound reasonably accurate?"

"Well . . . yes," Henry replied. Molly nodded.

"Now," Roger continued, "I'm going to ask you a number of questions about Josh when he was little, beginning with when he was born. These questions may seem silly to you, since Josh is 13 now. Some of these questions you answered last year with the learning disabilities staff, when Josh was evaluated for their program. But I want to make sure we cover all bases today. Is that all right with you?"

With the Peterson's permission, Roger proceeded to take a detailed "developmental history" of the boy, including information on Molly's pregnancy; the birth process; Josh's general disposition as an infant;

his feeding habits; sleeping patterns; how old the boy was when he first sat up, walked, and talked; weaning and toilet training processes, etc. All were normal. That was important. If, for example, Molly had had a difficult pregnancy with a long and difficult labor and then Josh had suffered with colic for his first several months of life, such difficulties might have served as evidence of some kind of early problem that might be manifesting itself in the present. However, Molly had had a healthy pregnancy, an easy delivery, and Josh had been a sturdy, healthy baby.

"Well," Roger Steinberg said at last, "we have covered all the questions I had in mind for this afternoon. Thank you so much for your time and information, both of you. You have been very helpful. Is there anything else you think would be important for me to know in assessing Josh for special education services?"

"I can't think of anything," Henry Peterson replied. "Can you, Molly?"

"No," the mother said, "but what do you think, Roger? Is Josh emotionally disturbed?"

"Well, I don't like to give an opinion without time to evaluate with the team at school," the social worker replied. "As you know, we'll have a multidisciplinary team meeting including the classroom teacher who referred Josh, the E.D. teacher who observed him, myself, and both of you if you wish to attend. Before that time our psychologist, Mr. Meyers, will do some testing. He'll be at the meeting, too. We'll come to our conclusion jointly. But just for my own curiosity, what do you two think?"

"I think Josh is a normal little boy adjusting to growing up," said Molly.

"I think the kid has a problem," said Henry. "Look at this picture." And with that, he got up and pulled a photo album from a nearby bookshelf. He opened it right to the page he wanted, as if he'd done it often. There Henry revealed a picture of Josh taken by the school photographer at the end of the previous year.

"Look," the father said with great feeling. "Look how strained Josh's face looks. Look at that mouth clamped shut and those eyes. They look almost haunted."

Roger looked at the picture. He saw a pale freckled face staring back at him, with a set of large, scared gray eyes and a small, tight jaw. Wispy, fine, almost colorless light hair gave the tense little face an additional aura of frailty. Roger couldn't help but agree with the father's words. But the social worker found his mind dwelling more on Henry than on the boy. The compassion in the man's voice surprised and touched him. This father, who had been severely critical of his son only a few moments before, must hold other feelings as well somewhere within.

"What a touching photograph," Roger said at last. "They say a picture can be worth a thousand words, and I think it's true." After a short silence he continued, "But we don't know exactly what this one means, and we'll have a chance to discuss what, if anything, we can do for Josh another time. I think we've done enough for today." Roger rose, realizing as he did so that he was very tired, and was getting hungry for his dinner.

"Thank you both very much for your time and thoughts."

"You're welcome, and thank you, Roger," said the parents, and they showed the social worker politely to the door.

CHAPTER 4

JoEllen's First Case

Late on a Wednesday afternoon, the same day that Roger Steinberg conducted his interview with Molly and Henry Peterson at their country home, JoEllen Madsen strolled nervously into the Family Therapy Training Institute. Her experience as a student therapist was about to begin.

The institute required a heavy investment of time from its students. Classroom and clinical training took two years to complete and, in addition, if a trainee hoped to qualify for the coveted status of "Clinical Member" of the American Association for Marriage and Family Therapy, that trainee had to complete 1,000 hours of clinical work supervised and documented by AAMFT Approved Supervisors (Approved Supervisors receive substantial additional training to achieve that status). The institute itself could not provide nearly that many clinical hours for its students. Many of the trainees, of course, were able to complete them at their regular place of employment.

Classes on family therapy theory at the institute were held every Friday afternoon, beginning right after lunch and often continuing as late as 6:00 in the evening. All students were required to attend. JoEllen, like most of her classmates, had to obtain special permission to leave work early on Fridays, and her employer required her to make up the hours she missed. In addition, discussion groups were held every Monday from noon until 2:00 P.M. Students were expected to attend these regularly as well, even though most, like JoEllen, had to take time from work to do so and then make up the work hours later.

Evenings at the Family Therapy Training Institute were reserved for clinical training. The institute had been established as the training wing of a nonprofit social service agency. The agency made its regular office space available to trainees in the evenings. Certain prospective agency clients were referred to students rather than to regular agency staff. These were the people who called to make appointments and who had no insurance, or who had depleted their insurance, and who also said that they would have great difficulty paying agency fees out of pocket. Prospective clients who agreed to work with institute trainees could receive services free of charge.

JoEllen and a group of three other trainees met at the institute on Wednesday evenings for their clinical practice. Together, they constituted a training team, or consultation team. JoEllen felt especially lucky, as the supervisor who worked with her team was none other than Dr. Kurt Knaak, director of the Family Therapy Training Institute, with whom she had had her admissions interview. Dr. Knaak was a clinical social worker by background.

JoEllen was not assigned clients of her own for the first few weeks. Newcomers had the luxury of beginning their therapy training by observing the ongoing work of more experienced students. Two members of her consultation team were in their second year at the institute: John Kinsman, a Ph.D. psychologist, and Sandra White, a school guidance counselor with an M.A. in educational psychology. JoEllen and one other trainee, Kevin Lord, an ordained clergyman with a master's degree in divinity, were both newcomers.

Observation of ongoing therapy was possible due to equipment installed in a special office used for training purposes. The special office was outfitted with an enormous one-way mirror that filled most of an entire wall. Behind the mirror was an observation room, tiny and crowded, for the trainees. The special office was equipped with video equipment and a sound system. Students in the observation room could thus hear every word spoken in the therapy office, and they could view the session clearly, not only through the one-way mirror but also via a video screen mounted high in one corner. Videotapes made during therapy sessions could be used later to review a trainee's work.

When clients entered the special training office, the one-way mirror and the video equipment were immediately obvious. A large telephone, wired directly to another phone in the observation room behind the mirror, was also prominently displayed. Members of the consultation team used the special hookup to call in suggestions to the student therapist. Asking permission of clients to use the equipment was not only a legal necessity but a human courtesy. Clients at the institute were obviously "guinea pigs" to some extent and deserved an explanation of what was going on! Some clients responded that they were pleased to provide training services in exchange for the help they sought for themselves. Those who refused, at least initially, were seen in a regular office. Although that might have felt safer to them, in fact these clients lost out on the direct assistance of the team, including the skilled supervision of its experienced leader.

Once new trainees were oriented to the procedures of the institute, they were assigned clients of their own. Only one hour's work for each trainee could be performed "before the mirror" on any given evening, however. One hour per trainee added up to four hours of clinical work for the team "behind the mirror." Teams usually observed therapy sessions from 5:00 P.M. until about 9:00 P.M. Then at least half an hour longer was spent reviewing various cases. Obviously, dinner for team members was a brown-bag affair, hastily gulped at odd moments!

JoEllen immediately learned that team participation in therapy work was considerable. Telephone calls to the trainee during a session were frequent. JoEllen wondered how she would respond when her interview with a client was interrupted by the telephone. She was afraid she would lose her train of thought. And she wondered how she would feel when every word she uttered, every facial expression she exhibited, every gesture she made was under observation by others, especially her supervisor. To JoEllen, it seemed too much like operating in a fishbowl. She couldn't help but hope that her first client would schedule at a time when another trainee was working before the mirror. That way, she could begin her counseling work in privacy. If she made mistakes, nobody would know.

As a social worker, JoEllen had conducted client interviews throughout her working life. She felt quite confident about her skills in this area. Her interviews as a social worker were usually geared toward collecting information in a supportive manner, much like Roger Steinberg's interview with the Peterson family. JoEllen assessed client strengths and areas of need, and then linked her clients with resources that could bolster their strengths and help meet ongoing needs. When JoEllen's professional assessments indicated a need for serious changes in her clients' personalities or in their family relationships, she referred them to therapists with special training. Working to change the dynamics of family systems was not JoEllen's area of expertise. But now she was about to learn to do this work herself.

During JoEllen's fifth week at the institute, she was assigned her first client family, at last. And as she had hoped, the family was scheduled to be seen at a time when another student was assigned to the special training office. JoEllen would be able to begin her work in privacy, in a regular office. She would not be observed. She could not help but feel relieved.

The assignment took her by surprise, however. JoEllen had rushed into the institute from work without a moment to spare, expecting only to observe that evening. However, as she trotted past the agency's front office with a hurried wave, the young receptionist, Kelly, called out her name. Kelly knew that JoEllen had been eager for her first client, so she grinned as she announced, "Hey, JoEllen, your time has come. Your first family is waiting right over there." And she pointed toward a small group seated across the large waiting room. Kelly handed JoEllen a referral slip on which a few sentences of basic information were written, along with a blank intake form.

JoEllen looked over at the family and made immediate eye contact with the mother across the room. She didn't feel quite ready to meet her new clients. She hadn't had a moment's preparation. But here they were, and contact was already established with one of them. JoEllen felt embarrassed to turn away now. The mother looked as if she had something to say at this very moment, urgently. So without taking time to read any of the referral information, the trainee trotted over to meet the family.

"Hello, I'm JoEllen Madsen, your therapist," she introduced herself primarily to the mother, with whom she still held eye contact. "And you are ______?"

The mother introduced herself and her family: Lucy Callan, her husband Warren, and their son John, who, by his size and dress, appeared to be a teenager. The boy's face looked twisted because of a pronounced harelip.

"Follow me," said JoEllen, wondering where she was going to take the family. She remembered a pleasant office on the second floor. She wasn't sure if it would be available, but she set off to find out, walking rapidly with the family filing along behind her. In JoEllen's haste, she didn't notice that John was limping and having difficulty keeping up.

Therapist and family filed past a very pleasant indoor atrium filled with trees and flowers, but this evening JoEllen hardly noticed. The family had no opportunity to enjoy the unusual display because their therapist was moving so quickly. When JoEllen reached the office she hoped to use, she found the door shut tight. The room was clearly already occupied. JoEllen turned to the family apologetically.

"Sorry," she said. "I'd hoped to use this office, but it's full. We'll try another one around the corner."

Again, the trainee set off nervously at a fast pace. The next office she hoped to use was also occupied. Two doors down the hall, however, a smaller one stood empty. JoEllen invited the family to enter, and then realized there were only two chairs available for their group of four. There wasn't a lot of extra room for more, either. She thought for a moment, asked her clients to wait, and then ran down a long corridor to the seminar room used for institute classes. There she collected two small metal folding chairs. She knew they would fit into the limited space available.

By the time JoEllen returned, Lucy and Warren Callan had seated themselves in the two comfortable armchairs in the office, one usually used by the client and the other by the therapist. John Callan stood awkwardly in a corner. Now JoEllen saw that one of his ankles was taped almost to his knee. She could see the bulge under his pant leg. She opened a folding chair for the boy and the other for herself. Both sat down. The metal chairs were hard and cold.

JoEllen tried to look as if everything were happening as it should. Trying not to gasp for breath too obviously, she smiled more anxiously than she knew. Her words rushed out.

"Welcome to the family therapy clinic. I'm sorry I haven't had a chance to read your intake form yet. Why did you come here tonight?"

The mother spoke immediately. "I wanted to see somebody today, because this is getting just impossible. Your clinic was the only place I could find that had an opening right away. Besides, we've used up our insurance."

"So coming to a free clinic was important to you?" responded JoEllen.

"Of course it was," interjected Warren Callan. "But don't get the idea we couldn't pay. I work, and so does she." He jutted his chin toward his wife.

"That's true for lot of people," said JoEllen in what she hoped to be a reassuring tone. "Nowadays husbands and wives often work and bring home double incomes but still, paying for counseling out of pocket can be difficult."

"But we could do it if we thought it was worth it," Warren returned loudly. JoEllen noticed his voice was rough, aggressive. He was a large man with a balding head and a pot belly, not particularly pleasing to look at. And what did he mean by, We could do it if we thought it was worth it? That sounded as if he thought counseling was a waste of time. JoEllen felt a moment of discomfort and dislike. She then ignored the statement.

"So," she said brightly after a long moment. "Here you all are. How can I help you?"

"We don't know if you can help us," said Warren.

Lucy Callan spoke then. She was a small woman with wispy hair and a tight, gaunt face. "We're here because Warren's being unfair to John," she said, glaring angrily at her husband.

"How is Warren being unfair?" asked JoEllen, secretly agreeing with the wife already.

"He is a terrible father. He took away John's motorcycle keys today. He's saying he won't let the poor kid ride his own Harley anymore. John's Harley is practically all the kid lives for, and I don't think it's right. John earned the money for that bike himself. So I called to make this appointment. I told Warren if he didn't come, I was leaving him this time."

"The kid's just plain ugly," said Warren. "And I don't mean just his ugly face. I mean he's got an ugly temper and he's a bully to other kids. He uses that motorcycle to act like a big shot, and I don't like it."

"He's not trying to act like a big shot," responded Lucy Callan angrily. "John just wants to have something special that other kids want, too, so they won't make fun of him so much. The poor kid—he can't help it if he has a harelip. He was born that way. He only acts like a big shot because other kids pick on him."

JoEllen took a long look at John. The boy's face seemed set in a perpetual sneer. It was hard to tell how much of the sneer was the harelip and how much was just facial expression. John's hair was unkempt and greasy, his body slight, his stature short. Multiple oil stains marred his clothes. Like his father, nothing about the teen was very pleasing to look at. Moreover, while the father at least had a large, manly sort of physique, poor John looked like he might fall over if someone pushed him very hard.

John caught JoEllen's eye for a moment and then looked away. JoEllen, uncomfortable with her own thoughts, turned to the father.

"What do you think about that, Mr. Callan?" the trainee asked.

"About what?" the man responded.

"About John's harelip, that he needs the Harley to make up for it," JoEllen returned.

"You mean he needs the bike to keep other kids from picking on him? Sure it helps," the father replied. "But John can't handle a Harley. And he took it out on the road today against my orders."

"But it's *his* bike," Lucy insisted.

"In the first place, the kid is only 15, and he's not supposed to be driving *anything* on the road," Warren Callan growled at his wife. "In the second place, he's costing me a fortune." He turned back to JoEllen.

"Why do you think that ankle of John's is taped?" Mr. Callan continued. "The kid fell with the bike today. Lucy thought he might have broken his leg, so she took him to the emergency room. Lucky it was just a sprain and a lot of bruises. But our insurance charges a damned big deductible if you use the emergency room."

"Warren, all you care about is money," Lucy Callan cried out.

"So you think your husband cares more about money than he does about his son, Mrs. Callan?" JoEllen inquired.

"I'm sure of it," the mother replied. "That's why we're here tonight."

"That's ridiculous," the father sputtered.

Lucy continued to talk to the therapist. "Warren has to hear from an authority that his son needs him, not to yell at him all the time but to understand him. John has a tough life. Kids tease him terribly because of his harelip. You know kids, they're awful that way. So John needs extra acceptance at home. Warren won't listen to me, but he might listen to you."

Warren Callan also addressed the therapist. "Somebody has to provide the discipline in this family, and since my wife won't do it, I have to be the one."

JoEllen looked from mother to father to son. John was squirming in his chair. The trainee could empathize. The hard metal chair she was sitting on wasn't very comfortable either. How to respond? She wasn't sure. She knew that an important role in family work involves facilitating communication. However, this set of parents seemed to be communicating clearly—they just disagreed. Although JoEllen couldn't help empathizing more with Lucy than with Warren, she realized the father had a point. An undersized 15-year-old really shouldn't be driving a huge Harley out on the highway. Not only was it against the law, but John had indeed already been hurt. The boy probably wasn't strong enough yet to handle such a big machine, and the highway was a dangerous place.

Uncertain how to proceed, and since each parent seemed to have a reasonable point of view, JoEllen suddenly wished strongly that she were conducting her interview in front of the one-way mirror. How she could use a telephone call from the team right now. But she was on her own.

JoEllen suddenly realized that John hadn't said a word so far in the interview. There he sat in a corner of the office looking terribly uncomfortable. The boy was physically shifting from side to side in his chair and his eyes darted from one parent to the other to the floor. His sneer seemed even more pronounced than usual. Probably it was time to bring him into the discussion.

"What do you think about all this, John? Do you agree with your mother or with your father?" the trainee inquired. JoEllen expected John to agree wholeheartedly with his mother. What she certainly didn't expect was what actually happened next.

"What the ______!" John cried out a string of incoherent expletives and jumped up from his chair. Despite a marked limp he moved fast across the floor of the little office, past JoEllen, past his parents, straight out the door.

Lucy Callan jumped up, gave JoEllen a quick glance in which distress was evident, and then followed her son.

"What the hell," said Warren, rising also. "Well, I told you I didn't expect any good to come out of this." And he stalked out of the office after Lucy and John.

JoEllen sat frozen. What should she do? Go after the family? Stay put and wait? Maybe the parents would catch up with their son and bring him back.

After a few minutes it was clear that the family was not going to return. JoEllen decided to follow them, but by the time she reached the receptionist's desk, her clients were out the front door and gone.

Kelly's expression was one of amazement. "Hey, JoEllen," she said, "What happened? Your family just left the agency practically on the run!"

JoEllen felt as if she were living out a therapist trainee's nightmare. So much for working with her first clients in privacy, so that if anything went wrong, no one would know.

CHAPTER 5

❀

Consultation with the Team and the Discussion Group

After JoEllen's debacle with the Callan family, she joined the rest of her team behind the mirror. Members were engrossed in work taking place in the training office, however, so that it was not until much later that she could tell them what had happened.

Team members were concerned both for JoEllen and for the Callan family. Yet it was growing late in the evening, past 9 o'clock, as a result of the length of time some of the sessions in the training office had required. Kurt Knaak said the consultation team could review JoEllen's case briefly and determine what immediate steps to take. Then she should bring her experience to the next Monday noon discussion group for a more complete review.

"Oh great," thought JoEllen. "Now absolutely everybody in the institute will know about this disaster."

"First," said Kurt, "it's important that you contact the family again. Offer to see them next week, and if they sound hesitant, offer the services of a different student therapist. Any of your teammates can take them on at this point; just be sure to schedule the family at a time when we can see them before the mirror."

"OK," said JoEllen, although calling the Callans was about the last thing on earth she wanted to do. She realized, however, that Dr. Knaak was right. It would not a be a good idea to leave this family hanging after such an experience.

"Have you got the necessary information to call them?" Kurt asked.

JoEllen suddenly wanted to drop through the floor. She remembered she had never taken time to fill out the agency intake form, where the numerous lines and spaces were laid out specifically to record telephone numbers, addresses, and the like.

Now what? As she was about to dissolve in embarrassment, JoEllen remembered the referral slip that Kelly, the receptionist, had handed her. She reached into her purse to find it. Thank heavens, it was there. And mercifully, upon the slip was listed a telephone number for the family. In addition, a brief sentence noted John Callan's motorcycle accident. And then the sentence: "Caller reports ongoing conflict with husband unresolved by marital therapy last year." Shamefacedly, the trainee read the note to the team, admitting she hadn't taken the time to read it before meeting with the Callans.

"Don't worry, JoEllen," Kurt responded. "Beating yourself up tonight won't do a bit of good. Besides, this is an excellent, if painful, introduction to the systems perspective for working with families. You have a situation here where there is obviously conflict between the parents. That's probably at the root of the problem, not the particular incident involving the son that brought them here this evening."

"Oh," said JoEllen lamely.

"I want you to take this case to your Monday noon discussion group and review it in detail," said Kurt. "Write a brief note about what happened tonight for the agency file, but write a process recording for purposes of consultation on Monday. It can be very informal, just for your own use, not for any permanent record. Do you know what a process recording is?"

"Yes," responded JoEllen. She knew a process recording would be time-consuming, but she also knew that Dr. Knaak's request was reasonable, under the circumstances. She would have to write out what had been said in the Callan interview word for word, as well as she could remember, along with observations of nonverbal responses, her own and those of her clients.

Before leaving the agency that evening, JoEllen carefully placed an intake form for the Callans, only part of which she could complete, the referral slip, and a brief, dated record of her session with the family in a file that Kelly had provided. "Case notes" were routinely kept by agency employees and students alike. They served to remind therapists about what had happened during previous sessions and also provided useful information for those who might substitute during a colleague's absence, or who might be assigned the same clients in the future.

JoEllen telephoned the Callans from home the following evening. She reached Lucy Callan. To her dismay, the woman refused to schedule another appointment at the institute. She told JoEllen frankly that she was not satisfied with the service she had received. She said she was considering returning to her prior therapist, despite the cost. JoEllen lamely encouraged Mrs. Callan to do so, while inviting her to return to the institute if she should change her mind in the future. JoEllen explained that the family could meet with another, more experienced trainee, if they wished. The mother thanked her politely. That was the end of the conversation.

The new trainee, of course, felt terrible about the whole affair with the Callans. She spent a couple of evenings writing down the sequence of questions she had asked during the interview to the best of her recollection, and recording how the various family members had responded. So she was ready for her discussion group the next Monday, eager for feedback, although still very unhappy and ashamed about what had happened.

Discussion groups for students at the Family Therapy Training Institute included different participants than the teams that consulted behind the mirror every evening, but their purpose was basically the same: consultation and supervision. The groups were conducted by different leaders, however, and provided more time for individual attention. The leader of JoEllen's discussion group was Dr. Madeleine Sweet, a clinical psychologist. Dr. Sweet brought a wealth of skills and experience to her assigned role. An older woman and longtime employee of the agency, she provided a safe harbor for trainees to express their disappointments, fears, achievements, and learnings. An AAMFT Approved Supervisor, she doubled as a consultation team leader behind the mirror for a different group of students during the week.

Madeleine Sweet had a keen mind and was a compassionate and patient person as well. She remained almost invariably calm and soft-spoken. Trainees soon learned they could take many personal and professional risks with her. She usually opened her weekly discussion sessions by asking which trainees wanted time that day for consultation, and approximately how much each needed. The two hours available were then budgeted so that each student had time who requested it, with room left over for lesser concerns when possible. JoEllen asked for 20 minutes. She would have requested more except that there were five trainees in the group and all wanted time that day.

When JoEllen's turn for consultation arrived, Madeleine asked her if she had a videotape to examine. JoEllen explained that she did not, as she had interviewed her clients in a regular agency office. She explained, however, that she had prepared a process recording of her session, at Dr. Knaak's request.

"Excellent," said Madeleine. "That should be very helpful. How about beginning with a short summary of what happened?"

JoEllen did so, beginning with the hurried events in the waiting room, which continued during her search for an office. She described John's dramatic exit from the interview followed by both parents. She then explained, looking rather dejected, that Mrs. Callan had refused to return for another session due to dissatisfaction with the service she had received.

"Good grief!" exclaimed Gretchen Young, one of the other trainees in the group, an M.S.W. "And this was your first case here at the institute? What a tough way to begin!" The humor and support evident in Gretchen's voice were reassuring.

Another trainee, Bob Smith, a psychiatric nurse, spoke up as well.

"Something like that happened to me just the other day at my regular job. I had to tell a patient he had AIDS, and he walked out on me. He was extremely angry. I felt terrible."

"Well, you can be sure I felt terrible about what happened here," JoEllen responded. "I still do."

"No problem," quipped Harry Hannum, a Protestant clergyman with a dry sense of humor. "We'll just kick you out of the institute as a complete incompetent." Everyone laughed, and then JoEllen admitted she had worried about just that.

"Nonsense," reassured Madeleine. "This sort of thing happens to everybody from time to time, even experienced family therapists. Now—you say you've brought a process recording of the session with you. What did you learn as you wrote out the recording?"

"Shall I read it?" asked JoEllen.

"No, that would take more time than we have today. As Dr. Knaak said, the record is primarily for your own use, a learning tool that you can keep to look at later as well. I want to hear what you learned as you wrote it. Then the group can give you additional feedback."

"OK," said JoEllen. "The first thing I learned is to slow down. Had I taken time to find an office, check the chairs available, and read the referral slip before meeting with this family, I might have gotten off to a better start."

"Could you do that now? You said you felt almost compelled to walk over to that family right away."

"I think so. I could have introduced myself and then asked the family to wait for a few minutes, or I could have asked Kelly to inform the family I'd be with them in a few minutes. After all, at work my clients have to wait for me from time to time. I just became flustered here because I wasn't expecting clients of my own."

"Good," said Madeleine. "You might also consider calling the institute from work during the day to find out what your schedule looks like for the evening."

"That's a good idea," responded JoEllen.

"What else did you learn?" asked Madeleine.

"Well—to fill out my intake sheet, at least the client's name, address, and telephone number, at the beginning of the interview. And to observe my clients more carefully. I completely missed the fact that John's ankle was taped until he was sitting across from me in the office. The poor kid probably had a hard time keeping up while I was running around looking for a place to have an interview."

"Good point," said Madeleine.

"What I'm still not sure about is why the kid ran out on me," JoEllen mused. "I was just starting to talk to him, and all I did was ask for his opinion."

"Ah," said Madeleine. "That's an important question. We know now something that you didn't know then, and I expect it's related."

"What's that?" asked JoEllen.

"Check with the group for their ideas," responded Madeleine. She enjoyed teaching as well as consulting, so she routinely involved her students in the consultation process.

Rose Salazar responded first. She had recently earned her M.A. in Psychology and moved from another state to participate in the institute, due to its accreditation by the AAMFT. She spoke in her usual straightforward manner.

"I'm not sure if this is what we're looking for," she said, "but didn't you say, JoEllen, that you learned after the family left that Lucy and Warren Callan had unresolved problems in their marriage? You read it on the referral slip?"

"Yes," said JoEllen. "Actually, I could probably have found out about ongoing marital conflict much sooner if I'd picked up on several clues early in the interview. While writing out my process recording, for example, I remembered that Lucy told me she had made an appointment at the institute because 'this' was becoming impossible. She went on to say something about needing free services because they'd used up their insurance benefits. I pursued the money thing, asking something like 'was free service important to them.' That only put Warren Callan on the defensive."

"What would you do differently now, JoEllen?" asked Madeleine.

"If I could do the interview over again, I'd ask Lucy Callan to tell me exactly *what* was becoming impossible. What did she mean by 'this?' She might then have said something about ongoing problems in her own relationship with Warren, not just her dissatisfaction with Warren's performance as a father. I'd also ask if anyone in the family had been in therapy before. After all, somebody *must* have been, since their insurance benefits were used up."

"Good thinking," said Madeleine. "I believe we're headed in the right direction. Marital difficulty is the clue I think we need that can help us answer JoEllen's previous question, 'Why did John Callan run out of the therapy session?' "

Bob spoke up. "You know, as a nurse, I can't help but view the kid as the primary patient here. I know that doesn't follow the track our group is taking right now, looking toward marriage problems as the major issue to examine. But I can't help but notice that nobody even *spoke* to John during the first part of the interview—not even you, JoEllen, when you saw that his ankle was bandaged. I think the boy must have felt like he was being completely ignored."

"You're right, Bob," responded JoEllen. "I noticed that later, too. I left the poor kid standing on an injured ankle when I ran after extra chairs and I never even asked him whether he was hurting." JoEllen felt a twinge of shame and promptly lost her train of thought, picturing in her mind how pathetic John had looked with his scarred and twisted lip, his messy hair, and greasy clothing. She really hadn't known how to relate to the boy and so she hadn't tried.

Harry spoke up then. "You know, maybe JoEllen should have paid more attention to John earlier, but so much else was going on in the encounter with this family that it's not surprising. That's what makes family therapy both difficult and exciting. So much happens all at once that it's very hard to pick up on all the important clues. Probably impossible, even for the experts."

"Of course," said Bob. He and Harry both turned to grin at JoEllen. It was clear to the new trainee that her colleague's comments were aimed to assist her in understanding the case, not to put her down.

"Thanks, both of you," she said.

After a pause, Madeleine spoke again. "There are clearly a number of factors at work here. JoEllen, you know from your reading that taking time to 'join' with clients is very important. What would you do differently with John to gain his cooperation if you could redo the session?"

"Well, of course, on hindsight I realize I should have spent time getting to know John as a person early in the session. First of all, I'd have offered him a chair right away! Then I'd ask how he hurt his leg, how much pain he was feeling, how he felt about coming to therapy, what he wanted to talk about in session, that sort of thing."

"That's the idea," said Madeleine. "Every therapist probably has a slightly different way of creating working relationships with clients, but I think the term *joining* describes well what has to be done. A favorite technique many therapists use is to ask all family members to introduce themselves at the beginning of the session and then to explain what brought the family to therapy from their own point of view."

"OK, that makes sense," responded JoEllen.

"Now," continued Madeleine, "while Bob has a good point, that John probably needed attention early on, I believe the conflict between his parents was the major reason he ran out of the therapy session just when he did. Does anyone in the group have an idea why I might think that way?"

Gretchen spoke up then. "In my job at a shelter for runaway children, I often notice that when a child's parents come to visit, or a parent and a significant other, their kid goes haywire for a time. This seems to happen most when the adults are having disagreements. Sometimes they pull the kids into their fights by asking them to take sides. It seems to me that that puts youngsters in an impossible position. No matter who they agree with, they alienate somebody important to them."

A beam of understanding flashed through JoEllen's mind. "Oh my gosh," she said aloud.

"What are you thinking, JoEllen?" asked Madeleine.

"That's exactly what I did to John. I thought I was being considerate of his point of view when I asked him whether he agreed with his mother or his father. But what I did was ask him to alienate one of his own parents."

"That's very probably correct," said Madeleine.

"So John had to run away to avoid being put in a position that would be harmful to him," said JoEllen.

"That's right," said Madeleine. After a pause, she continued. "One of the goals of family work is to help parents keep doing the work of parents: making the major family decisions themselves, establishing the basic rules of discipline, and standing behind those rules. The kids may not like what their parents decide, but that's much better for them than being forced to 'parent the parents.' Playing the role of parents is much too scary for kids, even teens; they aren't ready for that kind of responsibility."

"How could I be so dumb?" lamented JoEllen.

Rose broke in. "Dumb? This is why we're all here! To learn how to work with families as interactive systems!"

Madeleine smiled and continued her mini-lecture. "Family systems theory can help provide a perspective that guides therapists to assess families as whole entities. From the point of view of linear problem solving, JoEllen, you thought you were dealing with a reasonably straightforward problem: 'Should John Callan be given back the keys to his Harley.' You got lost in trying to weigh the pros and cons of that concern. But you were more probably dealing with only a single symptom of Lucy and Warren Callan's overall unhappiness with their marriage. The extent of their unhappiness is unknown to us at this time, but you can be sure the two parents express their discontent with each other in many ways. Disagreeing over how to discipline John is only one."

"Let me see if I understand you," said JoEllen. "You're saying that Lucy and Warren are probably unhappy in their marriage as a whole. Disagreeing over rules for John is just one way they express their unhappiness with each other."

"That's right," said Madeleine.

"I guess that makes some sense to me," said JoEllen. "But didn't you also imply that John's misbehavior itself might be a symptom of the parents' marital problem?"

"I meant to do more than imply that idea. A systems perspective guides me to want to check out such a hypothesis very carefully. From my practice experience as well, I strongly suspect there is a connection between John's misbehavior and his parents' unhappiness with each other."

"What kind of connection do you suspect?"

"Look at it this way. If John seriously misbehaves, what will his parents probably pay most attention to, his escapades or their own unhappiness with each other?"

"Why, John's escapades, of course. Falling off a motorcycle and landing in a hospital creates a crisis!"

"Of course it does, and oddly enough, the crisis, or a series of them created by a very resourceful child, can help stabilize a troubled marriage. John may not be consciously aware of what he's doing, but when he misbehaves, his parents direct their attention to him rather than to their unhappiness with each other. That can prevent or at least delay a divorce."

JoEllen looked confused. "OK," she said, "I can accept that interpretation as a possibility, I guess. But at this rate, John could kill himself on that motorcycle! Harleys are enormous, and he's just a little guy!"

"That's a realistic worry in this case. In fact, children all too often sacrifice themselves to prolong their parents' marriage. Symptoms more commonly involve truancy, school phobia, poor grades—things like that. But the purpose is the same: to try to keep the parents together. To a youngster, the parents' impending separation is often experienced as a direct threat to personal survival. The whole world feels like it's falling apart. Due to stress alone, a kid can start acting crazy."

"So," responded JoEllen after taking this in for a few moments, "according to a family systems perspective, John Callan's behavior probably isn't going to improve until Lucy and Warren Callan resolve their marital difficulties."

"That's right. John will probably continue to misbehave so that his parents are more upset with him than with each other. That just might keep Lucy and Henry Callan an intact, if unhappy, marital pair."

"Whew. That's complicated," mused JoEllen.

"No problem," quipped Harry. "It's all explained in your reading assignment for next week. The rest of us understand everything perfectly already."

The discussion group ended with a hearty laugh and a few more good-natured jokes enjoyed by all.

CHAPTER 6

❀

Another Referral for Family Therapy

"Decisions, decisions, how do we make decisions in this case?" mused social worker Roger Steinberg, as he walked toward the school conference room. A multidisciplinary team (M-team) was about to meet to discuss little Josh Peterson. Roger was glad he would not be the only staff person responsible for determining what to do about the boy.

Josh's parents, Molly and Henry Peterson, were both planning to attend the M-team meeting. While parental attendance at M-teams was officially encouraged (parents had to be offered the option by law), staff usually felt constrained when parents were present. They felt a need to choose their words more carefully, for fear of causing offense. Roger Steinberg suspected that today's meeting would be particularly awkward because one of the parents who would be present was also a long-term colleague—Molly.

According to Roger's professional social work assessment, Josh Peterson did not meet the qualifications for special education placement as a child with emotional disturbances. Josh exhibited certain kinds of disturbed behavior at school, to be sure, but Roger believed the boy's behavior at home and in the community, as described by both parents, fell well within the norm for a 13-year-old boy.

Yet Roger also knew that Henry Peterson thought his son had a serious problem, and he knew that Josh was continuing to get in trouble at school. Just recently the boy had defied his English teacher by telling her she could make him sit in class, but she couldn't make him do the readings she assigned. Josh was right, of course. The teacher couldn't force the boy to read. All Josh had to do was shut his eyes or stare out the window. Josh was a perceptive and intelligent young fellow. However, he was using his intellectual gifts in a self-defeating manner. Roger hoped the team would be able come up with a plan that could help the boy. The social worker had several ideas to offer for consideration.

Roger entered the school conference room quietly and took a seat. Almost everyone expected was present except for the parents: the English teacher, Mrs. Anderson, who had referred Josh; the E.D. teacher, Mrs. Henke; the school psychologist, Mr. Meyers; and the assistant principal, Mr. Roman. Roger greeted his colleagues and looked questioningly at Martin Meyers, who in his position as director of pupil services formally chaired most M-team meetings. Martin looked around inquiringly and then said he was expecting the Petersons momentarily. Just then both parents arrived, and the next few minutes were spent in introductions. Martin then began the formal part of the meeting.

"We welcome you all here today," he said cordially, "especially Molly and Henry Peterson. It's not often one of our colleagues attends a meeting like this in the role of parent, and I'm sure it isn't easy for you, Molly." He looked over at Molly and smiled. Molly returned a serene, composed, tight little smile of her own.

"Thank you, Martin," she replied in a dignified manner.

"Henry," Martin continued, "I want to thank you for your presence here today, too. So many fathers leave this sort of meeting for the mothers, and I believe input from both parents is important. Fathers have their own points of view, which should be heard and considered. Have you any questions before we begin?"

"No," said Henry Peterson, "but I want everyone here to know that I understand my son has a problem and anything you can do for him here at school will be OK with me."

"Thank you, Henry," Mr. Meyers replied. "Now let's move on to the teacher who referred Josh for evaluation. Mrs. Anderson, will you describe Josh's behavior in your classroom? Specifically, what behaviors caused you to refer Josh to special education?"

"What behaviors!" Mrs. Anderson exclaimed in her hearty voice. "It's more like what *lack* of behaviors led me to refer the boy! I felt I needed to earn my salary by teaching Josh something, and he just won't let me."

"Can you be more specific, Mrs. Anderson?" Martin felt a grin tugging at his lips. The psychologist liked Josh, and he had recently observed the boy in the classroom as part of his assessment for the M-team. Mrs. Anderson's words brought an amusing picture of the boy to mind: a thin, freckle-faced little fellow cleverly extending enormous effort not to do any class work. One almost had to admire him. Josh had a certain intensity about him and he seemed earnestly to be trying to accomplish something by avoiding doing anything—but just what was it?

"Yes, specific behaviors," continued Mrs. Anderson. "Let me see if I can describe them for you. It's not so much what Josh does do as what he doesn't do. He doesn't interact with other kids. He never tries to get anybody else to misbehave or anything like that. He just doodles and stares out the window all the time, and won't do his schoolwork. He dawdles. That's about it."

"Does he become verbally defiant?" asked Martin.

"No," Mrs. Anderson replied. "Well, yes, I suppose you could say he does sometimes. But only when I really get after him to read or do some other assignment. Then he tells me I can't make him, in an angry voice. Otherwise, he sits quietly at his desk. You know, I do like the child. He's bright, and I think he's artistically talented. You should see some of the doodles he makes. The drawings are excellent, usually of cars, trucks, or other machinery."

"How do you feel about the boy?"

"I guess I feel sorry for him. He seems miserable somehow. I suppose he doesn't like school—that must be why he's late all the time. I wish I could do something for him. That's the reason I referred him. When I talk to Josh alone without pushing him to do his schoolwork, he's a very nice little boy. It's a shame he's wasting his time the way he does."

"How do you think special education services could help Josh, Mrs. Anderson?"

"I don't know, to tell you the truth," she replied seriously. "Josh is certainly not one of those kids with severe disciplinary problems—at least he isn't if you leave him alone. But then, if you leave Josh alone, he doesn't do any schoolwork. I thought maybe our classroom for children with emotional or behavioral disturbances could help him because it's small and highly structured. He could have regular one-on-one attention in the E.D. classroom. Maybe that would motivate him to learn something. Even one-on-one sessions with E.D. staff in the regular classroom might help."

"Yes, but," his mother spoke for the first time. "Yes, but you know the kids who are labeled as "emotionally disturbed" are all looked on as problem kids. People view them as different, and they take on a reputation for being bad, whether they deserve it or not. Josh isn't bad, and I don't want him labeled as different, either."

"Molly, you're just not being realistic," Henry Peterson broke in. "You know Josh is a problem at home. He never does his homework, and he's always sloppy with his chores."

"So you two disagree on whether a placement in special education would be helpful," Roger Steinberg spoke up to highlight the difference between the parents for the benefit of the other staff at the meeting.

The Peterson parents shifted and twisted their bodies uncomfortably. They didn't look at each other. Henry spoke then.

"I guess you could say Molly and I disagree," he responded. "I think the kid has problems, and if you can fix him at school, I'm for it. Molly's too easy on the boy. She was too easy on George, too, and you remember where that got him."

Some of the school staff took a deep, collective breath at the mention of George. Josh's older brother was a real if unseen presence in today's meeting—up until this moment unacknowledged. Everyone remembered George's prolonged struggles through high school. All feared Josh would follow in George's footsteps. This was another, if unspoken, reason for the special education referral.

Martin Meyers spoke to the parents. "You know," he said, "I think the staff here mirror your disagreement. I don't think people here have reached a unanimous conclusion on whether a special education placement would be appropriate for Josh. Let's hear what others think. Mrs. Henke, you are the E.D. teacher who observed Josh in the classroom. What kind of behaviors did you observe? Do you believe they would warrant placement in a special classroom, or provision of special services in the regular classroom?"

"My observations were similar to those of Mrs. Anderson," replied Mrs. Henke. "Josh is simply not learning in school right now. He was on-task for only six minutes during the first hour I observed him. I observed him twice more on different days and his percentage of on-task behavior was consistent—about 10%. That is extremely low. I believe placement in the E.D. classroom would be appropriate, for at least part of the day. We might want to mainstream him for nonacademic subjects like art and music."

Mrs. Henke was referring to the fact that most children accepted into special education programs spend only part of their school day in a special classroom. They are "mainstreamed" (placed in regular classrooms) as much as possible, according to their individual needs as assessed by the M-team. The purpose of mainstreaming is to reduce the labeling problem that so worried Molly Peterson, and to provide children with "special needs" more normal role models in the classroom. Mainstreaming also maintains children in the least restrictive environment possible, as required by special education law.

A "least restrictive environment" is a setting that provides the least possible interference with normal life patterns while still meeting a child's special needs. Some schools implement the least restrictive environment provision very literally and mainstream all children with special needs in regular classrooms. Special supports, such as tutoring or counseling, are provided to individualize services according to each child's special needs. However, Josh's school maintained a special classroom for students determined to have emotional or behavioral disturbances, staffed with a specially trained teacher.

"Thank you, Mrs. Henke," said Martin Meyers. "And what are your findings from your conference with the parents, Roger?"

Roger cleared his throat. He looked toward the parents before he began, noting that Molly's face had assumed a smooth, guarded expression. The father appeared pleased, probably in response to the recommendation for placement in special education by Mrs. Henke, the E.D. teacher. Henry seemed certain his son had a problem and that it was the school's place to do something about it.

"Well," Roger began, "I had a helpful discussion with the Petersons in their home a few weeks ago. Molly and Henry," he said, turning toward the parents, "I'm going to summarize what I learned from you. Please feel free to add any new thoughts you may have at the end of my report." Roger took a deep breath, because he didn't think his report and recommendations would please Henry Peterson. He paused, and began to speak quietly.

"The Petersons agree that Josh doesn't have any problem in the neighborhood or community. The neighbors like Josh, and no one outside the family or school has ever complained about his behavior." Roger looked over at the Petersons. Both nodded.

"Molly and Henry disagree, however, on the seriousness of problems Josh displays at home." Roger continued. "And as we all know, this disagreement is significant. In order for a special education placement to be made, there must be evidence of disturbance in an environment other than the school—specifically, in the home or the community. Does anyone have a question about this?" There was general silence.

"Molly and Henry disagree over whether Josh displays disturbed behavior at home," Roger repeated. Then he went on to explain his findings about Josh's behavior in that setting. Roger concluded with his professional assessment that Josh's behavior at home was not different enough from the norm to warrant placement in special education.

Martin Meyers spoke up then. "Thank you, Roger," he said. "Mr. Peterson," he said glancing in Henry's direction, "I see you have a question. Would you mind holding it until I've given my report? Then we'll open the meeting for general discussion." Henry nodded his consent and Martin continued.

"I've retested Josh's IQ. He consistently scores well above average. The fact that this boy isn't doing his work at school has nothing to do with his intellectual ability. So I decided to do some other kinds of tests, to help understand Josh's emotional condition. I administered the Rorschach test, a projective measure in which patients tell stories in response to ambiguous, abstract pictures. According to my assessment of Josh's responses to the Rorschach, the boy is clearly suffering from feelings of depression. That might suggest a need for special education services. But I am also concerned that placing Josh in special education might increase his depression. We all know how sensitive children are to being labeled 'different.'"

"We now have some difficult decisions to make," continued Martin. "We all agree that Josh is having problems at school. We would like to help him. What are our options? First, we could recommend some type of special education service here at school. Or, we could determine that Josh is not an appropriate candidate for special education. Either way, we could recommend counseling, either individual or family." Martin paused, looked around, and then continued.

"We're here today to work as a team, to determine the best possible plan to help this boy. Let's put our heads together."

Roger cleared his throat, then spoke. "As I indicated in my report, I do not believe that special education is an appropriate placement for Josh. His disturbed behavior seems limited to school or school-related activities, such as homework."

"How can you say that," Henry Peterson spoke up, "when I have so much trouble with this kid? Josh does a lousy job on all his chores!"

Molly spoke then, hastily responding to her husband's words. "You're the only person who thinks Josh has problems at home, Henry, and he tries *so* hard to please you. You just can't see it. Josh doesn't need special education, he needs a father." There was an awkward silence.

Henry responded in a pained voice. "What do you mean, Josh needs a father? I have high standards for the kid, and that's the way it ought to be! Josh has to learn to obey, and to follow my instructions."

Martin Meyers interceded. He spoke carefully. "You know," he said, "often it's the most committed parents who disagree with each other. It means they care deeply. Thank you for telling us your different points of view." There was a brief silence, and then Martin continued.

"Does anyone else have a recommendation they'd like to make?" In this way Martin helped the Petersons avoid airing more of their own disagreements in front of Molly's colleagues, which he feared would embarrass the woman deeply later. He tactfully moved the meeting on to a different topic.

The next input was a surprise. Mrs. Anderson spoke up in her usual hearty tone.

"You know," she said, "this may sound surprising from the one who made the referral to special education. You are all aware that I think Josh has some kind of problem. But I'd also hate to see him labeled as emotionally disturbed. Maybe counseling would be the way to go for now. I'd feel happy if I knew the child were getting some kind of extra help as a result of my referral."

Martin Meyers agreed with Mrs. Anderson. Mrs. Henke disagreed; she felt she could help Josh in her small, tightly controlled classroom. Mr. Peterson agreed with Mrs. Henke. Mr. Steinberg and Molly Peterson agreed with Mr. Meyers. The meeting went in circles for a while, as the same evidence was interpreted in different ways by different people. Then Mr. Roman, the assistant principal, spoke.

"I haven't said a lot today because I am here primarily to represent administration, and I generally support the recommendations of the professional staff on the M-team. But since there is disagreement among us, I'll put in my 2-cents worth. Compared to the kids that get sent to my office, this boy hardly sounds like a disciplinary problem. Certainly not here at school, and he doesn't sound like he behaves all that badly outside of school, either. So why not go the middle route and recommend counseling for now? If counseling alone doesn't work, we can always reconsider the boy for an E.D. placement later."

"That sounds good to me," said Roger Steinberg, "with one modification. I suggest that the team recommend family counseling, rather than individual."

Roger paused, choosing his words carefully. He knew that the idea of family counseling frightened many parents, because they feared they might be blamed for their children's problems. So the social worker wanted to frame the service in a positive, nonthreatening way.

"We all know that parents are the best experts on their children," he began. "So parents taking part in counseling along with their children can sometimes make the difference between success and failure. Parents can offer information and insights about their children that are exceedingly important." Roger stopped and made full eye contact with each parent. Then he smiled. "Sometimes counseling together can even be fun!" he joked.

"I support Roger's recommendation," Martin Meyers said in a thoughtful tone. "And," the psychologist continued, "I believe it would be best to refer the Petersons for counseling outside of the school setting. After all, Molly is one of our own faculty, and I expect she would feel more comfortable consulting with counselors who are not also colleagues." There was a short silence.

"I think it would be a good idea for Josh to go into counseling," Molly said at last. "I know it helped his brother, George. And I guess we could find someplace to go outside of the school." Her sensitive face looked almost sad for a moment, then she smiled as she tried to joke: "I suppose Martin Meyers deserves a break from the Peterson boys. Anyway, I guess we could use our teacher's union insurance plan—does anyone know what kind of coverage we get for counseling?"

"Our insurance program is administered by a managed care corporation that limits mental health counseling to about six or eight sessions, Molly. You'll probably have to pay out of pocket if you want more than that." Roger spoke from his considerable experience in referring families for counseling.

"However," the social worker continued, "in a situation where a child's future is at stake, I think the cost is worth it. Will you consider entering into counseling as a team?"

"As a team?" Molly replied, looking confused.

"Yes, as a team," Roger continued patiently. "The Peterson team, to be specific."

Martin Meyers spoke to the assembled group. "Let's clarify the recommendation to make sure everyone here is indeed in accord. Roger and I are recommending family counseling, rather than individual, for Josh. We both believe input from his family can help the boy in the counseling process. Is this recommendation supported by the M-team as a whole?"

One by one, the other staff members agreed: Mrs. Anderson, Mrs. Henke, and Mr. Roman, in turn. Martin then turned to the Petersons.

"This is what Roger means by entering counseling as a team. This M-team recommends that the Peterson family team work together in counseling to get to the bottom of Josh's problem." There were a few moments of solemn silence. Finally, Roger spoke.

"You know, there is an excellent resource for family counseling not far from here. It's called the Family Therapy Training Institute. Services are free for people without insurance or for people who want to continue with counseling after their insurance benefits are exhausted. All the trainees are experienced professionals with at least a master's degree, and they are supervised by experts."

Henry and Molly looked at each other.

"Why, but that's crazy," Henry Peterson spouted suddenly in a loud voice, shattering the somber atmosphere. His blue eyes were intense and a red flush began to spread along his narrow jaw. "Here I have this kid with some kind of problem, and you say I need counseling, too. Are you trying to tell me there's something wrong with *me?*"

"This is Josh's problem, not the family's," Molly supported her husband, speaking firmly. "You say this is a family problem, but I tell you it is not. Sure, we all know George used to have a problem but he's doing well now; he's been married for over a year and he has a full-time job. Our daughter Charlotte gets excellent grades and she has more friends than any other kid in high school. Except for Josh, this family is doing fine." Molly's usually serene face was stormy.

"Josh is the one with the problem. He's the one who needs counseling." Henry Peterson reinforced Molly's words. The two parents moved closer to one another, shaking their heads and speaking almost in unison. "No, we won't accept a recommendation for family counseling."

Roger and Martin exchanged glances. Both were disappointed. They had hoped for a different result. At last, Martin spoke.

"Let me ask you to reconsider."

Roger looked at the parents' set faces and sighed. "I know our recommendation involves some inconvenience for you, even some risk," he said. "No one can predict with certainty what the outcome of counseling will be. We can say, however, that we believe the best chance for helping Josh involves your participation and help."

"We certainly want to help our son," Molly said, struggling to recover her usual serene, dignified smile. "We are willing to pay for counseling if necessary. But Henry and I agree that Josh should go by himself. No 13-year-old would want to have his parents listening in to his private thoughts, anyway!"

More discussion ensued among the school staff and the parents, without reaching agreement. Finally, Martin Meyers ended the meeting by tactfully summarizing the conclusions of the school M-team and the preferences of the parents. The M-team, he said, would recommend that Josh remain in regular education classes and attend counseling with his family at a resource outside of the school. It would be up to the Petersons to decide if Josh would actually go into counseling, and if so, what kind.

Everyone went their separate ways, and the atmosphere at the end of the meeting was cordial.

CHAPTER 7

❀

Precipitating Events

Molly went home and picked a fight with her husband that evening. It happened right after Josh and Charlotte went to bed.

"You know, Henry," she began suddenly, surprising even herself, "they think something is wrong with this family down at the school—you know they do. And I agree. It's your fault, and you know it."

"Oh, Molly, quit it," Henry replied. "You're upset. It's been a long day. They're just looking for somebody besides themselves to blame down there. Josh is a smart kid. They said so themselves. He ought to be getting better grades. If they treated him right, everything would be fine. He's bored at school, that's all. I had the same problem when I was a boy."

Molly whispered back in a fierce tone. "Josh may be bored, but that's not the real problem. The problem is that you don't treat any of us very well at home. You don't speak to Josh for a week at a time, and sometimes you ignore me too. You're always off teaching those dancing lessons at night. You're hardly ever home in the evenings. Why don't you take me with you once in a while?"

"Molly, the students in the dancing classes don't want the instructor's wife around. Half the fun for those folks is dancing with me themselves. I entertain them. I give them a good time. It's therapy for some of the single gals."

"You used to take me along. You used to let me help you teach new steps."

"That was only in the beginning, before—"

"Before what—before the children came?"

"Well, yes. And you know that Charlotte is better at teaching now, anyway. If I need another instructor, I can bring Charlotte along. She's young, she's a lot of fun, and all the women in the classes like her."

"Where does that leave me?" Molly fumed.

"You're my wife, Molly," Henry replied sincerely. "You are my primary relationship. You're more important to me than anyone else in the world. You should know that. I couldn't live with anyone but you." Henry's voice was warm, his tone charming. Molly could feel a lovely, familiar sense of security begin to calm her fears. Then Henry continued.

"But that doesn't mean I want to be with you all the time. I get bored seeing the same face day in and day out. I have to bring new people into my life."

Molly's budding sense of security bolted immediately. A tense silence occupied the next few moments. Then the woman spoke candidly.

"I'm worried, Henry. Where do you go those evenings when you aren't teaching classes? Who are the new people in your life?"

"Shh, shh, you'll wake the kids," Henry put her off. I'm tired. It's time for bed. You know I'm always home by 10:00 or 11:00 every night. You have absolutely nothing to worry about."

Molly was silent. Her eyes filled. Tears began to pour down her face. She let Henry see them.

"Come on, cut it out, Molly," Henry responded sharply. "Stop acting like a baby."

Molly's tears gradually subsided and her eyes took on a vacant look. Slowly her lips curved slightly in their customary smile. She took a deep breath and let it out in smooth control.

"Well, what should I do about Josh?" she said, changing the subject.

"Call your teacher's union and find out how to make an appointment for him."

"Just for Josh?"

"Didn't we already agree that was what we wanted to do?"

"Yes, but I thought maybe you and I might—"

"No way I'm going to talk to any stupid counselor. Forget it. Good night."

Henry stalked off to bed. Molly slipped into the bathroom and turned on the water in the tub. She let her tears flow freely then, muffled safely by the running water. She soaked her tired body for a long time, pushing soap bubbles idly into mounds and patterns. By the time she joined her husband in the bedroom, Henry was sound asleep.

The next morning, during study hall duty at school, Molly contacted her union and was referred to a mental health clinic that the union insurance plan approved. She made an appointment for Josh with a psychologist, Dr. Lang, who specialized in working with children. She took Josh to his first session about a week later, staying only long enough to fill out the required forms.

Josh told Molly little about his sessions with Dr. Lang, but he seemed somewhat happier after the first few appointments. The mother felt a sense of relief that an experienced professional was helping her son. Molly believed that male attention alone could benefit the boy, as Josh got so little from his father at home.

Suddenly, however, Molly's sense of respite was shattered by a call from Dr. Lang. "I don't want to alarm you, Mrs. Peterson," the psychologist began, "but there is something you need to know."

Dr. Lang explained to Molly that normally, information between psychologist and client, even a child, is confidential, but an exception is made by law in circumstances where a client might seriously injure himself or others. Dr. Lang then reported that in their previous session Josh had told him about recurrent thoughts of suicide.

Dr. Lang said he had questioned Josh carefully to determine if the boy had an actual plan, a method he was considering using. Fortunately, Josh did not, so Dr. Lang didn't believe he was in immediate danger. However, the psychologist continued, teens all too often do take their own lives, so Josh's suicidal thoughts must be taken seriously. Molly burst into tears on the telephone.

Dr. Lang talked with Molly at some length, describing how he intended to work with Josh for the next few sessions specifically to help the boy find compelling reasons to live. He advised Molly not to tell Josh about his call at this point. Josh might view it as a betrayal of trust and stop confiding. Dr. Lang told the mother to call him immediately, however, if any unusual behavior should alarm her. Josh could be hospitalized for his own protection if necessary.

Molly was devastated by the news. She told Henry about it as soon as possible. He returned late that night, as usual, but the two then whispered together in the dark, shoulder to shoulder, for a long time. Henry was as concerned as Molly. The parents agreed not to tell Josh about Dr. Lang's call, as they wanted the boy to feel free to confide in the therapist. But they wanted to help the boy.

Molly suggested that Henry praise Josh the next time he mowed the lawn, no matter what Henry thought about the imperfections, and the father agreed to do so. Molly said she would cook Josh's favorite meals for supper. She asked Henry not to criticize no matter what the boy ate. Henry agreed. This was an emergency. Henry even began staying home several evenings a week after supper, building crackling fires in the fireplace and listening to his favorite lively music. Sometimes the whole family danced around the living room in the firelight.

The next few weeks brought welcome changes in Josh. Molly received feedback from his teachers that he was doing better at school. Mrs. Anderson told Molly in a delighted tone that Josh completed a reading assignment in class and wrote a creditable book report. The math teacher reported a series of carefully completed assignments. "Maybe," Mrs. Anderson said to Molly, "we were wrong on that M-Team. Maybe individual counseling is just what Josh needed, not family counseling after all. This is the sort of situation in which I love to be proved wrong."

The crisis was over. Josh finished out the eight sessions with Dr. Lang that the insurance would pay for. Dr. Lang told Molly he felt it would be appropriate to terminate counseling at this point, as Josh reported being happy with himself and his progress at school. Josh himself told Molly that he felt he could get along all right on his own now. The boy's good-bye to his counselor was reluctant, but he was in good spirits and agreed to call Dr. Lang if he felt a need to talk with him in the future.

The family breathed a collective sigh of relief. Then it began to drift back toward its old ways. Henry began to keep more normal hours, which meant he went out dancing again after dinner most nights of the week. Sometimes Henry took Charlotte with him when he taught classes. Molly began to argue with Henry again about the amount of time he spent away from home. Arguments resurrected about the amount Josh ate, about who paid the food bills, and so on and so on.

One evening Molly was sitting at the kitchen table, working on lesson plans for school the next day. Henry was out dancing somewhere. Josh was keeping Molly company. He had finished his homework and was building a model airplane at the other end of the table. Molly found herself looking around at the dusty household furniture and at the kitchen floor that needed washing. She felt resentful. Henry had commented on the dirt in the house before he went out after supper, and his voice had sounded annoyed. Now it was 9:30 in the evening and Molly didn't feel like cleaning. She had been working all day. Yet in addition to her full-time job, somehow the household cooking and cleaning tasks all fell in her domain.

Molly wondered uneasily where Charlotte was. The girl had declined to go out with her father that evening and had left home soon after dinner to visit a friend. She should have been back by now. Charlotte, always obedient, never broke a curfew. She was supposed to be home by 9:00 unless she was with her father. But tonight she was late. Molly asked Josh anxiously if he knew where his sister was. He didn't.

By 10:00 P.M., Molly was distinctly anxious. She turned to Josh and asked what he thought she should do. At the boy's suggestion, Molly called the friend that Charlotte was supposed to be visiting. The telephone was answered by the friend's mother.

"Yes, Charlotte was here earlier," the mother replied, "but my husband and I thought the girls were over at your house. They left here more than an hour ago!"

Now there were two anxious sets of parents awaiting their young daughters—or rather, one anxious set of parents and one anxious mother, comforted by her anxious son.

At 10:30 P.M., Henry Peterson returned home. Charlotte and her friend were still missing, so Henry called the friend's father. The two men discussed calling the police. They decided to wait until 11:00 P.M., because the friend's curfew wasn't until 10:00 and it was "still only a few minutes after that," the fathers assured each other. "The girls just must have lost track of time."

Eleven o'clock approached, and Molly was almost sick with worry. Josh was worried too, wondering what could possibly have happened to his nearly perfect older sister. Henry was reaching toward the telephone when it rang. He expected to hear the voice of Charlotte's friend's father, telling him the girls had come home.

"Mr. Peterson?" A loud male voice inquired. It was definitely not Charlotte's friend's father.

"Yes, this is Henry Peterson," the man replied.

"This is the police," the loud voice said.

"The police?" Henry nearly lost his calm. "The police?"

"Are you missing a daughter?" came the terse reply.

"Yes, my Charlotte was supposed to be home by 9:00 this evening," Henry said. Then, anxiously, "Have you seen her?"

"We have, and your daughter won't be home tonight unless you come down to the station to bail her out. She's been caught shoplifting at the mall."

"Oh no," Henry said. "You can't be talking about my daughter. She's never been in any kind of trouble, and she's been visiting a friend this evening."

"Is your daughter's name Charlotte Peterson?"

"Yes."

"Does she have long blond hair and brown eyes? A little over 5 feet tall, maybe 100 pounds?"

There was a silence. Henry replied in a quiet tone. "Yes, that sounds like Charlotte."

"I'm sorry to have to tell you this, Mr. Peterson." The man's voice softened slightly. "Your daughter was caught by a security guard, so there's no mistake. She was stealing earrings—took six pairs off a rack, put them in her pocket, and tried to leave the store along with her friend. The security guard stopped both girls, but only your daughter had anything on her. We let the other one go."

"Thank you, officer," said Henry after a few long moments. "We'll be right down to get Charlotte."

Henry hung up the phone and sat stunned, lowering one clenched fist to the table and then the other. Molly stared at her husband silently. She had heard enough of the conversation to know the gist of what had happened. Josh was the first to speak out loud.

"Charlotte?" he chortled. "Charlotte stole something? Tonight? She must be crazy! Besides," he continued somewhat illogically, "she'd never do anything like that!"

The rest of the evening was memorable. When Henry and Molly arrived at the police station to pick up their daughter, they found a thoroughly disconsolate child who looked a great deal younger than her 16 years. Charlotte's eyes were streaked from crying, and her face and hands were smudged with fingerprinting ink. Her long blond hair was dishevelled. She was afraid to face her parents but was desperate to go home with them. The police let Charlotte go on Henry's signature.

"Why did you do it, Charlotte?" her father asked the moment he had his daughter in the car. "Why on earth did you do it?" His tone was as reasonable as he could make it, but he was angry.

"I don't know, I really don't know," was all Charlotte could say through her tears.

"Did you plan this?" Henry asked, suddenly furious. "You wouldn't come with me tonight when I asked you to help teach dancing."

"No! No! I didn't plan anything. It just happened."

"Something like this can't just happen. You have to go into a store, reach out and take something with your own hands. That's stealing. Deliberate stealing."

"Was this your friend's idea?" Molly rushed in to protect her daughter. She was sure Charlotte would say yes. Molly wondered if she should begin screening her daughter's friends.

But Charlotte said no, it was her own idea, or rather, impulse. The urge to take something at the store had come upon her suddenly and it was too strong for her to resist. Later, the friend confirmed that only Charlotte had taken anything.

Henry took Charlotte down to the scene of the crime the following morning and made his daughter apologize in person to the store manager. The man reprimanded the girl in fine style and then, when Charlotte's deluge of tears and wretched words of apology convinced him she was not a hoodlum, he told her the store would drop all charges if she promised never to take anything again. Of course Charlotte promised, with appropriate gratitude. Her criminal career was over. She was genuinely ashamed of what she had done. She seemed confused, almost appalled at her own actions.

The store manager and the legal system let Charlotte off lightly, but her parents didn't. They grounded the girl for the rest of the school year (the last quarter of her junior year was just beginning at the time of the shoplifting incident). Henry threatened to ground Charlotte through the entire summer if she didn't shape up. The girl responded by neglecting all of her schoolwork and actually failing two subjects, chemistry and French. Because she was not promoted into her senior year, she was to be grounded all summer. Her parents told her she had to go to summer school.

Molly was beside herself. Charlotte was the family's model student, Molly's own pride and joy in her work at the school. Henry, the proud father, couldn't understand what was happening either. Molly decided something had to be done. With great courage, she decided to talk to Roger Steinberg, the school social worker. She knew Martin Meyers better, of course, as Martin had worked with her at the school for several years. Roger was relatively new. Molly felt embarrassed, however, about things her older son, George, might have told Martin Meyers in counseling.

Molly intended to talk with Roger as soon as she realized Charlotte would fail her junior year, but it took time to work up the nerve.

Molly waited, in fact, until a few days after school was out. Many teachers were still completing their records, emptying their desks, and organizing their classrooms for the following year. These were days of joyful transition, summer vacation being right around the corner. An atmosphere of relief and happiness pervaded the school, but it was lost on Molly. She dragged herself to work and could barely look at Charlotte's chemistry teacher when they passed along the hallway.

Finally, on the last possible morning, Molly stopped at Roger Steinberg's office. She felt a wave of embarrassment sweep over her, and tried to hide it in her careful smile and her controlled tone of voice. She arranged her features smoothly and worked hard to sound light, casual. Then she began.

"Roger, I'm so happy that Josh is doing better." It helped to begin on a prideful note.

"I'm very happy about Josh, too, Molly. The teachers tell me he's really come around in the past few months." Roger's tone was warm, welcoming. As he smiled at Molly, his eyes invited her to say more.

"But something's wrong with Charlotte." The mother let it all out in one simple, rushed sentence. There was a long pause. Then, at last, "I'm sure you know already. Charlotte's just failed her junior year. She's always been an excellent student before. Can you recommend anything?"

Roger was in the middle of completing his end-of-year reports and he wanted to finish up his work and go home as much as anyone else. But instead of giving Molly a hurried reply, he invited her in to have a cup of coffee. He said he needed a moment to think. There was a hot pot in his office, and Roger made a great show of fussing with the cup and the fixings, intentionally giving his colleague time to calm herself. The social worker could sense, from the taught smile and the tight voice, how much Molly's visit was costing her.

By the time Molly Peterson left Roger Steinberg's office, she had the address and telephone number of the Family Therapy Training Institute. The family could be seen there right away, Roger believed, and the service would be free of charge, since the family's insurance benefits for outpatient mental health had been depleted through Josh's individual therapy with Dr. Lang.

CHAPTER 8

Beginning the Therapy Process

JoEllen Madsen read her new referral slip carefully, to learn as much about the Peterson family as she could. She felt a little nervous about meeting with them—not that she hadn't had a fair amount of experience in treating families by now. She had been enrolled at the Family Therapy Training Institute for over six months. But this family was scheduled for an interview during the hour when JoEllen worked before the one-way mirror. Being observed always made JoEllen nervous, in spite of the fact that the consultation team provided support and assistance as well as professional critique.

The team behind the mirror phoned observations and ideas right into the therapy room during live sessions. The team's feedback was usually helpful, but sometimes it suggested—even required—a change of approach. And sometimes just the presence of the team felt intimidating to a trainee! Floundering unobserved is painful enough; it's truly embarrassing when monitored by a team. Most students at the institute felt nervous, at least at the beginning of an interview before the mirror.

JoEllen Madsen, a seasoned professional and now in her late thirties, was a reasonably typical trainee at the institute. She brought with her an advanced degree and several years of work experience. She thrived on the lively energy she found among the students. Ages of the trainees spanned more than a generation, ranging from the mid-twenties to the late fifties, and educational backgrounds were diverse as well, including social work, psychology, nursing, guidance counseling, and divinity. Conversations among trainees could be electric.

Students at the institute all agreed that the best hours of the week were those spent *behind* the one-way mirror, observing *other* trainees sweat it out! Team members behind the mirror consulted freely with one another, relying heavily on their leader's knowledge. All team leaders were AAMFT-Approved Supervisors. A special sound system carried the interview from the training office into the observation room. Sound was not supposed to carry the other way, but muffled noises occasionally came through. Team members thus tried to keep their voices low, a practice that lent a delightfully conspiratorial atmosphere to their deliberations. When the team reached agreement that a trainee should try a different approach, the team leader called the student on a special telephone hooked up between the two rooms.

Everyone also agreed that the toughest hours of the week were those spent *in front of* the one-way mirror. One's every move was scrutinized and critiqued. Although institute students were taught to treat each other with respect and consideration, there still were times when personal vulnerabilities were exposed for all to see. These areas were discussed by the consultation team and also, where appropriate, by the weekly discussion group to which each trainee was assigned. Weekly discussion groups included different trainees from the consultation teams, so every student at the institute had two separate groups of peers with whom to confer on a routine basis. Videotapes of interviews in the training office were frequently reviewed and critiqued by the discussion groups later in the week.

JoEllen Madsen knew well that she had vulnerabilities that could hamper her work with families. The impact of her divorce was not entirely over; she still grieved at times. She worried that some of her vulnerabilities might be exposed in her work before the mirror. Still, she knew that the team could help her and her clients if personal problems got in the way. And to JoEllen's pleasant surprise, once engrossed in the work of the session, she actually forgot the presence of the team. She felt almost as surprised as her clients when the phone rang during a session.

JoEllen grew to appreciate the support and guidance she received from the consultation team. She knew their input would have helped her greatly in her initial interview with the Callan family, and it probably would have resulted in a more successful outcome. Not all clients who came to the institute agreed to be seen in front of the mirror, of course. The first task of every student involved securing a family's permission in writing. This task became easier with time, as the trainees gained greater appreciation of the value of the team and the importance of making a videotape for later review.

Families generally agreed to work in the training office once they had received a full explanation of the role of the mirror and the videotaping equipment. Like the therapists, family members seemed to forget about the mirror and the camera in the ceiling very quickly once the interview began. Young children, of course, enjoyed making faces at each other in the mirror and were often quite distracted at first. But soon even they settled down.

As JoEllen pondered the new referral slip in her hand, she wondered if the Petersons would agree to be seen in the training office. She would soon find out. The room was ready and the team was assembled on the hard bench in the narrow observation room. Only the family was missing. It was not uncommon for a family to be a little late, especially for a first appointment. Suddenly, the telephone rang. The vivacious receptionist, Kelly, told JoEllen that the Peterson family had arrived and its members were assembled in the waiting room. JoEllen thanked Kelly, waved at the team behind the mirror, and hurried off downstairs to collect her new clients. Her heart began beating strongly and she breathed a little faster in anticipation.

JoEllen reached the waiting room just in time to hear a well-built, sandy-haired, slightly graying gentleman and a slim, lithe woman with dark curly hair instruct their two children to sit quietly. Apparently these parents had reasonably good control of their children because both were obeying, one slightly better than the other. The pretty blond-haired girl, who appeared to be of high school age, was sitting primly, examining carefully shaped fingernails, while the boy, smaller and apparently much younger, was squirming uncomfortably.

"I don't see why I have to be here," he was saying to his mother, in a whining tone. "Dr. Lang said I didn't need to see anybody any more unless I wanted to."

"Josh, just this one time . . . ," the mother was saying when JoEllen arrived in the waiting room. It was comfortably furnished with overstuffed chairs, a sofa, and small tables lost under piles of old magazines and children's books.

JoEllen introduced herself and encouraged the parents to introduce themselves and the children. After they did so, she asked if the whole family was present. She learned that everyone was present except an older son, George, who had been living on his own for nearly three years and was recently married. JoEllen nodded, pleased. Since family counseling is usually conducted with the people who live under one roof, George's absence would not be a problem, at least initially. JoEllen asked the Petersons to follow her upstairs to the therapy room.

Off they all trooped, along the glass walls of the enclosed inner atrium of the agency where large plants, a small fountain, and even a few tropical birds fluttered. The atrium had been carefully designed by a sensitive architect to provide a soothing atmosphere. JoEllen moved with her clients at an easy pace, allowing them plenty of time to view the unusual display. She chatted casually with the parents about their trip to the agency. Were they able to find it easily? How was the traffic? The weather? She was already working to establish rapport. She knew she needed to make contact right away because the family would probably be put off by the room toward which she was leading them.

As JoEllen led the family up a long curving staircase, down a hallway overlooking the lovely atrium, and into the therapy room with the one-way mirror, she wished the training room could be as attractively decorated as most of the other agency offices. But one entire wall sported the mirror, massive enough to intimidate just about anyone. The room was furnished reasonably comfortably with a multitude of chairs, but none of the soft stuffed kind and no big deep sofa. The furniture needed to be light and movable because of the nature of family treatment. Moreover, since the room was shared by a number of trainees, it simply didn't have that "personal touch." There were a few obligatory pictures on the walls, but no reassuring framed list of degrees, certifications and licenses and only a single, scraggly plant. A video camera projected from a corner of the room near the ceiling, and a microphone dangled from the ceiling down into the middle of the room.

Henry Peterson, being an industrial equipment salesman, immediately recognized the technology in the room for what it was and stopped in his tracks a few steps inside. He remained standing almost at attention. At his cue, the rest of the family froze in the doorway.

"What's that," Henry sputtered, pointing dramatically at the mirror. "And that," (pointing at the camera) "and that?" (pointing at the microphone). The man's voice was resonant and full and could be heard far down the hallway, JoEllen was sure. Oh no, she thought. She could imagine all the other clients and therapists in the agency pricking up their ears. The therapist-in-training smiled nervously.

"Find a comfortable chair and I'll explain," she said, attempting to keep her voice calm and matter of fact.

"That thing isn't on, is it?" Henry sounded uneasy. He made no move to take a seat. He pointed at the video camera.

"No, and it won't be unless you give us your permission," said JoEllen in a tone she hoped to be soothing. Actually, since she was nervous herself about how the family would react to the equipment in the room, her voice didn't sooth anyone. "I'll explain it all to you," she tried again, somewhat more firmly.

"What's that?" asked Josh in a delighted tone. He took a few steps into the room and stood beside his father, making faces into the mirror. Charlotte stepped in after her brother, looked herself over in the mirror and ran her hands through her long hair to smooth it. She pirouetted, she patted her skirt.

"Please, everyone, take your seats and I'll explain about the mirror and the camera," said JoEllen once more.

"OK, as long as that thing isn't on," Henry Peterson said at last, having made his decision.

JoEllen felt a wave of relief. The man selected the most comfortable chair in the room and pulled it into a position where he was looking toward the door, with his back to the mirror. He sat down. At this cue, Charlotte seated herself to her father's left, revealing her profile to the mirror. Mrs. Peterson pulled up a chair to the left of Charlotte, so that her daughter sat between herself and her husband. Josh chose a chair on the other side of his father, facing his mother and sister. He left a space between himself and Henry so that he could look directly into the mirror. He continued to make faces.

Behind the mirror, the members of the observation team found themselves exercising considerable self-control to keep from laughing out loud. Some of Josh's facial expressions were wonderful. JoEllen pulled a chair up near the door, facing her teammates behind the mirror. That wasn't the position she usually took, but it was all that was left.

How to begin? The trainee usually tried to develop a family's trust, to put the members at ease, to "join" with her clients, by continuing to engage in small talk for a short period of time. She usually chatted about the weather, the family's trip to the agency, or any other social pleasantry that seemed to fit the situation. This evening, however, because of the strength of Mr. Peterson's negative reaction to the equipment in the room, JoEllen decided she would begin with an explanation.

"As you know, this is a training clinic," she said, drawing a deep breath, consciously reminding herself not to talk too fast. She had been told many times by the team that she talked too fast when she was nervous. "We are fortunate to have the services of a team of therapists here. We work together to assist families in solving their problems."

She continued with a spiel that had become almost second nature to her. She explained how a team of therapists could be a valuable resource for family and trainee alike. She assured the family that the team would provide feedback over the telephone and in writing as well, at the end of every session. She also explained that videotapes of all sessions were confidential, to be viewed exclusively within the agency for purposes of supervision and training. The family could view their own videotapes if they wished.

After several minutes of discussion and to JoEllen's great relief, Henry Peterson decided he would sign the required forms. He said he wanted the family's videotapes erased, however, when the therapy process was completed. JoEllen agreed. Henry wrote this provision on the permission form before he signed. Molly signed also. She was not so surprised about the special equipment, as Roger Steinberg had previously explained to her that the institute was staffed by trainees and their supervisors. Being a teacher, Molly sometimes used special technology to assist in the learning process of her own students.

JoEllen looked at her watch. About 40 minutes remained for family members to talk about their reasons for coming to the clinic. She reflected quickly, however, that even with such a time constraint, she needed to take more time to "join" with this family. Establishing a beginning therapeutic relationship can make or break a counseling experience.

"There, that's done," the trainee began with a smile as she put the required permission forms aside. "We've accomplished the formalities. Now, before we get down to work, I want to let you know I'm glad you all came tonight. You'd be surprised how often families schedule a first appointment, and then lose their nerve and cancel at the last moment. I imagine it was hard for you to come here tonight."

"You're right," said Molly. The mother's face seemed fixed in a half-smile, which looked neither comfortable nor content.

"And I want you to know," continued JoEllen, smiling back at Molly, "that you've taken an important first step—one that many families never work up the courage to make."

JoEllen then took time to look at each family member in turn, acknowledging each with a smile, and each member returned the smile. Then JoEllen continued.

"Before we begin, are there any questions?"

"If you don't mind my asking," said Henry immediately, "what are your credentials? I'm frankly concerned that I'm bringing my family to see a student."

"I don't mind telling you my credentials at all," JoEllen replied. She then described her education and previous experience as a social worker. She was grateful she wasn't a new graduate student! She remembered how awkward she used to feel back then, when trying to answer such a question.

When the Petersons were satisfied, JoEllen continued the conversation in a cordial way by asking the parents about their own education and work experience; she also asked where the children were going to school. She took some brief notes that would help her fill out the agency intake forms later, including home and work telephone numbers and addresses. These questions began to move the family into the work phase of the session.

"I think the time has come," the trainee said, "to begin talking about the reasons you are here tonight. We've completed the formalities and introductions." She paused, taking time to make eye contact with each family member in turn.

"I know from reading your referral slip," JoEllen continued, "that Charlotte has been in some sort of trouble. But I'd rather hear from each of you directly what brings you to the clinic tonight. Let's begin with you, Mr. Peterson. Shall I call you Mr. Peterson, or would you rather that I call you Henry?"

When a father attends a family session, it is almost routine for many therapists to begin with the father. The father often takes a peripheral role in child rearing, and he is likely to refuse to attend family therapy at all. Addressing a father first highlights his position as a parent. Furthermore, respectful treatment often encourages a father to participate in therapy, rather than merely coming along physically just to "humor" his wife, or worse, dropping out.

"It's OK with me if you call me Henry," the man replied graciously.

"Fine. Please feel free to call me JoEllen."

"Well, JoEllen, I don't have the faintest idea why I'm here tonight. This is my wife's idea. Actually, I think it's ridiculous. We're wasting your time, and you're wasting ours."

Not an auspicious beginning! But JoEllen knew that many people who enter therapy do so under duress, on the insistence of others; they are not really "customers" yet. JoEllen noticed an odd incongruity about Henry's response. The tough, off-putting words were said in a tone that sounded almost jovial, delivered with a grin that could almost be described as debonair. Uncertain as to the man's full meaning, JoEllen reflected back to him the clearest part of the message as she understood it.

"Sounds like you'd rather not be here," she said.

"You've got that absolutely right," Henry replied. This time his voice and facial expression matched his words.

"What was the reason your wife asked you to come?" This second question repeated the first, but was stated in a different way.

"How should I know?" Henry replied. "She hardly ever tells me anything." Now the tone was complaining.

"That's OK. Why not imagine what might be the reason your wife brought you here," came JoEllen's response. "It doesn't matter if you're right or not. We can check that out later." The trainee could be persistent.

"Hell no!" The man said, annoyed now. "Molly has her reasons, but she's sure not going to tell me. Maybe she'll tell you. Why don't you ask her?"

Surprised at the strength of the man's refusal, JoEllen made a quick tactical change. She turned to Mrs. Peterson.

"May I call you Molly?" she asked.

"Of course," came the response—cordial, but not warm. JoEllen noticed that Molly's smile was carefully composed, the dark eyes guarded. Molly looked for a moment almost like china doll, the expression molded with care.

"Molly, let's begin with you, since the referral slip noted that you made the appointment for the family this evening. What brings you here?"

"I'm not sure," came the reply.

"Not sure?" JoEllen had the sinking sense that both these parents were going to be difficult to work with. She fell back on a simple counseling technique of repeating words with a questioning inflection.

"No, I'm really not sure." Was that a sudden expression of fear flashing over Molly's features? JoEllen didn't understand the reasons yet, but she was fairly certain of what she saw.

Molly indeed was feeling frightened. She thoroughly wished she hadn't come by now. JoEllen looks too darned young to me, the woman was thinking to herself. I'll bet she's never experienced anything like what I'm going through with Henry. She'll never be able to understand.

JoEllen, meanwhile, could see the tension in Molly's face and hear the anxiety in her voice. She could see a defiant, almost mocking expression on Henry's face as well. I wonder what's going on, she thought. Neither parent wants to be here. Of course, that's a pretty common experience for parents in therapy. Yet the resistance with these two seems unusually strong. I wonder if we'll be able to work together.

JoEllen knew that families usually ask for help from outsiders only under duress. Some sort of pain has become unbearable. Hardly anyone personally wants to change, however, because the old ways are at least familiar. Everybody wants somebody else to change instead. So therapy can be frightening, even if voluntarily sought. It can be quite a challenge for the counselor to reach an initial contract, or agreement on the problem for work, with new clients.

"Molly," JoEllen said in a sympathetic tone, "I know it is very difficult for families to come to therapy together. I want to congratulate you on your ability to persuade your husband and children to come here this evening. I assume you are the one who organized people to come. The referral slip lists your name as the person who called the institute."

"That's right." Molly seemed to let her guard down a little. Her smile looked just a little more real.

"Tell me what it was that convinced you to make an appointment just when you did, Molly," JoEllen tried again. There was a pause; then Molly replied.

"The school social worker told me he thought I should—for Charlotte's sake."

Henry broke in then. "The guy had this crazy idea that bringing Charlotte in by herself wouldn't help her, that we all should come. Molly believed him. It sounds nuts to me."

Molly added hastily, "I think Roger was wrong, now that we're here. I should have brought Charlotte in by herself. She's the reason I called for an appointment. Maybe we should leave her with you now? We can wait for her downstairs in the waiting room." The mother sounded almost eager. She twisted her head around and looked at Henry as if signalling that it was time to go.

Henry rose to his feet immediately, and Molly stood up after him. JoEllen was taken by surprise. She felt her stomach tighten in alarm. She didn't want to lose any more clients out her office door!

"Please sit down," she said immediately, groping for words but speaking in a calm, firm tone.

"Sit down, at least for a while," she continued when nobody moved. "I want you to stay. I need more information from you before I can work with either of the children." Molly looked hesitant but she sat down, followed by Henry. JoEllen began again.

"I know Charlotte has had a problem, but one of the things we learn in training is that when one part of a family is in pain, all the others are affected."

"What do you mean, 'in pain?'" Henry shot back. "Charlotte has been refusing to do her schoolwork lately, and she flunked her junior year. She stole some earrings from a store a while back. That's not what I call pain. That's irresponsibility, dishonesty. Charlotte needs to be straightened out, that's all—she's the only reason we're here."

"Often there are circumstances within a family as a whole that affect a child's behavior," JoEllen responded gently. "Our clinic works with families to help them learn what these circumstances may be in their own particular situation . . ."

"There you go again!" Henry was speaking even more loudly now. "A kid misbehaves nowadays and the parents get blamed. I knew that's what you were going to do before we came—blame me, blame my wife. Well, it's not our fault. I won't have it. That's enough." Henry stood up once more, quite dramatically this time. Molly looked at him, her expression distressed. She half rose as well. Charlotte and Josh seemed to freeze in their chairs, anxiety painted across their features.

JoEllen felt herself start to panic. Family work can place a therapist in a bind. Parents must be told that circumstances in the family as a whole can affect their children's behavior; otherwise they will see no reason to engage in therapy themselves. But the very act of saying such a thing can offend parents to the point of driving them away. JoEllen struggled for a response.

The telephone rang. Gratefully, JoEllen answered the call.

"JoEllen," it was Kurt Knaak, the team leader. Kurt began with his usual dry note of humor. "Maybe you're in luck tonight. Looks like you've almost lost this crew." His teasing tone helped JoEllen realize that no matter what happened, there would be support for her and an opportunity to learn.

"You're only too right, Kurt," she replied. She would have liked to say more, but now was not the time.

"Use a one-down approach, JoEllen," Kurt then instructed the trainee. "We think that might work back here. These parents, especially the father, seem to want to be in control. We think your best bet is to give them all the control they want. Go one down. Get confused yourself." He hung up.

Molly put down her end of the telephone, thinking rapidly. Just how could she go "one down" and still guide the session? That was the trouble with these darned team directives! They could give a trainee new ideas, but it was the trainee's task to figure out how to implement them. Kurt had given her a hint, however, with his statement, "Get confused yourself."

"Henry and Molly, wait, please," JoEllen said, her voice now humble in tone and revealing her real confusion. "You know I'm just a trainee here, and I'm not sure why your whole family has been advised to come myself yet. I need your help in figuring this all out." For a moment, the parents wavered.

"How can we help you? I thought helping was your job," Henry said sagely.

"I certainly hope I can be of assistance to you," JoEllen continued, "but I need your help to understand just what kind of assistance would be appropriate." She smiled graciously at Henry.

Henry stood still for a moment, then nodded and sat down with a gallant little bow. Molly followed his lead. A sense of relief was experienced by everyone, including those behind the mirror.

"Parents have such a tough job," JoEllen continued in a commiserating tone. "I don't think the work they do for their children gets nearly enough appreciation from the community as a whole. All the community seems to do is complain when something goes wrong."

"Boy, you're sure right there," Henry said forcefully. His blue eyes flashed with a rakish charm. JoEllen felt herself warm to the man. Her smile in return was spontaneous and open.

"Then along come the so-called experts who try to tell you what to do with your own children," JoEllen's tone was teasing.

"That's right," said Henry, responding to JoEllen with a smile that reached his handsome blue eyes.

"And yet it's you parents who are the experts," JoEllen went on, serious now. "That's why I'm glad you're here. I need you. As the team suggested on the telephone a few moments ago, you are the only people who can help me really understand what's been going on with Charlotte."

Henry looked at Molly. Molly returned his look with a shrug. Henry drew a breath, and smiled.

"Maybe we can do that," he said, sounding amiable and important.

"But I'm not sure we know ourselves," Molly said suddenly.

JoEllen turned to Molly. "You're not sure, Molly?" she reflected. "That's OK. A lot of parents like you feel confused about problems with their children. I'm confused right along with you tonight. But maybe together we can make some sense out of this. Now—do we all agree that we're here this evening to work on Charlotte's behavior?"

Molly and Henry both nodded. JoEllen looked over at the children. Josh grinned and nodded, Charlotte frowned and looked away.

"OK," JoEllen said. "If both parents agree, that's our contract. Our contract for counseling together here at this clinic is to work on Charlotte's behavior, to improve it in a number of ways. Charlotte, you may not be happy about this contract, but you'll have a chance to give us your two cents' worth any time you're ready."

"Now," the trainee continued, "what was it that led you to make an appointment at the clinic just today, Molly?"

Molly seemed reluctant to answer, even yet. She sat silent, as if lost in thought. JoEllen took the cue. She turned back to the husband.

"What do you think is going on, Henry?" she said.

Henry suddenly came alive. "I just don't understand how she could do this to us," he said, and there was real feeling in his voice. "Charlotte has always been everything a man could want in a daughter. She's a great dancer and an excellent student. But all of a sudden she's letting us down."

JoEllen took note of the man's description of his daughter as a "great dancer," which he placed even before "excellent student." She felt a flicker of interest about the importance of this activity to the man. But she chose to ask first about the "letting us down" part of Henry's message. She guessed this was probably the presenting problem, or the reason the family was seeking therapy. It might or might not also be the precipitating event—the reason the family was seeking help at exactly this point in time.

A presenting problem and a precipitating event may or may not be the same thing. A presenting problem may have been going on for a considerable period of time, upsetting people but not to the point where they seek help outside the family. A precipitating event, on the other hand, is something like the proverbial "straw that breaks the camel's back": a relatively immediate trauma that actually pushes people to the point of reaching out for help.

"Specifically, how is Charlotte letting you down?"

And so, from Henry, JoEllen learned the story of the shoplifting. She learned how Charlotte had stolen the earrings, apologized profusely and sincerely, and then proceeded to neglect her schoolwork. She learned that Charlotte had just recently flunked the eleventh grade at school. This was behavior of a girl who had been an honor student only the year before. The shoplifting and poor school work was the presenting problem, as Henry described it; Charlotte's actual failure to pass her junior year seemed to be the precipitating event.

JoEllen found out by questioning Henry that Charlotte had never shoplifted before and had never done poorly in school prior to the shoplifting. In fact, she had been an honor student. These were strong clues that Charlotte was reacting to some new stress in her life. The stress might be something about the Peterson family, but there were other possibilities as well. For example, Charlotte might have been jilted recently by a boyfriend or ostracized from a clique at school. She might even have developed a drug habit. These possibilities would have to be checked out.

"Henry, from what you're telling me, these behaviors of Charlotte's are new, beginning only a few months ago."

"That's right."

JoEllen looked over at Charlotte, who looked away.

"Has anything changed lately in the family as a whole?"

"Nothing I can think of," Henry said.

Not much information there. As JoEllen was thinking about whether or not to probe further with Henry, the telephone rang.

"JoEllen," Kurt said, "you're moving in the right direction, checking out family issues, but it's getting late. Better get on to the mother."

"OK," JoEllen hung up.

"Molly," she said shifting her position to face the mother, "tell us your point of view about what is happening in the family lately."

"Well," Molly replied, "this is very poor timing on Charlotte's part because finally, everything was going well with Josh. I had hoped to be able to take it easy for a while."

So something new *had* happened in the family!

"Tell me more . . ."

"Josh was failing in school earlier this year. He didn't do very well last year either, or the year before. The school evaluated him last year to find out if he had a learning disability. I was sure he didn't and I was right. Josh came close to flunking last year, though. This year, he's finally gotten himself straightened out. He did well in most of his subjects, cleared up his detentions, and was promoted to eighth grade." Molly's voice now expressed genuine pride. "I knew my son could do it all along."

"That's wonderful!" JoEllen exclaimed, picking up on the mother's feelings. "I'll bet you are very proud of Josh."

"I am," said Molly, "and relieved." The look on her face was completely sincere; her strained smile vanished and her face suddenly appeared much younger. "I've been so worried about Josh. He's such a good kid, but he always looked so sad. He seems much happier now." Molly looked over at the boy and smiled. Josh glanced quickly at his mother and then looked down with a proud, shy grin.

"Did something happen recently for Josh that made a difference for him, helped him to be happier?"

"Well . . ." Molly began, and hesitated.

"He saw a shrink," said Henry sharply.

"A psychologist," corrected Molly. "The school referred him. They did a special education evaluation for emotional disturbance this year, but Josh wasn't emotionally disturbed. He just wasn't doing well in school for some reason. They suggested he see a counselor so we took him."

"Good for you, Molly and Henry, for arranging to get help for Josh. What you did seems to have helped him be a better student," said JoEllen.

"Yes," said Molly.

"And you said the counseling seemed to make your son happier, too."

"I'm sure it did," the mother said. "We made the right decision."

"What do you think, Josh?" JoEllen turned to the boy, who was all eyes and ears by now. "What do you think changed so that you can do better in school now?"

The boy spoke right up. "Dr. Lang let me talk about anything I wanted. He listened to me. He agreed with just about everything I said to him."

"How was that helpful for you, Josh?"

"He looked at things exactly the way I do. Then he helped me fool the teachers at school."

"Fool the teachers at school?"

"Yes. The teachers all thought they could make me do things I didn't like to do, but they couldn't. All they could do was give me detention, and they couldn't always make me go to that either. I told Dr. Lang and he agreed I was right."

"I guess you were, Josh."

"Then," the boy continued in an eager tone, "Dr. Lang helped me to fool the teachers. I started to do their silly assignments ahead of time, so they didn't have anything they could tell me to do. They couldn't even yell at me! It was fun!"

"Good for you, Josh! How do you like school now?"

"No problem," the boy said. "I like not having to go to detention all the time. Now I can do what I want after school."

"How does your family like your new behavior?"

"Oh, they say it's great. Mom's happy, and even Dad tells me he likes my work sometimes. He even tells me I'm mowing the lawn better than I used to. That's not really true. I'm not doing anything different with the lawn lately, but if Dad thinks I am, that's OK with me!"

"How about Charlotte?"

"Charlotte?"

"Yes, how do you think Charlotte likes it, the fact you are doing well and your parents are praising you more?"

"She likes it OK, I guess—she hasn't said anything that I remember, anyhow."

"So you aren't sure how Charlotte is taking it."

"Well . . . I guess I'm not."

"Maybe we should talk with her. What do you think?"

"Sure, that's OK with me."

"OK, Josh, thanks for telling me what's happening for you. Before I go on with Charlotte, do you have anything else you'd like to say right now?"

"Nope, that's enough."

"OK then, I'm going to talk with Charlotte now." JoEllen smiled toward the girl, who was carefully examining her fingernails again. "Charlotte, what do you think has brought you and your family here to the clinic this evening?"

Charlotte looked up, saw JoEllen's smile but didn't return it. Her face looked brooding, the brown eyes guarded, the voice sulky.

"Well, its about time you got to me. I'm the reason everybody is here, or at least they say it is." Here was a clear invitation to find out more about the family as a whole.

"Thank you, Charlotte. What do you mean by 'I'm the reason everybody is here, or at least they say it is?' "

"Everybody's blaming me for everything lately," the girl said. "Josh is so terrific all of a sudden."

"Everybody's been blaming you for everything lately. Please tell me what you mean by 'everything.' "

"Well, sure I stole some stuff."

"You did." The statement was a question as well.

"Yes, I did," she replied defiantly. "And you're going to ask me why. Everybody does. Don't bother. I don't know why."

At this point Charlotte's sulky tone shifted toward despair, and suddenly she was sobbing, digging her fists into her eyes like a young child. JoEllen waited, giving the girl time to cry. The therapist took a covert look at the other family members to see if anyone wanted to comfort Charlotte, but no one moved in the girl's direction. Henry looked distressed, but he didn't reach out an arm to hug his crying daughter sitting right next to him. Molly's face took on its fixed smile. Josh squirmed.

As Charlotte's sobs subsided, JoEllen reached over and put a box of Kleenex by her feet. She didn't want to interrupt the flow of emotion, but she wanted to give the girl some needed support. Charlotte reached down and took a tissue, blotting her eyes carefully to avoid smudging the mascara she had meticulously applied. At last JoEllen spoke.

"Tell me about your tears," she said to Charlotte.

"I don't know why I'm crying," responded the girl in a small voice. "I don't know anything, I guess."

"You said the family has been blaming you for everything lately. What do you mean by 'everything'?"

"Nothing feels right anymore. Mom and Dad fight at night when they think we can't hear them, but we do. Sometimes Dad gets mad at all of us, but mostly it used to be Josh. Now Josh is his pet and Dad's mad at me."

"How do people in your family fight, Charlotte? "

"How?"

"Yes, how. In some families certain people fight all the time, and the rest don't; in others, everybody fights. Some families fight a lot, some only rarely. Some make a lot of noise when they fight, others are very quiet. Some families hit, others don't. What is fighting like in your family?"

"Well, nobody hits. That's good, I guess. I have a friend who is afraid of her parents because her father hits her with a belt and her mother spanks her with a hairbrush. Nobody hits anybody in our family. Whenever I feel really bad, I think about that."

"That's very good. Your family can be proud. So how do people fight in your family? All families do fight, you know. That's not a problem, that's human. The important thing is *how* people fight."

"I guess in our family people fight all the time, but nobody admits it. Mostly, Daddy just stops talking. Sometimes it's for an hour or two, sometimes it's for days and days. Lots of times he goes out dancing to get away from us. Mom gets even madder when Dad leaves, but he still goes out."

"Then what happens?"

"Well, sometimes nothing happens. Dad comes home and goes to bed and I guess Mom's already asleep because we don't hear anything. Sometimes she's still awake, though, because we can hear voices through the bedroom door. Sometimes the voices are loud enough that we can hear the words."

"What do you and Josh do when your father and mother fight?"

"If it's late at night, we stay in bed and block our ears. Sometimes we can't go to sleep for a while."

"How do the arguments between your parents turn out?"

"We can't hear the words well enough to know exactly, but we can guess. If Dad doesn't talk to Mom for a couple days afterwards, then we know he's really mad. If he yells at Josh, then we know he's really mad too. Lately he's been yelling at me. If Dad goes out dancing, he might be mad; it's hard to be sure because he goes out dancing all the time anyway—he teaches classes. If Mom's mad, she'll jump on Dad at the supper table if he criticizes what Josh eats. That hasn't happened for a while, though."

This young woman clearly had a good idea of the fighting patterns in her family. She was describing very particular types of interactions between specific family members.

"You say that lately everything feels worse in the family, Charlotte, but yet you say Josh isn't getting criticized as much. What is it that feels worse to you?"

"Well, for a while things got better for everybody when Josh did his schoolwork, but then . . ."

"Then? Go on . . ."

"I just don't know!" Charlotte almost shouted, her voice suddenly angry and despairing once more. "Things got happier for a little while, but then they got worse again!"

Charlotte's emotion was strong and the temptation for JoEllen to explore it with the girl more fully was powerful. There was a practical problem in doing so, however. The time allotted for the therapy hour was coming to a close. JoEllen had gained plenty of information to explore in future sessions, and now she needed to achieve a sense of completion for this particular one. She needed to take time for consultation with the team behind the mirror as well. In short, the trainee needed to achieve a satisfactory closure for the evening, not probe into new areas of feeling that might take more time to resolve than the appointed hour could provide.

"Charlotte," JoEllen responded, "I can hear the pain in your voice. I think you have a lot of concern for your family and I'd like to talk with you more about your thoughts and feelings. But we can't do any more tonight. Our time is almost up."

She reached over and touched the girl reassuringly on the arm, something she had wanted to do for the past several minutes. She smiled at Charlotte, and Charlotte glanced up at her from lowered eyelids. JoEllen knew that the use of touch in therapy was risky; some therapists never touch their clients because of fear of malpractice suits, based on accusations of sexual impropriety. However, in this circumstance—comforting a confused young girl surrounded by her family—JoEllen felt the gesture would be accepted. It might also serve as a model for appropriate behavior to the watchful family members. Charlotte visibly relaxed a little.

"Now, then," said JoEllen sitting up straighter in her chair, "what have we accomplished this evening? We have heard from everyone about the problem that has brought you in tonight: Charlotte's behavior. We have learned that Josh used to have a problem with his behavior too, but fortunately he is doing fine now. We have begun to consult together as a problem-solving team to learn how to help Charlotte. Does that about sum things up?"

Everyone nodded.

"I'm going to ask one more question," JoEllen continued. "I don't know anything about the oldest child in your family, George. Did George get into any kind of trouble while he was growing up?"

Molly answered sadly. "George had trouble all along in school. He flunked his senior year." Then she brightened. "But he earned his diploma later, and he has a job now. He got married last year. George is doing just fine now. I always knew he'd make it."

"I'm glad George is doing well," JoEllen responded warmly with a smile in Molly's direction, "and of course, that's hopeful information with respect to Charlotte and Josh."

JoEllen decided not to pursue anything more about George just then. She felt the family had endured all the probing it could handle for the time being. Besides, she had the information she was looking for. It supported her working hypothesis that the family as a whole would be the appropriate client for therapy.

"Now, we have an important decision to make at this point," the therapist continued. "I believe all of us need to work together to accomplish constructive change for Charlotte, and perhaps for others in the family. Will you all come back at the same time next week?"

Henry and Molly exchanged glances. Molly nodded slightly in Henry's direction. "We'll come," Henry said.

"Very good," said JoEllen, outwardly neutral but inwardly pleased. "Now, with many families, this would be the end of our session. But because we have the advantage of a team to consult, I'm going to go talk with the therapists behind the mirror for a few minutes. I'll be back shortly to give you the team's feedback."

From behind the mirror, JoEllen and the team watched the family members as they sat alone in the therapy room. No one reached out to comfort Charlotte. The father sat back and closed his eyes. The mother looked warningly at Josh as he began to squirm and make faces into the mirror. Charlotte looked down at her nails and studied them in great detail. A few tears were still visibly running down her face but she made no sound.

"Here is a group of people who have not yet learned how to support each other," said Kurt, as team leader. "How shall we design our feedback? Remember, we want to begin with a compliment and end with a suggestion."

The message the team designed was simple: "We want to congratulate you for coming to the institute this evening. Your courage to take this risk tells us how committed you are to each other. This week, we want you to observe your family interactions and decide what you really like—what you definitely do not want to change."

JoEllen sent the family home directly after presenting this communication from the consultation team, so as to maximize its effect.

CHAPTER 9

❀

The Systems Perspective

Before the second session with the Petersons, JoEllen reviewed her notes of their initial meeting. Writing case notes as required by the agency sometimes felt like a chore, but the information could be very helpful later. The presenting problem for the Peterson family, JoEllen recalled as she reviewed her notes, was Charlotte's behavior, which apparently began to deteriorate several months ago. The shoplifting, fortunately, was a one-time event; but the girl's subsequent neglect of her schoolwork had become chronic. Still, no one in the family had responded by seeking counseling for her. The precipitating event prompting the family to seek assistance seemed to be Charlotte's actually flunking her junior year in high school.

As an experienced social worker, JoEllen had counseled people for many years. In some of her positions, she had even interviewed whole families. Before she had been trained in family therapy, however, she probably would have worked with Charlotte alone in this situation. She would have determined a diagnosis for her, using the DSM-IV (the APA's *Diagnostic and Statistical Manual of Mental Disorders,* Fourth Edition), as a guide.[1] A probable diagnosis would have been "Adjustment Disorder with Disturbance of Conduct." JoEllen would have determined such a diagnosis for two reasons. First, diagnoses may be helpful for therapists because they may serve as guides for treatment. Second, however, there is an overriding practical reason: insurance companies insist on specific diagnoses of "mental disorders" or they will not pay for treatment.

JoEllen never liked to label her clients as having "mental disorders," so she usually tried to determine diagnoses that were least likely to brand them in damaging ways. (Diagnoses can damage in at least two ways. First, clients can respond by giving up or getting worse because of the negative impact of hearing the label; and second, employers sometimes discriminate against potential employees who have received treatment for "mental illness.") "Adjustment" diagnoses are relatively innocuous, as compared with a serious illness like schizophrenia, and are appropriate if clients seem to be responding to psychosocial stressors that occurred within the previous few months. JoEllen believed that, somehow, Charlotte's unusual behavior was related to Josh's improvement at school and at home—a change in family circumstances that had occurred just prior to the girl's shoplifting episode. Any change, even a change for the better, may serve as a stressor.

The therapist trainee felt fortunate that, in this situation, she didn't have to assign a diagnosis to anyone in this family. While family therapists often do have to determine diagnoses for particular members to help families obtain insurance money for treatment, the service provided by the institute was free. More than that, JoEllen's training as a family therapist now led her to question the usefulness of assigning diagnoses to individuals. When a therapist works with a family as a system, the disturbed behavior of one member that brings the family to therapy is frequently found to serve the system as a whole. Oddly enough, it seems to help keep the system from breaking apart. The "sick" or "bad" individual acts sick or bad on the family's behalf, so to speak, although nobody in the family consciously knows this.

Therapists who treat families as systems often use the term *identified client* to designate the person whom families bring in for treatment as "the problem." For the Petersons, Charlotte was clearly the identified client. But had Molly and Henry Peterson agreed to undertake family therapy when Josh was doing poorly in school, Josh would have been the identified client. Had family therapy been sought even earlier, when George was having trouble, he would have held that honor.

Most families who bring identified clients to therapy include other members whose behavior is normal (what is considered "normal" varies according to the family, of course), or even exemplary. Family members who consider their own behavior normal do not like to be viewed as part of a client system that needs help. That relates to the fact that an even larger system, American society, tends to label as "bad" and to blame people who are experiencing difficulties. Nobody wants to be labeled and blamed. So most families in trouble wait a long time to ask for help, hoping the problem will go away. Usually it takes some kind of crisis to bring a family to therapy, and whoever precipitated the crisis is perceived as "the problem." Families then want that problem person to be "fixed" as soon as possible.

Families may be quite right, in that the problem behavior of one member *may* initially have nothing to do with the behavior of others. Every situation is unique. Therapists must confer with family members with deep respect and listen carefully to their ideas and perceptions. Peer pressure may be the reason for a child's sudden lack of interest in school, for example, or even the all too common phenomenon of shunning—a practice in which a group of children ostracizes another child. A severe thunderstorm in the middle of the night can precipitate a bed-wetting habit; an automobile accident can trigger anxiety regarding leaving home.

However, family therapists believe that work with families as a whole can often be the most effective means of solving individual behavior problems, even when the source of difficulty lies beyond the family. That is because one person's problem affects every other member of a family. A child's bed-wetting habit, even if precipitated by a thunderstorm, may lead to sleep-deprived, cranky parents who argue with each other about what to do about the situation. Another child in the family may begin to "act like an angel" in compensation, while a third may misbehave to gain attention. The whole family, once various members perceive the relationships among different behaviors, can form a powerful team to reestablish healthy patterns.

In addition, a family member frequently demonstrates a problematic behavior that does indeed relate to problems within the family system itself. In such circumstances, "fixing" one member's problem rarely solves the problem for the family as a whole. The Petersons' own experience provides evidence for such a predicament. George, the older son, had already been "fixed" by Martin Meyers; he had graduated from high school and had developed into an independent adult. Josh had recently been "fixed" by Dr. Lang; he was performing as a successful seventh grade student and his work at home was much more acceptable to his father. But now, suddenly, Charlotte was in trouble.

Could something be going on in this family that required a troubled child for the family to survive as a whole? And if so, *how* might the child's disturbed behavior help stabilize the family as a system? After all, such an idea is contrary to common sense. Molly and Henry Peterson were both very unhappy with Charlotte's behavior and sincerely wanted it corrected. Josh was having difficulty understanding his older sister, and Charlotte, who previously had enjoyed the enviable position of being her father's favorite child, was now suffering the embarrassment of arrest, school failure, and ongoing punishment from both parents.

Despite the apparent contrast to common sense, many systems theorists do believe that disturbed behavior of a single family member can help preserve the family system as a whole. In such circumstances, these theorists believe, entire patterns of relationships within the family need to be changed, not just the behavior of the identified client. Neither disturbed individuals nor the family as a whole should be blamed as "bad" or "sick," however. Such labeling is counterproductive and prevents families from seeking assistance and accepting the work of conjoint problem solving.

Engaging families in therapy can be difficult because of the unfortunate but realistic fear of being viewed by the community as deficient in some way. Parents especially fear being blamed for their children's problems. However, once a family does agree to accept the challenge, the family system itself will resist change vigorously, even if change would help its troubled individual members. Why? The answer to this question is both complex and surprisingly simple. It involves the fact that although life as usual may be difficult, at least it is familiar. Family life as a whole has achieved some kind of balance or steady state, even if unhealthy for a particular member of the family. The family as a system wants to maintain the balance or steady state because members believe at some level that that is their ticket to survival.

To better understand why family therapists believe that interactions among family members as a whole may need modification, even if only one member seems to be having a problem, it will be helpful to examine certain major concepts from systems theory. These concepts are introduced here not to attempt a definitive presentation but simply to provide a brief background for better understanding of the therapeutic techniques that student JoEllen Madsen struggles to master in her training as a family therapist.

General systems theory was originally developed by a biologist, Ludwig von Bertalanffy, who was deeply interested in the complex relationships between living organisms and their environments. Bertalanffy developed systems theory to help describe these complex relationships. The following is a summary of Bertalanffy's definition of a system:

> *Any entity maintained by the mutual interaction of its parts, from atom to cosmos, and including such mundane examples as telephone, postal and rapid transit systems. A Bertalanffian system can be physical like a television set, biological like a cocker spaniel, psychological like a personality, sociological like a labor union, or symbolic, like a set of laws.*[2]

As defined by Webster's *New World Dictionary*, a system is "a set or arrangement of things so related or connected as to form a unity or organic whole."[3] Defined more simply, for the purpose of this chapter, a system is a whole consisting of interacting parts. These parts are so interrelated that a change in any one part affects all the others.

Let us consider, as an example, a biological system: the human body. The human body is composed of many interrelated, interacting parts including the skeleton, muscles, blood, and so forth. What happens when one of these parts is disturbed in some way—say a bone in the skeleton is broken? Every other part of the system is affected. Muscles tighten, and blood circulation increases in the area of the broken bone. Nerves carry impulses to the brain that are translated as pain, and the pain in turn influences every other part of the body. The vocal cords may contract in response, for example, and the body utters a cry.

Another important characteristic of a system is that the whole is greater than the sum of its parts. Consider the human body once more. Obviously the body is made up of many interacting parts. The combination of all the myriad parts somehow exceeds the whole—at least, if the body is alive. Anyone who has ever witnessed a living person slip into death, though peacefully during sleep, will recognize that something fundamental has changed. The living biological system was clearly more than exactly the same collection of parts after death.

Each of the major parts of the system called the human body can themselves be considered systems: skeletal system, muscle system, blood system, nervous system, for example. These smaller systems are themselves made up of even smaller systems: organs, molecules, atoms, particles of atoms. Sometimes smaller systems within larger systems are called subsystems. What is considered a system or a subsystem depends only on where the observer decides to focus attention. The important concept to keep in mind with respect to systems theory is that of interrelationships: change in one part of a system affects all the others in some way. Smaller systems that are parts of larger systems in turn affect each another and the larger system as a whole.

The concept of larger systems takes us to the notion of *environment*. As described above, the systems approach examines the interactions between living organisms and their environments. What is an environment? Again, going to *Webster's*, an environment is "all the conditions, circumstances, and influences surrounding, and affecting the development of, an organism or group of organisms."[4] An environment, then, is simply a larger system, or suprasystem, surrounding a multitude of smaller systems or subsystems.

According to Alex Gitterman and Carel Germain, environments may be physical or social in nature: "The physical environment includes both natural and manmade structures and objects, and time and space. The social environment, which people have created and to which individuals must then adapt, includes institutions, organizations, and social networks."[5]

Ecologists have been working hard for the past two decades or more to demonstrate to the people of Earth that all the parts of the world are interrelated—in other words, that Earth itself is one large system. It is surrounded by even larger systems or environments, including the solar system and beyond through the universe. Though the physical and social environments can be distinguished conceptually, these aspects of environment themselves interact. For example, what people do with aerosol cans in their bathrooms, largely a social byproduct of advertising, physically affects the ozone layer of Earth's atmosphere, which in turn affects the cancer rates of living populations. What and how we eat, largely influenced by social custom, affects the condition of the forests of the world, which in turn affects the air we breathe, which then affects our health and our longevity. What we burn in our gas tanks, a byproduct of technology developed through human experimentation and ingenuity and encouraged by social custom, affects the air we breathe and ultimately our physical health.

To repeat, Earth itself is one large system, consisting of interacting parts (or subsystems) so interrelated that a change in one part affects all the others. It is itself part of a larger suprasystem called the solar system. The solar system is part of an even larger suprasystem known as the universe, too immense even to imagine. Beyond that, no one knows.

The potentially infinite numbers of parts and interactions of parts within systems makes it very difficult, if not impossible, to predict all possible effects. According to Margaret Wheatley,

> *scientists now emphasize the very small differences at the beginning of a system's evolution that make prediction impossible. . . . Edward Lorenz, a meteorologist, first drew modern-day attention to this with his "butterfly effect." . . . Does the flap of a butterfly wing in Tokyo, Lorenz queried, affect a tornado in Texas (or a thunderstorm in New York)? Though unfortunate for the future of accurate weather prediction, his answer was "yes."*[6]

How do the concepts of general systems theory pertain to working with families? As poetic as the idea of the butterfly's wing affecting the weather may be, this particular type of interactional effect is too tiny for practical use in family therapy! However, the concept of one small part of a system affecting the system as a whole is entirely applicable to family work. The cry of a small child at night will affect every family member who hears it, for example. Even the sleeping ones may incorporate the cry into their dreams in some way. Angry voices penetrating bedroom doors will leave their mark as well. The Peterson children often heard such angry voices.

Systems theory can help therapists remember to pay attention to interactional effects among parts of a system, but it cannot help much in the area of prediction. Just *how* will a given child react to angry parental voices, for example? And will another child respond the same way? Systems theory simply cannot supply answers to questions asking for predictions such as these. Therapists must approach each family with humility, constantly questioning, observing, and remaining open to new information and points of view.

Even the most experienced therapist will never fully understand how a family functions or how various factors will interact to contribute to whether therapeutic interventions succeed or fail. Myriad unknown factors constantly interweave and create unexpected effects. Causality, once believed to be linear ("A causes B") is now perceived to be more circular (A affects B which affects C which in turn affects A). Imagine circular causation in three dimensions and you have something like global interactional affects. Then recognize that a fourth dimension, time, interacts and has its affects as well.

Wheatley writes: "The world is far more sensitive than we ever thought. . . . In complex ways that no model will ever capture, the system feeds back on itself, enfolding all that has happened, magnifying slight variances, encoding it in the system's memory—and prohibiting prediction, ever."[7] Hence, systems theory, which helps explain how systems remain stable over long periods of time, also—as modified by chaos theory— helps explain the inevitability of unpredictability and change.

Even though systems effects are basically unpredictable because of myriad interactions of parts that can never be fully known, the family therapist can take heart at the knowledge that his or her efforts will make a difference, even with a family whose situation appears hopeless. The therapist, even as a lone individual, will affect the system in some way through presence alone because the therapist introduces at least a slight change in a particular family's condition. Effects of the therapist's action that may seem very slight in the beginning can amplify into substantial differences (hopefully positive!) in family functioning.

Humans are biological organisms, so they are part of the physical environment just as the butterfly, Earth, and the stars are. But people are also very much parts of their social environments. Systems concepts are as applicable to social environments as to physical environments. The social environment is also made up of systems of various sizes. Each particular social system may be visualized as surrounded and enclosed to some degree by larger systems. For example, the individual is part of a larger nuclear family system, which in turn is part of an even larger extended family system including grandparents, aunts, uncles, and often stepparents, step-grandparents, and so on. The extended family itself is part of a larger community system such as a village, city, or town, which is part of an even larger county, state, nation, and so on.

Since systems emerge in various sizes and shapes, it is necessary to find a way to distinguish particular systems so that they can be examined and discussed. Systems theorists have developed the concept of *boundary* to delineate a specific system. If the system in question is a single individual, one can easily picture its boundary; the boundary can be described as the individual's skin. But what about the boundary of a system like a family? That boundary is more abstract—a concept. To make the concept more real, a system's boundary can be visualized as a closed circle drawn around and enclosing the assorted parts of the selected system.[8] For example, a circle drawn on paper could represent the boundary of the Peterson family, within which the names of the various family members can be written, identifying them as members of that particular system.

One characteristic of a boundary is that the exchange of energy within the circle it encloses must normally be greater than that exchanged across the boundary. One can't simply draw a circle at random and label it a boundary. A circle inscribed around a family such as the Petersons is a true boundary because the energy exchanged within it—such as food, conversation, affection—is normally greater than that exchanged with outsiders.

A healthy system needs *semipermeable boundaries.* In other words, a system must exchange a certain amount of energy across its boundaries in order to meet its needs. Today, for example, the family system usually must obtain supplies of money from outside systems (such as from jobs, social security) to purchase provisions necessary to keep members fed and clothed. Families usually also must obtain medical care from other systems, and education, religious services, and the like. Even the wealthiest, most self-sufficient families depend on other systems, like banks and hospitals, for survival.

Systems boundaries can be more or less permeable or impermeable. A system is referred to as an *open system* if its boundary is relatively permeable; it is referred to as a *closed system* if its boundary is relatively impermeable. Systems with closed boundaries tend toward entropy, or disorder and dissolution. To understand this concept, consider the single human biological system. If the "boundary" of the human body becomes closed to outside resources such as air, water, or food, the body will die. There is no doubt about that. On a more abstract level, imagine a family so closed it refuses to allow family members to work outside the home or to purchase supplies from the outside community. For how long can such a family survive? What will happen when it runs out of food, or fails to pay the rent or mortgage or even the taxes?

No system can maintain itself without resources from beyond its boundaries. On the other hand, a system that is entirely open will not survive very long either. If the boundaries of a particular system are too permeable, the system will lose its special purpose and become no more than a collection of individuals. As an example, imagine the famous Mormon Tabernacle Choir deciding to take in anyone who wanted to be a member, regardless of ability to sing on key. The beautiful music for which it is so famous would soon exist no more, and many talented members would leave.

Every system has a *purpose,* or *goal,* toward which it is always moving. Goals vary with the system (for example, a choir's goal is to make music), but the fundamental goal of every system is maintaining its own survival. Words and phrases prevalent in common speech reflect this concept intuitively: people speak of the "survival instinct," the "will to live," the "life force." Almost everyone has had the experience of sudden and unexpected danger to life or limb, in which some part of the person has reacted so fast and so correctly to maintain life that the individual was later amazed. One's biological system seems to be prewired to maintain its own survival. Larger systems also manifest this basic goal of survival.

In addition to systems boundaries and systems goals, another concept important to systems theory is tension. *Tension* is considered to be characteristic of systems, an inherent condition. As various parts of a system interact, tension is produced, so that ongoing changes induce ongoing responses. In systems theory, tension is considered neither positive nor negative; it is simply a given.

Systems theorists view tension quite differently than psychoanalysts of the Freudian school do. Freud postulated that certain biological drives or tensions (especially sex and aggression) push every individual toward relieving tension. The ultimate goal of the individual organism from the Freudian point of view is satiation or quiescence of troubling biological drives, or a complete cessation of tension.

Satiation or quiescence is not the end goal of organisms according to systems theory; that goal, as noted above, is survival. Tension is necessary for systems to adapt to their environments and therefore to survive. The adaptations that tension helps create may be constructive or destructive, but the tension itself is a given; it is always there.

How tension acts to assist systems to adapt can be difficult to conceive. One way to think about effects of tension, from a systems viewpoint, is to imagine various parts of a system linked together with rubber bands. If you pull hard on one part of the linked system, that part will move, of course, but the rubber bands joining it to other parts must also stretch. Some bits of rubber band will stretch more than others, depending on their position with respect to the part being pulled. Various parts of the system will begin to bounce and bob in response to the tension in the stretched rubber bands. Whatever the response of any particular part, various adaptive movements will occur in every other.

Virginia Satir, a social worker (now deceased) who became famous for her innovations in family therapy, sometimes actually tied members of a family together with ropes to demonstrate how people affect one another. Then, for example, she would instruct a rebellious teen to physically move away from the family. Everyone in the family would then clearly feel the tension in the ropes and sense the necessity to shift their own positions to adapt to the new force.[9]

Another important concept in systems theory is that of *feedback.* Since all systems have goals, the major common goal being survival, systems need sources of information to track their progress. Are they moving toward attainment of their goals or not? Feedback is information to the system about goal achievement. If feedback informs a system that it is moving toward its goals, the system will tend to do more of whatever it is already doing. This type of feedback is known as positive feedback. If, on the other hand, the system is moving away from its goals, the feedback that so informs the system will be self-correcting, or negative. The system will then attempt to modify its behavior so that it can begin to achieve its goals again.

Webster's defines *feedback* as "a process in which the factors that produce a result are themselves modified, corrected, strengthened, etc., by that result."[10] Compton and Galaway offer the following more complicated definition: feedback is "a communications network which produces action in response to an input of information and includes results of its own action in the new information by which it modifies its subsequent behavior."[11]

The feedback process with respect to human systems can be very complex. Someone or something or some combination of persons and things must transmit (send) the feedback. Someone must receive the information that is being transmitted and assign it meaning and importance. The information must then be organized and evaluated according to its perceived importance with respect to goal attainment. Then, if the feedback is perceived to call for modifications in behavior, someone or something must take charge and change behavior in the direction of goal attainment. Change in the direction of goal attainment requires decisions and selection among available options.

Feedback is often conceived to occur in the context of a "feedback loop." In other words, information is encoded and sent by a transmitter to a receiver, which then sends feedback to the transmitter. Breakdowns in a feedback loop (transmitter to receiver and back again) are a constant hazard. For example, once transmitted, feedback calling for modifications in a system's behavior can be misperceived or misinterpreted according to the characteristics of the receiver. Feedback may be sent in a language unfamiliar to the receiver, for example. The receiver, for that matter, may be deaf or blind! Or the receiver may not wish to receive the feedback. How many times have people griped, "George (Georgia) only hears what he (she) *wants* to hear!"

Feedback loops within families may break down, as they may in any system. In colloquial language, such breakdowns are known as *miscommunication.* Every family experiences miscommunication from time to time. A strong, healthy family system can survive many an incident of miscommunication, just as it can any other accident or problem. The forces tying the various parts of the family system together (the most basic force being desire for survival) are strong enough to withstand many minor problems. But when miscommunication grows into a communication breakdown, the survival of the family as a whole becomes at risk. Often families wait this long before asking for help, if they ask even then.

Before returning to the Peterson family, there is another concept from systems theory that is important for the family therapist to consider. That is the concept of *steady state,* or dynamic equilibrium. A certain stability or balance is required for a system to maintain itself, to achieve its basic goal of survival as a unique whole. According to systems theory, all systems strive to maintain the steady state in order to survive as a unique entity. At one time the term commonly used to describe the steady state was *homeostasis.* Yet the term *homeostasis* implies that a given system stays just the same forever, regulated internally by some kind of control mechanism analogous to a thermostat in a home that keeps the temperature always at 70°F.

But systems are not static. As we have discussed before, their boundaries must remain open for the systems to survive. Information and resources constantly cross systems boundaries, so that while a given system maintains a unique identity fundamental to the steady state, it is also changing from day to day. For example, Molly Peterson is a system with a unique identity. She can be recognized as Molly Peterson today, tomorrow, next week, and many years from now. But she will not be quite the same Molly as she moves through her life span. And Molly in her mid-forties isn't much at all like Molly was as an infant or will be as an old woman.

Systems as wholes gradually change, so that a concept of dynamic equilibrium or steady state is more appropriate than homeostasis.[12] Systems must change, in fact, in order to adapt and survive. Families, for example, must adapt to ongoing changes in their children's physical maturation. Teenagers require very different kinds of care than infants do. If a family is to survive, parenting techniques must change, and spouses must also change their behavior toward one another, depending on ages of the children, differing work schedules, and so forth.

And despite the usual steady state that systems maintain for survival purposes, very small deviations within a system or in the wider environment can lead to unexpected, unpredictable changes in surprisingly short periods of time, as mentioned earlier. That is because a change in one part of a system reverberates throughout and can be amplified in unexpected ways through feedback mechanisms. Unpredictability, of course, makes life much more interesting!

Now let us return to JoEllen Madsen, family therapy trainee, as she reviews her first session with the Peterson family. JoEllen's notes remind her that the Petersons came to the Family Therapy Training Institute with a specific presenting problem: Charlotte's misbehavior. The precipitating event bringing the family to therapy was the girl's recent failure in school.

Without systems theory to guide intervention in a situation like this, many therapists would probably proceed to counsel with Charlotte alone. However, systems theory guides its adherents to suspect that Charlotte's family as a whole is experiencing difficulty, that something may be threatening its basic systems goal of survival.

In the experience of many systems-oriented therapists, when the survival of a family is in jeopardy, children pick up on the clues and adapt their behavior in an attempt to keep the system together. Anger between parents, for example, often frightens children. They may begin to worry about what will happen if Mommy and Daddy get a divorce. Their fear is not unwarranted, because if Mommy and Daddy break apart, the family as a whole breaks apart also. The world as the children have known it comes to an end. This is a cataclysmic event for children, who are vulnerable and unable to survive on their own.

As tension increases in a family, various parts of the system may respond in different ways. Some children may adapt by misbehaving, sometimes at home, sometimes elsewhere, perhaps at school. Other children may withdraw or, conversely, behave like angels to avoid tilting any further what feels like too shaky a wagon. Systems theory cannot predict how various members of a system in jeopardy will actually behave; it can only predict that adaptive behavior will occur.

Can children's misbehavior help a family system survive? On first consideration, such a hypothesis seems ludicrous. Misbehavior stresses the family further. Parents become increasingly upset and often bring their children in for therapy at this point.

However, the concepts of feedback and feedback loops can provide interesting evidence in support of such an idea. Imagine that a child misbehaves by accident, responding almost at random to an overload of tension between the parents. The child then notices (on some level, conscious or unconscious) that Mommy and Daddy begin to talk with each other about what to do. Their angry tones become directed at the child rather than at each other. Perhaps on an unconscious level, that child might then "decide" to misbehave again. The bad behavior results in Mommy and Daddy functioning together as a team, so the family as a whole doesn't feel so much like it might break apart.

Misbehavior unfortunately can grow worse and worse, as a child becomes part of a positive feedback loop: misbehavior prompts Mommy and Daddy to talk more with each other, so that survival of the family system seems to be enhanced. Positive feedback leads to more misbehavior, which prompts Mommy and Daddy to talk with each other again. Their original anger at each other becomes more and more diverted toward the child. The parents remain together, the family is "saved" as an intact system, but at immense cost to the child, who is then ironically blamed by the parents as the cause of all their troubles.

JoEllen's notes reminded her that all three of the Peterson children had had trouble in school and at home. This provided evidence for her that more was going on for these children than the serial eruption of three different intrapsychic personal pathologies. Was first one Peterson child and then the other misbehaving to distract the parents from a problem in their own relationship? After all, spousal unhappiness in a nuclear family system threatens the survival of that system. JoEllen strongly suspected that Molly and Henry Peterson's marriage was in trouble. That would be her initial working hypothesis. She would have to check it out.

CHAPTER 10

Marital Distress

As the time approached for the Peterson family's evening session at the Family Therapy Training Institute, the crew behind the one-way mirror fiddled anxiously with the buttons on the video machine. JoEllen Madsen stood in the middle of the therapy office facing the mirror, talking toward the invisible crew behind it.

"Testing, testing," she said, "tell me, is the mechanical monster working tonight?" She grinned foolishly as she searched for something more original to say.

The trainees at the institute were going through their routine evening testing of the sound and video equipment that connected the therapy room with the observation room. Everything, to everyone's dismay, was down. No image appeared on the TV screen, and no sound penetrated the mirror. There was a sense of minor panic in the tiny viewing room as each member of the consultation team tried to get the machinery working—people plugged and unplugged electrical cords, jiggled wires at the back of the video equipment, and consulted with each other in urgent whispers.

So began a typical evening for the team. At last, someone made some brilliant technical move and JoEllen's voice blasted into the space behind the mirror. At the same time, her image sprang onto the video screen. There was a collective cheer. The team leader turned the sound down, people began to laugh, and one of the trainees called JoEllen on the telephone to let her know all was ready. Now the only element missing was the Peterson family. Late again.

Another ring on the telephone. This time it was the receptionist calling JoEllen: "Your clients are here, sitting in the waiting room."

"Thank you, Kelly. How many family members have arrived?"

"Two parents and two kids."

"That's the right number. I'll be down in a minute."

No matter how many times JoEllen experienced this routine, she felt a sense of drama. Would the video equipment work this evening? Would the team members arrive on time? Would the family members keep their appointment? A sense of uncertainty lingered right up until the final phone call announcing the arrival of the clients. Then curiosity and anticipation would take over. What would happen this evening? One could imagine, but never fully predict. Surprises were the name of the game in family therapy. Every session was different.

Some family therapists refuse to meet with a family unless all members are present. The theory behind such a policy derives from the systems perspective: if a family comprises a system, then the entire family should be seen together. The Family Therapy Training Institute worked according to such an idea when first established. However, practical matters got in the way of this "purist" position.

The practical matters that initially intervened were simple. Often only the mother was willing to accompany her child, for whom she was usually the one to seek help. Should mother and child be denied service if father refused to participate? At first the answer was yes, supported by the belief that if the agency was firm in its position, father would come eventually. In many cases, he did, but certainly not always. Staff became concerned about mothers and children seeking service who were then denied. On humane rather than theoretical grounds, the policy was changed. Staff were urged to encourage entire families to come, starting with the secretary who scheduled appointments. But whoever came would be seen.

Later, given experience dealing with parts of families *as* parts of families and not as detached individuals, staff learned that often missing parts would show up in fairly short order. Perhaps systems theory could have helped therapists predict such a response. After all, whole systems not only affect their individual parts, but parts affect each other and the whole as well. If the repeated requests of mother and child didn't reel father into counseling, for example, sometimes their changed behavior at home did the job. New assertive behavior on the part of a wife may bring a husband in to complain!

This evening, the Peterson family was indeed late, but only by a few minutes. JoEllen viewed this as an auspicious sign. As she led the family members up the stairs toward the training office, she couldn't help noticing a different air among them. They seemed more relaxed this evening. Henry even told JoEllen a few jokes as they walked down the long hallway that overlooked the atrium. They were pretty good jokes, too. The trainee made a mental note to try to remember them. Again, she felt herself warming to the man.

Molly walked quietly behind Henry and JoEllen. The children ran ahead. JoEllen could hear them laughing in the therapy room. When she reached the office, they were making funny faces into the mirror. Charlotte looked almost as young as Josh as she scrunched up her face and stuck out her tongue, swiveling her shapely hips toward her reflection.

Family members sat down in the same chairs they had chosen the week before, pulling them into the same positions. Charlotte sat between her parents and Josh sat to the right of his father, looking toward his mother and into the mirror. JoEllen closed the office door and seated herself in the last remaining chair, next to the door, facing the mirror at a slight angle.

"Well, how is everyone tonight?" the trainee began.

Everyone smiled back and said they were fine.

"That's not obligatory," JoEllen teased. "I mean, one of the nice things about therapy is that it's different from a social get-together. In the typical social get-together, you know you're supposed to say, 'fine, thanks,' when somebody asks how you are. In a therapy session, you can tell the truth. So, how is everybody tonight? Let's start with you, Molly." JoEllen decided to begin with Molly because so far the mother had been quietest in the group tonight.

"Oh, I'm fine—really," Molly replied. "I think everyone's feeling fine tonight, in fact."

"That's good news," JoEllen replied. "In fact, I've noticed everybody seems to be in a pretty good mood this evening. Am I right?"

"Yes," Molly replied. "We've had a good week, I'd say. I think we probably don't need family therapy after all."

Molly's words about not needing counseling did not surprise JoEllen. They indicated that the normal "resistance" to therapy was alive and well in the family. Therapy is work, its outcome is uncertain, and it's not something the average family wants to undertake unless its current pain is unbearable. And the systems concept of steady state permits a therapist to predict that any system will resist change, whether in pain or not.

Given her systems training, JoEllen decided to "go with the resistance." This concept guides a therapist to identify, acknowledge, explore, even encourage whatever factors are holding a client back from fully engaging in the change process. After all, perhaps the family does not need to change after all. Perhaps its "steady state" is good enough. No system is perfect. Determining whether change is necessary is an important task of the family therapist. And oddly, a therapist's acceptance of a family's resistance to change can help them transcend it.

"Oh," JoEllen replied. "So you've had such a good week you have decided you may not need to come to counseling."

"That's right," Molly replied.

"Tell me more about that. Specifically, what have you identified that you like about the family just as it is? That was your homework from the team last week, if I remember correctly—to decide what you like about your family, what you do not want to change."

Molly's face, which had appeared rather composed this evening, suddenly underwent a dramatic change. Her dark eyes lit up, and her shapely lips spread into a wide smile. The woman's voice was animated, and she answered in an ardent tone.

"Oh, we do have fun together. This family has more fun together in a year than most families have in a lifetime. We would never want to change that. That's what we talked about all week."

Now JoEllen was surprised! Fun? This family where each child took turns failing in school, where the father was perceived as angry, judgmental, and often distant, where children said they often heard the voices of their parents quarrelling late into the night? Fun?

"What kind of fun do you have together, Molly?" The trainee tried to keep her voice tone matter-of-fact, but some of her surprise slipped through anyway.

"Oh, up until now I guess we've only told you the bad things," replied Molly, picking up on JoEllen's surprise. "But really, this family has a very good life together. We have lots of friends who think Henry and I are the ideal couple. We do a lot of things with wonderful people who look at us as the center of their group. We go biking, hiking, camping, dancing—all sorts of things together to have fun. We make a lot of people happy." Molly's words tumbled out fast.

"You say you do a lot of things that are fun and make many people happy. Do these things make you happy too, Molly?"

"Of course they do. That's what I just told you. WE ALL HAVE F-U-U-U-N." Molly accented each of her words and dragged out the last one until it seemed to have about six syllables. Her sincerity was evident and her smile enthusiastic and proud.

JoEllen smiled back and responded to Molly that having fun certainly was important. A vague uneasiness, though, led her to pause for a moment. The telephone rang.

"This may be important, Molly," said Kurt. "There may be more to this than meets the eye. Stick with it. Talk it over with Henry and the kids."

"It?" asked JoEllen. She didn't feel comfortable saying very much to the team in front of her clients, so she abbreviated her words.

"This group stuff she's calling *fun,*" said Kurt. "What's fun for one person may not be fun for another. Check it out."

"But Molly just said it *was* fun, for all of them." Now JoEllen was getting resistant herself, in her nagging uneasiness.

"You're right, JoEllen, she did," Kurt responded sharply. "The team thinks there's more to it, however. Talk to Henry. Find out specifically what he likes about the group activities."

JoEllen hung up the telephone and thought for a moment. Sometimes she shared the team's directives with her clients, and sometimes she didn't. This seemed to be a time when frankness was the most appropriate course of action. She turned to the husband.

"Henry," she said, "Molly has been telling me about how much fun your family has, doing lots of different things together with a group of people. The team wants to know what you in particular like about this group and its activities."

Henry flashed JoEllen a rakish smile, and then waved into the mirror as if enjoying the spotlight. He returned his attention to the trainee. His handsome blue eyes gazed at JoEllen warmly and long. His features arranged themselves in an expression of excellent humor. He slicked his graying blond hair back with both hands.

"Oh, I enjoy being with other people very much," the man crooned. "People are important to me. I teach ballroom dancing two, sometimes three nights a week, you know. I meet a lot of people that way. I invite the ones I like best home and we all become good friends. We do a lot together, like Molly said. Biking, hiking, you name it."

"So you are the person in the family who brings the group of people together socially, Henry?"

"That's for sure." For a moment Henry's face looked a little less pleasant. "Molly complains about it sometimes, but she really likes to be part of a group as much as I do. Without it, she'd be lonely."

JoEllen turned to Molly. "Is that so, Molly?"

"Well," Molly replied, "partly. I can certainly make friends on my own, but I do enjoy many of the people Henry brings home."

Henry spoke again. "A lot of folks we know look at our place as a second home. Molly cooks supper for whole bunches of people in the summer, when she isn't working. It's fun for her. And you know," Henry said, leaning forward dramatically, his eyes so intensely blue and fixed upon JoEllen's that her thinking process almost stopped, "we have about six dimes taped to our refrigerator. Can you guess what they're for?"

"Ah, no . . . I can't say as I—"

"Would you like to know?"

"Well . . . er . . . I, ah . . ."

"We've introduced several couples who have gotten married!" Henry announced proudly. "That's what the dimes are for! It's like tossing coins into a wishing well, only we tape them to our refrigerator instead. We do it for our friends who are looking for somebody to marry—mostly women looking for husbands, of course."

As Molly listened, fascinated, Henry leaned toward her even further, his voice tone taking on a conspiratorial air.

"JOELLEN!" He whispered intensely, "YOU SHOULD VISIT US! YOU SHOULD TAPE A DIME TO OUR REFRIGERATOR TOO! IT'S WORKED FOR A LOT OF PEOPLE!"

JoEllen felt herself blush with embarrassment. Her left hand throbbed with a sudden awareness of its emptiness, devoid of the wedding ring she had worn for so many years. She felt vulnerable, exposed. The memory of the rejection she had experienced with her husband blasted back into her psyche, nearly paralyzing her.

Another example of the wounded healer—wounded, *would-be* healer, she reminded herself wryly, recognizing on some level that she was stuck. She felt as if she were suspended somewhere in space. She wished the telephone would ring.

Henry's blue eyes continued to pour into JoEllen's gray ones invitingly, his voice rich and smooth as silk. His smile was engaging, hypnotic.

"You'd probably like doing other things with our group, too. Do you know how to dance? I can give you a special rate for lessons . . ."

The man looked so alluring, his voice sounded so hearty and warm. He was obviously so interested in JoEllen's well-being. As Henry leaned toward JoEllen, his eyes peered deeply into hers. The woman felt drawn to the man once more, as she had when he began telling jokes in the hallway on the way to the office. She found herself smiling back, confused, not in control. She ran one hand through her long brown hair and smoothed her skirt repeatedly with the other, grinning foolishly. Her mind felt muddled, and her heart was beginning to pound.

JoEllen's professional training raced to partial rescue. Forming social relationships with clients outside of the therapy office was not ethical behavior. JoEllen knew that absolutely. The fact had been instilled in her as an undergraduate when she first studied the social work code of ethics developed by the National Association of Social Workers. Dual relationships with clients were too likely to interfere with the objectivity required for professional intervention.

Still, the trainee as a person was often lonely, especially during the long, quiet hours in the evening. JoEllen couldn't help feeling drawn to the idea of belonging to a congenial group of people talking around the dinner table on a lovely summer evening, Henry paying rapt attention only to her. . . . JoEllen's mind began to wander as if in a dream. She caught hold of herself, shocked, pulled herself back into the therapy room with effort.

"Henry—I'd like to Henry, really I would, but—" she fumbled.

Mercifully, the telephone rang.

"JoEllen." It was Kurt, his voice sounding urgent.

"Yes?" she responded, a little breathlessly.

"What are you feeling *right now?*"

JoEllen felt herself gasp, redden. She opened her mouth as if to speak but made no sound. She wasn't sure exactly how she felt, but she certainly wouldn't want Henry or anyone else in the room to hear what she *thought* she felt.

"No need to tell me," said Kurt on the telephone. "Just take time to tell yourself. Remember, clients often act toward their therapists in the same ways that they act toward others in their life. Their actions are aimed to produce particular responses, although usually that aim is unconscious, outside awareness. What you are feeling right now is probably what most women who interact with Henry Peterson feel. Pay attention."

There was a pause, while JoEllen silently assessed her emotions: she felt vulnerable, exposed, and attracted to Henry all at once. *Attracted?*

"He's seducing you," Kurt said bluntly over the wire. "He's inducting you into his normal operating system with women he likes. Do what you need to do as Henry's therapist, and then check what's happening with Molly." There was a click as the team leader hung up.

JoEllen took a deep breath to compose herself. When she spoke again, however, she was still rattled.

"Henry," she said, trying to sound firm but sounding stilted instead, "thank you very much for your concern about me. You have obviously noticed that I am single. In fact, I am divorced. But I also need to tell you that we are taught in our training program not to mix business with pleasure. So I must decline your offer."

"I don't see why," Henry smiled persuasively, sounding like the salesman he was. "We probably won't be in counseling with you after tonight. I want you to feel free to visit us anytime, JoEllen. You'll have fun, I guarantee it. We'll all be happy to see you again."

"Thank you, Henry—and no, that wouldn't be appropriate behavior for me. We'll talk more about it later if we need to. But right now, I want to talk with Molly."

Here, JoEllen made a choice. She could have chosen to work on her relationship with Henry right then, the feelings his messages seemed geared to elicit, her responses, and how to utilize them for a therapeutic purpose. At some point certainly, Henry's seductive behavior would have to be confronted. But JoEllen decided to explore instead the feelings Henry's behavior might be eliciting in Molly. This choice was reasonable, particularly as JoEllen had been guided to do so by the team. It's also possible that the trainee took the easy way out, since she was still very flustered!

"Molly," JoEllen said rather abruptly, "how are you feeling right now?"

Molly seemed to have disappeared deep inside herself while Henry made his pitch to the trainee. As JoEllen turned to face this attractive wife, mother, and teacher, the woman looked a million miles away, her eyes focused vacantly somewhere out of sight, her expression remote.

Gradually, however, Molly's features assumed their familiar smooth, waxen semi-smile.

"Why, just fine, of course," the woman replied in a cordial, correct social tone.

JoEllen was not surprised at Molly's response, although she didn't believe the words for a moment. On a flash of intuition she turned to the daughter.

"Do you believe your mother, Charlotte?"

Charlotte rolled her eyes and made a face into the mirror. She turned to look at JoEllen and made another face, lifting her eyebrows and squeezing her mouth into a tight little bunch of muscles and lines.

"Charlotte?"

"What?" The lips unbunched, curled downward into a pout. The eyebrows fell back down also, drew low over the eyes. Charlotte looked much younger than 16 right then.

"What do you think your mother is feeling?"

"How should I know?"

"Take a guess."

Charlotte shrugged, her facial features settled into a more normal position, and she sighed, "Mom isn't happy, that's for sure."

"What makes you think she isn't happy?"

"She gets really mad at home about this stuff."

"Tell me about the stuff that makes your mother mad at home."

"Dad!" Charlotte cried. "What Dad does!"

"What does your father do that makes your mother mad?"

Silence. JoEllen probed again.

"Tell me what your father does that makes your mother mad sometimes, Charlotte."

"He flirts." The words were whispered.

"Like he was flirting with me a few minutes ago?"

"Yes." Barely audible. Then, "That's why I didn't want to go to dancing class with him anymore."

"That's why you didn't want to go to dancing class with your father?" JoEllen was taken aback, not expecting this information. Her inflection invited Charlotte to say more.

"Yes. The night I got caught shoplifting, Dad asked me to go to dancing class with him again. But I knew if I went I'd have to watch him and that other lady."

"You mean you'd have to watch your father flirt with some other lady?"

Very softly: "Yes."

"Dad flirts all the time!" This came unexpectedly, almost in a shout, from Josh. The boy glared at his father for a brief moment, then turned to look into the mirror and shook his fist. "He leaves Mom alone! That makes her sad!"

"With whom does your father flirt, Josh?"

"Well, with you, right then."

"How did you feel when that happened?"

"MAD!" Josh shouted.

"I'm sorry about that, Josh," JoEllen said sincerely, "because what just happened here in the office between your father and me made you unhappy and mad. You and Charlotte are brave to talk about it. Flirting between your father and a woman like myself who is not your mother can be upsetting. You said flirting makes you mad. How do you think it makes your mother feel?

"VERY SAD! AND MAD!"

"Just a minute!" Henry Peterson broke in, his voice tone smooth as honey and his facial features arranged to appear utterly reasonable. "There is absolutely nothing wrong with a little flirting. Flirting is the way a man lets a woman know he thinks she's attractive. It's a compliment. It makes everybody feel good."

"Everybody?"

"Everybody. You heard Molly just now. She said she was fine. She knows she's my primary relationship, that I'd never leave her. That's what's important to her. Believe me, Molly knows I put our marriage first."

"Let's check that out with your wife," JoEllen said. "Molly, you've heard Charlotte say that Henry flirts with other women. He just flirted with me. Josh says the flirting makes him mad. He thinks it makes you sad and mad. But Henry says it isn't a problem for you. What do you say?"

Molly's face was a study in mixed responses, her lips still curved in smile, her jaw muscles clenched so that a little muscle quivered in her neck. She didn't answer. JoEllen could see the woman was struggling. She decided to give her time.

Seconds passed, tension mounted. JoEllen fought the desire to fill the silence with sound, any sound. Charlotte, seated between her parents, leaned her shoulders slightly toward her mother and sighed. She leaned toward her father then, and aimed an appeasing little smile at him. Then she examined her shapely finger nails, intently. Josh stared at his toes, wiggling them at the end of his sneakers, and made faces at the mirror.

"You see," Henry said loudly, "Molly agrees with me."

"I haven't heard anything from Molly yet," JoEllen said in a stern tone. "Henry, please wait for your wife to speak. It's her turn."

More seconds passed. The tension in the room became palpable. And then Molly spoke. Her voice tone had a rawness to it now. Her words were abrupt, the content so changed they came as a shock to JoEllen even after Henry's flirtatious behavior.

"I've often thought of leaving," the woman said. Her words hung in the air. JoEllen nodded gravely, waiting for more. Then Molly continued.

"But I have to think of the kids. Everything would be OK if Henry would just stop flirting in front of me and the kids, I think . . . it's so embarrassing." She stopped, caught her breath, then continued in a nearly frantic tone, "But we have SO MUCH FUN!"

Tears poured down Molly's cheeks while part of her smile held firm. She seemed to waver between a sob and a smile for several long moments. Then the sobbing sounds took charge, and the smile was gone. JoEllen glanced over at Henry's face and saw his features harden in annoyance. The children looked at the floor. JoEllen placed a box of Kleenex at Molly's feet. Molly took a tissue, blew her nose, and continued.

"When George was a baby, once I walked and walked around and around the block carrying him most of the night, trying to find the courage to leave Henry. We were all living with his mother then. But where could I go? What could I do? My own mother would have taken me in but she had a new man in her life and she lived halfway across the country. I thought about my father. Thinking about him made me realize that nothing in my life with Henry was as bad as it had been with my father. So I decided to stay with Henry. My husband doesn't drink and he doesn't beat anybody up."

"Are you saying that when you were a child, Molly, your father drank too much and was violent at times?"

"Yes. I used to hide in the attic when he got drunk. I climbed up through a trap door in my bedroom closet. The problem was, I could still hear all the terrible sounds. I felt horrible when I hid, because I could hear my father hitting my mother and my older brother, Ben. Mother stayed with father only on account of Ben and me. My brother died in high school, no one knows quite how. Now, I think my father may have caused internal injuries during one of their fights. Mother left Dad right after I went away to college."

"How is Henry like your father?"

"Henry like my father! Good heavens, he isn't anything like my father. That's what attracted me to him. Henry doesn't drink, and he's basically a good man. He never hits anyone and I love him very much."

"I'm glad to hear that, Molly." JoEllen's voice was gentle. Then she probed: "But just what *was* your husband doing that made you consider leaving him when George was a baby?"

"The same as he's doing now."

"Which is?"

Molly looked around uneasily. She looked especially at her son and daughter.

"The children are here . . ." she said haltingly and then stopped.

"Oh, Mom, we know!" Charlotte burst out angrily. "You think we don't know what you mean by all those dumb words you use when you're mad at Dad at home?"

"What do you mean, Charlotte?" Molly spoke quietly, her tone almost threatening.

"When you tell him to stop it, that there's no wrath like that of a woman scorned."

"That means I'm angry with your father. When he flirts too much with other women."

"Yeah, sure," Charlotte said. "And what about when he's been out screwing around?" The teen's eyes flashed as if she dared anyone to challenge the words she used.

There was a moment of stunned silence. Josh rose suddenly and began to whistle and make faces into the mirror, dancing and waving his arms. Then he pirouetted around the room like a small wild man. "Nyah, nyah, nyah," he chanted.

Henry stood up also and moved toward the office door. "This is ridiculous," he said. "I think it's time we took this show on the road." Josh fell in step behind his father, still pirouetting and chanting.

Molly sat frozen in her chair, staring at Charlotte. Charlotte started to stand up, then looked helplessly back and forth between her mother and her retreating father. She took a small step in Henry's direction and hesitated. JoEllen realized she might lose the whole family. Not again! Shades of the Callans! Time seemed to stop. As if in a dream, she watched Henry move closer to the door, followed by his son.

Almost without thinking, JoEllen sprang to her feet and literally barred the door with her body. Her quick action brought her nose to nose with Henry. Or almost nose to nose—his was several inches higher than hers.

"Please sit down," JoEllen said, her voice as firm as she could make it. "Henry, Josh, both of you—take your seats. We haven't finished yet."

It seemed as if long minutes passed before Henry gave JoEllen a courtly sort of smile, bowed gallantly, and returned to his chair, followed by his son. It was probably only a few seconds. Charlotte sat back down as well. JoEllen remained on her feet by the door.

The telephone rang. Kurt spoke briefly. "Good work. Stay on your feet," was all he said, and hung up.

JoEllen had previously learned that standing up was a way a therapist could gain more presence, more authority, in a session. Since hers had just been challenged, this seemed like good advice. She needed to reestablish control.

"Josh," she began, looking down at the boy sternly, "you just tried to rescue your family from having to talk about something that is very hard to talk about. I wonder how you were chosen for that role."

"What?" the boy said.

"In some families," JoEllen continued, "when people are about to talk about something that's hard for them, one person manages to stop the discussion. You tried to do that just now by clowning around and distracting everybody. Did you know that's what you were doing?"

"Not exactly," Josh said.

"You see, Josh," said JoEllen, for the boy's benefit and also for that of all the other listening family members, "for some reason this family doesn't want to talk about what you began to talk about, your father's flirting, and maybe other things he does with women. Would you agree?"

"Well, yeah," Josh said. "But Dad won't change, he's said so a thousand times."

"That's the kind of thing we're here to discuss," said JoEllen. "I'm going to ask your mother now what she'd like to change if she could. Would that be all right with you, Josh?"

Josh looked into the mirror. This time he didn't make a face, he just looked sad. He glanced over at Charlotte, who stared back at him with a frightened expression. He did not look at his father.

"OK," he said.

Henry spoke up. "I don't like what you're doing, JoEllen," he said in a firm, annoyed voice. "You keep asking my wife, even my kids, what they don't like about me, but you don't give me a chance to tell you what my problems are with my wife."

JoEllen turned to Henry. "That's a fair statement, Henry," she said. "But we can't do everything at once. Your turn is coming."

Henry sat still for a moment, his lips in a frown. "OK," he said at last, with another little bow from his chair. The man certainly had style.

JoEllen took a deep breath and sat down. Though she recognized that standing up gave her more authority, she felt awkward and preferred to be at eye level with her clients. She turned to Molly.

"Molly, let me be frank. Charlotte is 16, Josh 13. Most teenagers aren't experts on sexual behavior, but they've certainly heard a lot about it, at the very least. They're curious, sometimes scared. It's OK to talk about sex by name here, if that's what's going on."

"But they're just children!"

"They are children who seem to think your husband is 'screwing around.' That sounds to me like they think he's having sexual relationships with people besides you. Is that right, Charlotte?"

The graceful 16-year-old let most of her long flaxen hair fall into her eyes. She curled her shoulders forward until her face seemed almost to disappear behind the wavy mane. But when she spoke, her words were loud enough to hear.

"I guess so," Charlotte said softly.

"What makes you guess so, Charlotte?"

"Because Dad is usually late when he comes home, and Josh and I can hear him and Mom arguing through the bedroom door. Sometimes they're still arguing at breakfast, sometimes at supper, and that's when Mom uses silly words like 'a woman scorned' but we know what she means."

Molly looked over at Henry.

"Did you know what your children were thinking, Henry?"

"I knew what Charlotte was thinking," the man answered to JoEllen's surprise.

"You did!" the trainee responded, letting her surprise show.

"Yes," Henry said in a calm, forthright manner. "It was our little secret from her mother."

"Your little secret from Molly?"

"Yes, Molly didn't think Charlotte knew, and Charlotte didn't want Molly to know she knew."

"What secret did you and Charlotte share?"

Now it was Henry's turn to look around—first at his wife, who was staring at him with an odd, hard expression on her face, then at Charlotte, finally at his son.

"Molly wouldn't want me to say this in front of the children," he said at last.

"You might as well, Henry," Molly said grimly. "We've come this far."

"Well, then," Henry said and cleared his throat with firm, important noises. To JoEllen's surprise he smiled, his expression almost jaunty. "Charlotte asked me a few months ago if I was having an affair. I decided she was old enough for an honest answer. I'm much more realistic about the kids than Molly is."

"What was your honest answer?"

"I told her that I was having an affair, of course. As I said, Charlotte is old enough to know and I'm an honest man. I also told my daughter that her mother and I agreed it was OK for me to have affairs. I'm not deceiving Molly and I'll never leave her."

Molly turned to Charlotte.

"Charlotte, what was it that led you to ask your father if he was having an affair when you did, a few months ago?"

Charlotte peered out from behind her haven of hair, her dark eyes wide. She looked almost proud of herself.

"Oh, Dad takes me to help him teach dancing classes sometimes. I could see he had a crush on a lady there. When he came home late one night, I asked him if he had been with her. He said yes. Then I asked him if he was having an affair. You see, Mom," she said firmly, "I know what that means. He said yes."

Henry spoke up then. "I believe it is important for a man to be honest with his daughter. When she is old enough to understand, of course. I believe it is important for a man to be honest with his wife, too. I've never deceived Molly."

"Henry," JoEllen inquired, "you said a few moments ago that you and Molly agreed it was OK for you to have affairs. Let me ask you specifically; do you mean sexual affairs?"

"Yes, we agreed."

There was a low yell of anger from Molly. JoEllen looked over to see a change in the woman's face. No longer the waxen smile molded for public appearance. Now Molly was showing her feelings openly in her snapping eyes and furious frown.

"Agreed!" Molly yelped. "Agreed! When Henry told me about his first affair, I cried my heart out. He got very mad at me for showing my feelings and blamed *me* for taking it the wrong way."

"Yes," Henry said, remarkably at ease in this discussion. He was in excellent humor now, his face smiling, his voice resonant and persuasive. "Molly did take it the wrong way. She thought I was going to leave her. But that's not the kind of man I am. I'll never desert Molly; she's my primary relationship."

"Henry, you've said before that Molly is your primary relationship. What do you mean by 'primary relationship'?"

"Molly is the only woman I want to live with. All the other women are short-term only, and I tell them that from the beginning. Molly is the person with whom I plan to spend the rest of my life."

"What's the reason for your extramarital affairs, then?"

Henry's features took on the satisfied appearance of a debater about to deliver a punch line.

"Molly can't give me all I need—and I'm not talking just about sex. I'm talking about companionship, too. It's not Molly's fault, it's just the way she is. She doesn't like to do all the things I do, or even have the time."

"Yes," JoEllen said a bit dryly. "I understand your wife works full time as well as being mother to your children. And if she's like most women, she probably does the bulk of the housework too."

"Yes," said Henry without skipping a beat. "My job hasn't worked out as well as Molly's, so I have a lot more free time than she does. She should be happy I meet a lot of my needs outside the marriage. My having special relationships with other women provides me with extra energy, which I can bring back to give to the whole family."

JoEllen found herself thinking that the man sounded like an advocate for systems theory. To remain healthy, a system must exchange energy across its boundaries. Maybe all Henry was doing, as he said, was replenishing his resources from outside to enrich the family system as a whole. Certainly that shouldn't be a problem. JoEllen felt herself starting to get lost in a web of painful memories, old debates. A dialog with Chip turned on in her head and pushed the present interaction out of focus.

Reading confusion on the trainee's features, an intuitive Henry pressed his point: "Molly just shouldn't be so jealous, she shouldn't be so insecure. That's the real problem in this family."

JoEllen felt weary. She had been here before. But she dragged herself back into the conversation with Henry.

"You think that the major problem with your having affairs with other women is that Molly is too jealous and insecure."

JoEllen reflected Henry's words as a statement, not a question, and she found herself knowing what she would hear in response. Chip's words—a deja vu right in the therapy office. And maybe the two men were right. Lord knows, she'd been insecure enough in her failed marriage. Lord knows, she'd been horribly jealous. And maybe, maybe if she'd just been a little stronger, tougher—maybe then she'd still be married to Chip, enjoying his warmth and companionship. JoEllen began to drift down currents of personal pain, loss, uncertainty. She only vaguely heard Henry's next words.

"That's it exactly, JoEllen. You've got it right. Molly shouldn't be so jealous and insecure. She shouldn't pay any attention to my affairs. I'm not about to leave her."

JoEllen felt herself continuing to drift as in a trance. An inner dialog with Chip began to pound in her head again. And she recalled again from an anthropology course that polygyny (one man, multiple wives) is the preferred form of marriage throughout the world. It is legal in many lands. JoEllen took pride in trying to be open-minded.

"What about venereal disease?" she asked Henry suddenly, jolting herself back to the present. This was the clincher for monogamy nowadays.

"I'm very careful," Henry said in a matter of fact tone. "I don't want a disease any more than Molly does. I always take precautions."

JoEllen found herself wondering who was right. Maybe Molly did just need to grow stronger, as JoEllen wished she had been able to do herself. Jealousy and insecurity are ugly emotions. Growing beyond them is an admirable achievement. The trainee lost touch with the moment, deep in memories. The telephone rang.

"JoEllen, what is going on?" asked Kurt in a sharp voice. "Come behind the mirror for a few minutes."

That woke the therapist up! JoEllen felt a surge of embarrassment. Leave the therapy room now? Before the end of the session? She must really have blown it. How to cover for herself? There was really nothing she could do now. Awkwardly, feeling like a naughty child, she excused herself and left the office, explaining she would be back shortly.

The trainee was greeted by four curious faces in the observation room. Oh great, a full audience. Did she really expect to be bawled out in front of the other trainees? Oh yes, JoEllen sighed to herself, you still do have that insecurity problem.

"JoEllen," Kurt greeted her in a quiet but urgent tone, "it looked to us as if you were drifting off in there. What was happening for you?"

JoEllen grinned in embarrassment and looked down at her hands. She didn't answer.

"Was it something personal, JoEllen?"

"I guess so," she said, looking and sounding exactly like a resistant client.

"It looked to us as if you were buying a lot of what Henry was saying in there, and then getting lost in it."

"I guess I was," JoEllen said, "but you know, a lot of what Henry said makes sense."

"For example?"

"Well, what he said about getting energy by having affairs outside of the marriage, and being able to bring that energy back to the family for everybody's benefit. It's true that if Molly weren't so jealous it could work that way."

"You believe that?"

"Ah, yes, well, partly I do."

"What part do you believe?"

"Well," JoEllen took a deep breath and took the plunge. She knew the team knew of her failed marriage; they had consulted together before about how her personal problems might affect her work as a therapist. She trusted the members.

"This feels like a deja vu to me," the trainee explained. "My former husband sounded a lot like Henry. Our marriage didn't work, but still, what my 'ex' said made a lot of sense to me then, and it still does."

"You believe your husband had a right to have affairs? That your jealousy and insecurity were your problems only, and that if you could just have gotten over them your marriage could have worked?"

"Right. And I failed. And so I've lost Chip."

"That's what I thought I remembered from a previous consultation," Kurt replied. "So you're still working on the arguments pro and con affairs."

JoEllen flushed. "Yes, I guess I am," she said.

"If I remember correctly, your husband fell in love with the woman in his last affair and left you."

"Yes."

"In spite of your efforts to conquer your insecurities."

"Yes, although I could probably have kept him as my husband if I'd been able to get over my insecurity—and jealousy," JoEllen added candidly. "I think Chip would have stayed with me if I could have just let him have his affair."

"JoEllen, let's look at this from outside the perspective of 'right' and 'wrong.' Let's look at it from the perspective of systems theory. Yes, a healthy system needs to exchange energy across its boundaries. But remember, if the boundaries of a system are *too* permeable, the system loses its purpose and identity."

"OK," JoEllen responded. "But how does that pertain to the Peterson case?"

"Extramarital affairs aren't socially sanctioned in this culture," Kurt continued. "For that reason alone, they usually result in a great deal of pain and anger between a husband and wife."

"Yes, but they apparently work in other cultures."

"We don't live in other cultures, though. Other cultures may have traditions we don't understand that can help people cope. No matter—we don't have them here."

"Ah . . . well, I guess that's true."

"In this culture, if one member of a marital pair has an affair, the other will almost always feel angry or hurt. At the same time that this couple needs to deal with that anger or hurt, the energy normally available to the marriage pours out into the new relationship instead.

Too little energy is invested in the marriage itself to resolve its problems, especially by the partner involved in the affair."

"I've certainly experienced that dynamic," reflected JoEllen wryly.

"So," continued Kurt, "the marriage is likely to dissolve. To use a systems perspective, sexual activity outside of a marriage is probably a sign that the boundaries of the marriage are too permeable for the marital system to survive in this culture. Regardless of what Henry, or your former husband for that matter, believes, considerably more energy pours out of the family system than is brought back in that way."

"I guess I haven't looked at it quite that way before."

"Well, give it some thought," Kurt instructed.

JoEllen experienced an unexpected surge of mental excitement, as Kurt's answer to a question from her own past clicked into place. This new perspective was worth the cost of the institute's tuition! The trainee remembered how much energy she had expended to conquer her own jealousy in marriage, without success. Perhaps she should have expended her energy instead to close the system's boundaries. Or, failing that, in getting herself out of the marriage before so much of her self-esteem had been shattered.

It was 20/20 hindsight, but a relief as well. Perhaps the end of her marriage wasn't a tragedy, after all. Perhaps it was simply a necessary step so that JoEllen could move on to something better in her life.

"Then again," Kurt continued his mini-lecture, "just as important in guiding a therapist's actions in a case like this is the concept of triangulation."

JoEllen struggled to pay attention.

"Murray Bowen's theory?" she finally asked, remembering a recent homework assignment.[13]

"That's right. How do you think that might apply here?"

"Well, Bowen feels a two-person system is unstable, and that under stress it will pull in a third person, who is vulnerable in some way, to form a triangle."

"Does pulling in a third party solve the original dyad's problem?"

"No. It just allows the two people to avoid dealing with whatever caused the stress between them originally. Energy that should go into problem solving for the couple gets siphoned off into the relationship with the third person, like we were saying a couple minutes ago."

"See any evidence of triangulation with the Peterson family?"

"Good heavens, it's everywhere! With the kids, with the women Henry has affairs with."

"Right," said Kurt. "Now go back into the therapy room and do what you need to do to close the session constructively. We're getting near the end of the hour. We'll need to do our final consultation shortly to develop the team's message to the family."

"OK. Thanks, by the way," JoEllen smiled slightly to acknowledge the crucial assistance of the team. She then returned to the therapy room.

"Hello again," she said to the family. "The team felt it was important to talk with me in some detail. My apologies for keeping you waiting."

"That's OK," Henry said politely, serving as the family spokesman.

"Thank you, Henry. I need to ask you a question, Molly," JoEllen turned toward the wife. "Henry said a little while ago that you agreed to his affairs, that the only problem was your jealousy and insecurity. What do you think about that now?"

Molly's smile was shy, like a small child's.

"I've been thinking about that since you left the office," she said. "There's a lot to what Henry says—I can't deny it."

"Tell me more, Molly," said JoEllen.

"I try so hard to control my jealousy, but I usually fail. Henry says I'm too insecure, and he's right. I guess the troubles we have are mostly my fault. We both have a lot of fun with the people he brings home. He only has sexual affairs occasionally. I should try to make the best of it."

"You should try to make the best of it?"

"Well, I guess I have to. Henry says he'll leave me if I don't stop bugging him about his other relationships. Our marriage has lasted over 22 years; his affairs never last more than a few months. I know he really does love me the most." Molly's words spilled out in a confused jumble of self-deprecation, resignation, and pride.

"Molly tries to control me," Henry spoke up suddenly. "That's when I think about leaving her. But if she understands what I need, I'll always be there for her."

"Henry, we're getting near the close of the session," JoEllen interjected. "We'll talk about your issues with Molly next week. Right now, I want to continue talking with your wife. Molly, I hear a lot of pride in your voice when you say that your marriage has lasted over 22 years."

"That's right," Molly said firmly. "I know so many people whose marriages have broken up. We've made ours work, in spite of our problems."

"Yet you have struggled with feelings of jealousy and insecurity for years."

"Yes, I know I need to learn to handle those feelings better."

"Maybe, maybe not," said JoEllen. It was Molly's turn to look surprised.

"Have you ever considered," JoEllen continued, using the new insights she had just gained in consultation, "that your feelings of jealousy and insecurity could be a warning that your marriage is in danger?"

Molly stared at JoEllen. She was not expecting to hear anything like this.

"Have you ever considered that your feelings could be appropriate under the circumstances? That expressing them could be an act of courage, not weakness? That they could be your very good friends?"

Molly looked confused. "But my feelings make Henry so mad," she said.

"That's true—you have told me that, and so has Henry." JoEllen looked over at Henry.

"You're darned right they do," Henry said. "Molly's insecurity drives me crazy."

"Henry, I admire you for being so honest," JoEllen said. "You express yourself well and you are obviously sincere. But look at things from a different point of view for a moment. OK?"

"What do you have in mind?" said Henry.

"A concept in family therapy called triangulation."

"What?" Henry asked, looking startled.

JoEllen heard Josh and Charlotte giggle nervously. The two children had been silent for a long while, but they were listening intently to the interchange between the therapist and their parents.

"You mean like a love triangle, like in the novels?" asked Charlotte.

"Something like that," JoEllen smiled in Charlotte's direction and continued. "The team reminded me about triangulation when they called me behind the mirror. They suggested I talk with all of you about it."

Henry had a sense of humor and he quipped: "As long as you don't mean strangulation. Occasionally my wife has threatened me with something like that, and it makes me nervous."

Everyone laughed. The tension in the room eased a little. The therapist searched for words.

"*Triangulation* is a fancy term, but it's a relatively simple idea. The term was coined by a man named Murray Bowen to describe a process where two people under stress involve a third person in their relationship. It helps stabilize the system."

"That makes sense," said Henry. "When I get mad at Molly, I talk to somebody else and it helps a lot."

"To some degree it may help for a while," answered JoEllen. "But if that is all you do to ease the stress, the problem that caused it will not be resolved in the long run."

"What do you mean?" Henry asked. JoEllen could see Molly listening carefully.

"Henry, when you draw a third person into your relationship with Molly, you drain off energy toward the new person. When that happens, you have a tendency not to take the time you need to resolve the problems with your wife."

"So what? Maybe two people can just forget their problems if somebody else is around who is interesting and distracting."

"It isn't quite so simple. The two-person system originally under stress, say a couple like you and Molly, is now a three-person system under stress. The three-person system has to be under stress because at least one member is unhappy. So it tends to pull in another person and then another. You end up with a series of interlocking triangles. Relationships become impossibly complicated." JoEllen was engaging in outright education as a part of her therapeutic efforts.

"Are you telling me you think this—this triangulation—is happening with us, with Molly and me?" Henry asked.

"You've got it," JoEllen said, unconsciously repeating Henry's own words from earlier in the session.

Henry sat silent for a moment. Then Molly spoke.

"I think JoEllen's right. Henry, do you remember when you got mad at that woman you were seeing last year? Before very long you were seeing somebody else and then those two got mad at each other—and you as well!"

"Don't be ridiculous," snapped Henry. "People can have disagreements and they're just disagreements."

"Still, Henry," Molly said softly, "I think JoEllen has something."

"Think about it, Henry," said JoEllen.

When Molly spoke again, there was a childlike quality to her voice. At last, someone was telling her something she wanted to hear. She wanted to hear it again.

"You say," Molly spoke slowly and carefully, "that when Henry has an affair with somebody, he's draining off energy into that relationship that he should be using to work things out with me instead?"

"That's what the theory suggests," said JoEllen. "You could even say that the jealousy and insecurity you experience when Henry is having an affair are your good friends. They are informing you that energy that should be going into your own relationship is being diverted elsewhere."

"That's not fair!" Henry spoke up loudly. "You're giving my wife ammunition against me!"

"Perhaps, Henry," JoEllen responded quietly. "But look at it this way. If one member of a two-person system uses triangulation, the other will too. Can you think of an example where Molly might use triangulation when you think she should deal directly with you instead?"

"I sure can," Henry said immediately, looking somewhat mollified. "I think she triangulates with the kids. George and Josh especially. She always uses them against me."

"Henry, given that you are an observant man with a keen mind," replied JoEllen, "I expect you may be right. We can talk about that next week." She knew the man needed a compliment, and she hoped her comment would involve Henry in looking for additional evidence to support the concept of triangulation, rather than putting his energy into disputing the theory.

"Now," the therapist continued, "it's almost time for our session to end this evening. I'm going to leave you all for a few moments to consult with the team. I'll be back shortly."

Behind the mirror, the team noted with satisfaction that Molly and Henry began arguing with each other almost as soon as JoEllen left the office. Molly told Henry angrily that she had always thought her jealousy was justified under the circumstances, and Henry told Molly angrily that she had better not try to control him. Their messages to each other were irate and not at all fun. But their words were spoken directly to one another, not diverted through the children or through the women with whom Henry had his various affairs. The team believed that Molly and Henry's arguing with one another was a necessary step in the right direction, dealing with their disagreements directly.

The message to the family from the team at the end of the session read as follows: "Henry and Molly, we congratulate you because you clearly show intense passion for one another. Not many couples who have been married for 22 years have been able to maintain the level of passion that you possess. It allows you to become very angry at one another yet continue to live together as a married couple.

"The team believes that the members of your family all have keen and inquiring minds. This week we ask each of you, including Charlotte and Josh, to use those good minds to gather information about triangulation in your family relationships. Don't try to change anything, just observe and gather data."

"We wish you well."

CHAPTER 11

Consultation and an Analysis of Family Structure

JoEllen thought a good deal about her session with the Petersons during the next few days. Since some of the family's issues, particularly sexuality, were issues she was dealing with also, the trainee decided to ask for further consultation from her weekly discussion group. JoEllen had been feeling depressed for the past few days, and she wasn't sure why. She knew she still grieved the loss of her husband; she knew that the material on triangulation reminded her of that loss. Still, she sensed something else was going on for her as well.

Fortunately, the interview with the Petersons in the training office had been videotaped. JoEllen previewed the tape, making sure it was clear and deciding which sections she wanted to review with the discussion group. Then, at her meeting at noon on Monday, she asked for half an hour of time. Madeleine Sweet granted the request after checking with other members about their needs that day.

When JoEllen's turn came, she fast-forwarded her tape to the section where Josh began to act like a clown. The discussion group complimented the trainee as she acted swiftly to keep Henry and Josh from leaving the therapy office. They applauded how decisively and effectively she had responded to such a serious challenge. JoEllen felt a glow of pride and thanked her colleagues.

She then fast-forwarded the tape to the point where she began feeling drawn into Henry's seductive behavior. The tape blasted out the sound of the telephone call from Kurt, the consultation team leader. It picked up the image of JoEllen's downcast, crestfallen face as she headed toward the office door and disappeared to consult with the team according to Kurt's instructions.

"What kind of feedback would be useful for you from our discussion group, JoEllen?" Madeleine asked.

"I'm not sure," came the young woman's reply. "I feel as if I learned a lot this week professionally, but what I learned affected me personally too, and I'm still sorting it out."

"Tell us more."

JoEllen described for the group the feedback she received from the team behind the mirror about extramarital affairs and triangulation from a systems perspective. She described the personal insights she had gained with respect to her former marriage. Her facial expression was flat, however, unusual for her, and her voice carried a troubled undertone. Group members listened with interest.

"You seem to have accepted some perspectives on sexual affairs that are new for you, yet I sense something's still bothering you," Madeleine probed.

"You're right, something *is* bothering me," JoEllen responded. "I'm not sure what it is, though. The application of systems theory to my own life was a revelation to me. It felt exciting the night it happened, and it gave me direction for working with the Petersons. But then I started feeling depressed."

"Depressed?"

"Yes."

"Any idea as to what the depression is about?"

"No, not really."

"Take a guess," Madeleine probed again.

JoEllen sat silently, then shook her head, embarrassed.

"I have a hunch," Madeleine said at last. "Would you be willing to hear it?"

"Of course."

"I have a hunch that you've told us the safe part of what happened for you last week, the professional part. I think the 'something' you are struggling with is less safe, more personal."

JoEllen sighed. "You know already that my former marriage ended with an affair. I was thinking about that as the family discussed Henry's sexual behavior. Still, I felt good about the new outlook I gained from my consultation with the team. At least I thought I did at the time. Now I feel as if I have unfinished business rolling around in my stomach."

Another trainee, Bob, spoke up. "I couldn't help but feel for you when you got called out of the training office by the consultation team leader, Dr. Knaak, JoEllen. You looked so unhappy in that last video scene, slinking out of the office like a kid called out for a spanking."

JoEllen's face took on a startled expression. She sat silent for a moment.

"I wonder if that's it," the trainee pondered then aloud. "I felt terrible when Kurt called me out of the office. I felt like I blew it and everybody knew."

"Ah," said Madeleine. "You felt like a failure, a bad little girl."

"Yes, I did. And I know it's crazy because we all get called out of the office sometimes. Well—most of us do," she added hastily.

"We *all* do, so there's no need for you to try to take care of the rest of us!" Gretchen teased with her usual good humor.

"JoEllen, would you be willing to do some personal work with me in the presence of the group?" asked Madeleine.

"I guess so," said JoEllen.

"You spoke just then about having a feeling of unfinished business rolling around in your stomach."

"Yes."

"We can begin with that if you're willing. That may give us insight as to what's behind your depressed feelings. Are you willing?"

"Yes."

"Right now?"

"Yes."

"Then pay attention to the place in your stomach where the unfinished business is rolling around. Put your hand on it."

JoEllen put her hand across the lower part of her abdomen.

"That place is right over your navel."

"Yes."

"Where the umbilical cord once was attached."

JoEllen's facial expression changed. Her previously tense features seemed to transform themselves into a much younger arrangement. Younger and softer.

"Yes," the trainee said in a small, childlike voice.

Madeleine waited as JoEllen's face continued to grow even younger.

"How old do you feel right now?"

"Oh, about 3 or 4."

"How safe do you feel, as a 3- or 4-year-old child?"

"Not safe. Not safe at all." Tears glistened at the edges of the young JoEllen's eyes.

"Where is your Mommy?"

"She's right here, but she's mad at me."

"How do you know she's mad at you?"

"She's always mad at me."

"How do you know?"

"She always tells me my hair is messy, my skirt is on crooked, my shoes are muddy, my socks don't match, and I look really awful. Besides, I've gotten a spot on my blouse."

"When is she telling you these things?"

"She tells me these things ALL THE TIME." JoEllen's voice was tense, hurt, angry.

"So you are a little girl, and Mommy criticizes you a lot."

JoEllen clutched her stomach with both hands, bent over toward the floor as if in pain and cried out, "YES!" Her long brown hair dropped almost to her toes and her shoulders began to shake. She covered her face with her hands and cried. Through long sobs she could be heard to gasp, "Mommy doesn't like me, Mommy doesn't like me," over and over.

Madeleine let JoEllen cry until the sounds subsided on their own. Then she handed the trainee a box of Kleenex.

"Where are you now, JoEllen?" she asked.

JoEllen smiled weakly, wiping her tears. "I'm back," she said.

"What have you learned?"

"I tend to fall apart when I'm criticized, because it reminds me of when I was a little girl. When I expect to be criticized, I feel like a scared child, ashamed of myself in advance."

"So even though your mother probably didn't *really* criticize you all the time, a part of you feels that way. When the team told you to come talk with them behind the mirror, your scared 3-year-old emerged and you expected to be overwhelmed with criticism."

"That's pretty close, I think," JoEllen responded. "I sure felt like I had done something awful, and was about to be punished. I guess I still feel like I blew it. "

"That makes sense," Madeleine said. "Now I want to do another exercise with you, JoEllen," she continued. "Are you willing?"

"What kind of exercise?"

"I believe that all of us have the resources we need to help solve our problems right within us. I believe a part of you needs nurturing and support now. Other parts of you are fully able to provide that nurturing. What I have in mind is a brief exercise sometimes called 're-parenting.'"

"Reparenting—I've heard of that."

"Good. Now as you know, parenting in general requires both nurturing and critical functions. Sometimes the functions get out of balance. Your inner parent seems very critical. Will you participate in an exercise to increase your inner nurturing?"

"No problem!" JoEllen responded. Her voice sounded interested and pleased.

Madeleine began her instructions in a firm, gentle tone.

"JoEllen, remember you are an adult now. Allow your mind to remember many important skills you have learned as an adult. You can close your eyes if you want to, to let yourself remember more clearly. Give me a nod when you are ready."

JoEllen closed her eyes and settled back in her chair. After a few moments, she nodded. Madeleine continued.

"Now remember especially all the nurturing skills you have learned as an adult. For example, you know how to hug a child in need, you can talk in a soft voice, you can even sing if you want! Take a few moments to remember all the nurturing skills you have today."

Madeleine paused, and the room was silent except for several sighs from the other trainees. JoEllen appeared to be concentrating her attention within herself, and at last she nodded again.

"Now, go back in your mind's eye and see the little JoEllen, the one who is 3 or 4 years old." There was a short pause. Then, "Have you got her in your mind's eye now?"

"Yes." Softly.

"Does the little JoEllen see you?"

"Yes."

"Is she willing to meet you? Ask her directly."

There was another pause, and another nod.

"Is the adult JoEllen willing to help the young JoEllen?"

"Yes."

"Then let grown-up JoEllen go over to little JoEllen, and introduce yourself. Ask the child if you can help. If little JoEllen says yes, give her the nurturing she needs, using the skills you have today."

Several moments passed. JoEllen's facial expression changed almost imperceptibly. All the residual tension in her features relaxed slowly, very slowly; after a few minutes a gentle smile transformed her face. Then the trainee opened her eyes, stretched, and yawned widely.

"There. How was that for you?" Madeleine asked.

"It helped. I feel much better now. Thank you."

The other trainees clapped. A few sighed as well. It had been a moving experience for everyone.

"Boy, did that remind me of some of my experiences with my own mother," Rose said.

"Me too," said Harry.

"This type of exercise is called self-parenting or reparenting," said Madeleine. "It's something we can all do for ourselves and for our clients. It's a way we can use our own skills in the present to take care of unfinished business from the past." She paused for a few moments. "Now, JoEllen, do you want to talk more about the Peterson case?"

"Yes, I do, but I'm not ready just now. Can you go on to something else, and come back to me?"

"Sure."

The next half-hour or so was spent on a case with which Bob was working. When the group turned it's attention back to JoEllen, she was prepared.

"What would you like feedback on now?" asked Madeleine.

"Family structure," answered JoEllen immediately. "I think I understand how the subsystems are organized in the Peterson family, but I'd appreciate input from others. Did anybody notice anything in particular about family structure from the videotape?"

Bob spoke immediately. "What stood out for me," he said, "was Charlotte's sitting between her parents."

"Yes," Gretchen reflected, "and she nearly followed her brother and father out of the office. In the last glimpse I got of her in the first section of the tape you showed, she was half standing, half sitting, looking back and forth between her parents. She looked torn between them."

"Josh seemed to be taking responsibility for family survival through his acting as a clown, diverting everybody's attention so that they wouldn't actually have to talk about Henry's affairs," Rose contributed.

"The parents do not present either a strong spousal subsystem or a strong parental subsystem. They appear divided, and the children seem to be pulled back and forth between them."

"Both children seem to feel responsible to do something to hold their parents together. But these children don't present a unified subsystem either. Josh acted like a clown to get his parents out of the office, and he might have succeeded if the sibling subsystem had been strong enough for Charlotte to have followed him."

"This appears to be an enmeshed family, where the children take on skewed roles under stress to hold the spousal subsystem together. Of course, they don't consciously know that's what they're doing."

Thoughts like these came thick and fast as group members brainstormed with one another. An enmeshed family is one where boundaries between subsystems are weak and easily crossed. For example, children may act like parents, and parents like children.

As the voices died down, Madeleine asked JoEllen, "What do you think of these ideas?"

"They make sense to me," responded the trainee. "I also suspect Charlotte and Henry constitute an enmeshed subsystem, and Molly and Josh as well. That's because Charlotte and Henry go off dancing together regularly. Henry even described his most recent affair, which Charlotte knew about, as 'our little secret.' Molly gets left at home with Josh, and I suspect she leans on the son for company that Henry ought to be providing."

"We didn't see much evidence of those subsystems on the sections of tape you showed us, but your ideas make sense," said Madeleine. "They're worth checking out. OK? Have you had enough feedback from the group for today?"

"Yes, and thanks," responded JoEllen. The discussion group went on to talk about other issues briefly, and then adjourned for the week. Several members took time to congratulate JoEllen afterward for her courage in exposing herself so personally in the supervision process.

CHAPTER 12

Family Therapy in Systems Perspective

Before going further, it is important to remember that this book is not intended to serve as a basic text on systems theory or on systems-based family therapy. The book's main purpose, instead, is to describe the experience of a family therapist-in-training in the context of an AAMFT-accredited program. However, for a better understanding of the practical therapeutic interventions presented throughout, major concepts in systems theory were introduced in Chapter 9. Similarly, several major systems-based approaches to family therapy are introduced in this chapter.

Many family therapists today use a systems approach in conducting their work. Systems theory, as explained previously, was originally developed by biologist Ludwig von Bertalanffy. A systems perspective was later adapted by social scientists for their own use because it seemed to help explain otherwise bewildering behavior patterns exhibited by social systems, such as families.

Many contemporary marriage and family therapists ground their work in systems theory, but they do not all do so in the same way. The number of different "schools" of family therapy may be partly due to the fact that the pioneers perfected their methods and techniques when systems theory was still being conceived. Some therapists worked with entire families without ever being aware of formal systems theory. Interpretation and application varied widely among those who were aware of it. Bertalanffy himself had little contact with early family therapists.[14]

It is interesting to note that the pioneers in family therapy began to work with families in toto at about the same time, in the early 1950s. Contemporaries who were aware of these pioneers' efforts viewed them as mavericks. Mainstream therapists in the 1950s worked primarily with individuals—a result of the pervasive influence of psychoanalyst Dr. Sigmund Freud. Freud's efforts were directed toward analyzing intrapsychic processes (processes occurring within the mind or psyche of the individual person), rather than interpersonal processes (processes occurring between two or more people). Not surprisingly, the work of the first family therapists was ignored or even ridiculed. Only later did systems theory help validate and provide a theoretical framework for their efforts.

This chapter will begin by describing some of the contributions of three pioneers in family therapy: Don Jackson and Virginia Satir—both associated with the MRI, a famous family research project in Palo Alto, California—and Murray Bowen, who was not part of the MRI. The chapter will then discuss the later but deeply influential work of Salvador Minuchin, who developed the "structural" school. Finally, it will briefly review contemporary trends in family therapy, including contributions of the Milan school, components of the feminist critique of family therapy, and challenges to the systems approach to family therapy from constructivist theoreticians.

Many, many other family therapists and schools of family therapy deserve to be discussed here as well, but an adequate job would require volumes. The reader is encouraged to explore the many fine texts that compare and contrast various historical and contemporary approaches to family therapy. Excellent ones have been written by Herbert and Irene Goldenberg, Michael Nichols and Richard Schwartz, and Arthur Horne and Laurence Passmore, among others. These texts include extensive bibliographies including original works (see the Notes for specific citations of these texts in this chapter).

Don Jackson

Don Jackson worked extensively with Gregory Bateson in Palo Alto, California. Bateson, a distinguished anthropologist, began research on human communication there in 1952, and in 1954 he began investigating the relationship between family communication patterns and schizophrenia. In the process, he developed his famous concept of the "double bind" (to be described later). Bateson was not a family therapist but a researcher and theoretician. He developed an interest in Bertalanffy's newly emerging general systems theory and introduced it to his colleagues. Bateson was soon joined by Don Jackson, who was a psychiatrist by training. Other well-known members of Bateson's project were Jay Haley, John Weakland, and William Fry.[15]

Bateson's team soon began observing family communication patterns as part of its research. Jay Haley and Don Jackson began developing techniques for treating families as well, based on systems concepts and analysis of communication patterns. Don Jackson founded the Mental Research Institute (MRI) in Palo Alto in 1959, where he invited Virginia Satir (among others) to join him. Jackson's group continued to maintain close association with Bateson's research team.

Jackson and the MRI staff conducted ongoing family therapy as well as research. Treatment was based on theoretical constructs from general systems theory, which Jackson adapted to family work. He focused on interpersonal, or systems-based, behavioral causation (as opposed to intrapsychic), and he concentrated on the present time frame. Jackson developed the concept of family homeostasis, or balance. As systems, he theorized, families must automatically attempt to maintain homeostatic balance. If this balance were threatened, he hypothesized, feedback mechanisms would become activated to correct the imbalance.

Jackson theorized that homeostatic mechanisms could help explain otherwise puzzling behaviors. Consider a child's bed-wetting, for example. Viewed in systems perspective, bed-wetting can help a family regain homeostasis. For example, if a child's parents have been fighting with each other, family homeostasis is disturbed and the survival of the system is thus threatened. The child's bed-wetting can function to divert the parents' anger, and they begin to collaborate on ways to solve the child's problem. The family system's balance is reestablished, at least temporarily.

Jackson developed many other concepts that family therapists later found useful, but his concept of family homeostatic mechanisms was especially widely adopted. Jackson also speculated that, due to these mechanisms, improvement in the symptom of an "identified patient" (a person brought by the family to be "fixed") might result in a family as a whole getting worse. For example, the identified patient's improvement might result in *negative* feedback to the family system, such as more fighting by the parents (since their anger at each other is no longer diverted by the child's problem). This would prompt the system to correct the new imbalance. Homeostatic mechanisms might induct another family member into the role of "identified patient."[16]

Jackson's view of systems interactions was that they were relatively machinelike. Disturbance in homeostasis activated feedback mechanisms, which in turn prompted behaviors that led to restoration of homeostasis. Jackson, in collaboration with Bateson, was a major player in the development of family systems theory. His work as a therapist was essentially theory-driven.

Virginia Satir

Virginia Satir worked closely with Bateson and Jackson for several years and clearly adopted many concepts from systems theory. She viewed all parts of a family as intimately connected and affecting one another, for example. However, Satir had already recognized this reality in her own practice *before* formal exposure to systems theory. Perhaps for that reason, her view of systems dynamics never became mechanistic, as did Jackson's. She remained fascinated with the inner thoughts and feelings of individuals, and she never doubted they made a difference. She explored the development of family problems over time and routinely asked for three-generational family histories.

Satir was educated as a social worker. Social work as a profession recognized early the impact of families as wholes on individual members. Social workers intervened with whole family units from the earliest historical roots of the profession. Before the turn of the twentieth century, for example, Jane Addams worked to strengthen families as part of the settlement house movement; Mary Richmond, at approximately the same time, recognized the importance of families in her leadership of the Charity Organization Society movement. Richmond's classic text, *Social Diagnosis,* written in 1917, by its very title asserts that the process of "diagnosis" requires going beyond the individual. Perhaps it was the fact that most social workers were female, while most psychoanalysts were male, that led to the initial overshadowing of social work practice perspectives by Freudian theoretical constructs.

Virginia Satir's education in social work took place in the 1940s. In the style of the time, her clinical training, even as a social worker, was Freudian. People were to be seen in therapy as individuals; if families were considered, they were viewed primarily as a source of pathology.

However, Satir soon rejected Freud's pessimistic, deterministic theories and maintained a growing conviction that every person has potential for growth. Toward the end of her long career, Satir called her therapeutic approach "The Human Validation Process Model." Its very name expresses Satir's optimism about the positive potential of humankind.

Satir's family therapy approach was drawn originally from her own private practice, which she began in 1951. Initially she treated children alone, but then she noticed that their symptoms, which she had thought resolved, returned in the presence of the parents. Thus Satir began bringing parents into the therapy process. Working with families was so unusual at the time that she initially felt very alone. When she read about Murray Bowen's work with families (to be described below), she went out of her way to visit him. She received the first professional validation for her work from Bowen, who was also essentially working alone.

In 1959, Satir moved to California. She contacted Don Jackson there, as she had read that he also worked with families. Jackson invited Satir to join the MRI, which he was just opening at the time. Satir did so. She soon found she was more interested in practice than research, however, and began the nation's first formal training program in family therapy in Palo Alto that same year.[17]

Satir came to believe, as do most systems theorists, that every system's primary task is survival. The key to family survival, in her view (beyond the basics such as food and shelter), is self-esteem. If parents' self-esteem is high, they have the resources to nourish a child. While certain systems theorists such as Murray Bowen apparently viewed any triad as negative, Satir believed that a coalition could be formed within a triad "*for* a third person as well as against that person."[18] In a well-functioning family, in fact, that is what parents do for a child.

Satir observed from her work with troubled families that self-esteem was often in short supply. People seemed to marry one another hoping to find someone who would be an extension of self, only stronger. Each spouse hoped the other would take care of all his or her needs. Unfortunately, each spouse soon found that the other was not an extension of self but had different likes, dislikes, and so on. Experiencing these differences led to disappointment, fear, and resentment, but those feelings were rarely expressed directly for fear of rejection. Instead of "I feel angry when you watch football and ignore me," a wife who felt neglected might say, "That Uncle Joe likes sports too much." Obviously, problems cannot be resolved by people who do not know what their significant other is trying to tell them.

Satir found several characteristics common to most troubled families, which she viewed as closed systems. Family rules were fixed yet out of date and inhuman, and the rules were covert, thus unable to be negotiated. She believed that rigid rules were often invented to protect the parents' self-esteem, and not to meet the needs of a growing, changing family.

Satir believed the growth-impeding practices of troubled families were maintained by rigid communication patterns. Her emphasis on communication was probably an outgrowth of her connection with Bateson's Palo Alto project, yet her contributions were unique. She observed that members of troubled families characteristically assumed communication styles of blaming, placating, computing (being super-reasonable, as if one lived in one's head only), or distracting (irrelevant, clownlike).[19]

Satir used extremely creative means to help family members recognize and change the patterns of communication and rigid rules in which they were stuck. For example, she instructed members to role play their customary communication styles, and then she had members consciously swap styles to experience the difference. To help people learn by exaggeration, she instructed placators to get down on their knees as they pleaded with blamers, who were told to stand on chairs and point long fingers at their victims. In a like manner, she had whole families "sculpt" themselves into physical arrangements representing their patterns of communication. She used ropes to tie family members together so they could feel physically what happened when members tried to change position.

Congruent communication was also an explicit goal of Satir's therapeutic process. To this end, she taught people to send messages in which verbal and nonverbal cues agreed. Confusing double messages could thus be avoided; for example, with a verbal message of "I love you" stated in an angry tone with a frown, the receiver cannot be sure what the sender means to convey. Satir instructed clients in the art of using "I" statements as well, speaking directly for the self about one's own feelings and experience. An example of an "I" statement delivered in a congruent manner would be "I feel angry when you watch football and seem to ignore me," with facial expression and voice tone demonstrating corresponding anger. The recipient of such communication might not like the message, but at least both the message and its source would be clear. Thus the issue causing discomfort could be openly addressed.

Satir also taught families about the problem of the "double bind," a type of double message in which no matter how the receiver responds, the sender will criticize. An example would be a father who insists, on the one hand, that all good children should keep their toys picked up, but on the other hand tells his son that "real" boys are tough and messy. The child who receives such a contradictory message will be unable to please his father whether he keeps his toys neat or messy. He may develop otherwise inexplicable symptoms, such as tantrums or emotional withdrawal.

Satir believed that increased self-esteem was fundamental for troubled family members to develop the faith and courage to change, to communicate more congruently, and to negotiate the flexible rules required for the growth of all family members. Thus her style of therapeutic work involved enormous quantities of nurturing and caring. She actively encouraged her clients to cultivate their own unique selves, to recognize and honor their own differences, and to speak their own truth as best they understood it. Here, her grounding in social work professional values is clear, in that the profession itself explicitly honors the worth and dignity of every person.

That Satir was a woman may be a salient factor in her bold emphasis on feeling as an important ingredient in the therapeutic process. Satir was anything but an uninvolved, distant therapist. Rather, she carefully nourished her clients and conducted her work with fervor and compassion. While utilizing a systems perspective, Satir never viewed systems processes as mechanical, as did most of her colleagues in the MRI in Palo Alto, all of whom were male. Two other males later analyzed Satir's highly effective communication processes and from them developed a lucrative school of psychotherapy known as "neuro linguistic programming."[20] Ironically, just as mechanistic utilization of systems theory was not the essence of Satir, neither was a psychotherapy based on "programming." That males focused on mechanical techniques and Satir on nurturing and growth may well be related to the sex-role socialization of the wider U.S. culture.

Murray Bowen

Murray Bowen, like Satir, was actively working with families as wholes even before Bateson's Palo Alto project in California began its research, though he never had any direct contact with that group. Independently, he developed a school, which he called family systems therapy, now generally known as Bowenian therapy.

Bowen was trained as a psychiatrist, and in that capacity he worked with people diagnosed with schizophrenia. He was initially fascinated by Freudian theory and worked with individuals, as was the custom of the time. Gradually, he wondered if family relationships might factor into the generation of schizophrenia. He began studying mother-child dyads, and later included fathers. From this work his important concept of triangulation was developed. Bowen, like both Bateson and Jackson, was a major generator of theory. His work as a therapist was cognitively based and theory driven. Bowen later perfected his theories by first analyzing various interactions in his own family of origin, and then utilizing the concept of triangulation to bring about change within it.

Bowen's major theoretical contributions to family work include: differentiation of self, triangulation, nuclear family emotional process, family projection process, multigenerational transmission process, sibling position, emotional cutoff, and societal emotional process.[21] Each will be discussed in turn.

Differentiation of self was of major importance in Bowen's theory. Basically, Bowen believed that one must differentiate one's self from one's family of origin in order to achieve genuine autonomy and to learn to separate thoughts from feelings. Bowen believed that sound mental health required the ability to generate and recognize one's own thoughts and feelings, not simply to accept those of one's family.

Triangulation occurred, according to Bowen, when two people in a relationship began to drift apart or to encounter some kind of stress. A third person—who may be a family member or an unrelated individual—would then be recruited as confidante, mediator, and so on. This process is normal to a degree; all relationships go through cycles of closeness and distance. But if triangulation of a third party becomes chronic, it tends to undermine the bond between crucial family dyads, such as the marital pair.

Bowen observed that families tend toward emotional fusion, or oneness, when there is a lack of differentiation among family members. He initially described the fused family condition as an "undifferentiated family ego mass." Later, he referred to the process that apparently maintains this fusion as the "nuclear family emotional process." Bowen also believed that parents transmit their own lack of differentiation to their children; this process he called the "family projection process."

Unlike Jackson and the Palo Alto team but similar to Satir, Bowen maintained clear interest in the development of family problems over time. He believed that children highly involved in family fusion processes move toward a lower level of differentiation, and that "identified patients" reflect problems not only taking place in the current family system but also those handed down by former generations. He described the process of transmitting emotional problems from generation to generation as the "multigenerational transmission process."

Sibling position was important in Bowen's theory because of children's potential to form triangles with their parents and with each other. He also believed that certain personality traits were related to sibling position, such as firstborns tending to take leadership roles, middle children to be skilled negotiators, and so on.

Bowen developed the concept of emotional cutoff to describe a mechanism that family members use to seek distance from their families, such as by physically moving far away. Bowen believed that the greater a family's fusion, the greater likelihood of cutoff by the children. Cutoff should not be confused with differentiation of self. Bowen believed that differentiation of self required objective analysis and conscious attention to dealing with one's family without becoming overwhelmed or triangulated. People who have simply "cut off," by contrast, remain emotionally bound, whether they are aware of that fact or not.

Later in his career, Bowen recognized that processes in wider society, such as sexism and racism, affect family life. He then coined the term *societal emotional process.* Bowen did not emphasize the concept in his work, however.

For Bowen, the goal of therapy was for the client to achieve genuine differentiation of self while still maintaining contact with family.

Unlike many systems-oriented family therapists, Bowen often worked with one person alone. Because of his personal success in differentiating from his own family, Bowen believed one person could achieve differentiation through systems-oriented analysis. The individual could then act as a fulcrum for family change.

Salvador Minuchin

Minuchin developed what probably became the most influential school of family therapy, the "structural school." An Argentinean born to a Jewish family, Minuchin served for a time as a physician in the Israeli army. Later he trained in psychiatry and Freudian psychoanalytic theory. Minuchin began to develop an interest in working with families after he was employed at the Wiltwyk School for Boys in New York, where his clientele was inner-city delinquent youth. Minuchin found that any improvement achieved through traditional therapy with these boys was usually lost when they returned home. About the time he was pondering this problem in the early 1960s, family therapy was achieving positive recognition. Minuchin invited (among others) Jay Haley, a member of Gregory Bateson's Palo Alto project, to work with him.[22]

Minuchin adopted a systems perspective, but he developed and utilized it in his own way. Probably because he worked with families who suffered from chronic poverty, discrimination, delinquency, and overall chaos and disorganization, he emphasized analysis of family systems using the present time frame. He intervened actively and directly to restructure families into what he believed would be healthier patterns of relationships. He frequently used strategies such as paradoxical intervention. In one well-known example, a mother brought her son to therapy to resolve their conflictual relationship. After careful assessment, Minuchin urged the mother to fight even harder with her son. He explained that in this way, she would not have to direct her anger toward her ineffectual husband, who was failing to provide for the family. Minuchin's intent was paradoxical, of course. The mother was expected to resist, and when she did, the child was relieved of his stressful position between his parents. Conflict was rerouted into the appropriate dyad, the spousal.[23] For such an intervention to work, however, the mother must not simply be urged to fight with her son;

she must also be made aware of the hidden function her fighting with the boy performs—avoidance of direct conflict with her husband.

Minuchin recognized that every family contains many interacting systems and subsystems, but he identified three subsystems that he believed were of primary importance: the spousal, the parental, and the sibling. He felt each had major but different functions to perform within the family. The spousal subsystem must protect itself as a crucial entity with executive functions and clear boundaries. Creating clear boundaries involved developing rules of interaction with other significant subsystems, such as in-laws and children, so that the boundaries would be respected. After children are born, a parental subsystem develops, which must provide nurture and discipline. But problems can occur if spousal and parental subsystems find themselves in conflict. For example, parenting demands can reduce the energy available to invest in maintenance and repair of the spousal subsystem.

When a second child enters the family system, a sibling subsystem is created. This subsystem is important because it provides the first context in which children learn how to interact with their peers. However, older children may be required to take on parental functions that interfere with their own needs, or they may be treated as much younger than their chronological age by parents unable or unwilling to let them grow up. Minuchin pointed out that families continue to develop and change over time as additional children enter the system and others become ready to leave the nest. Every family must constantly adapt, and professional assistance may be required to help them in the process.

In working with a given family, Minuchin analyzed its structure to determine whether the boundaries of the major subsystems were clear and defined. Instead, he was likely to find that they were too enmeshed (too close, as when a parent feels emotionally closer to a child than to the spouse) or too disengaged (as when spouses communicate only through their children). His goal in working with a given family was to restructure the family so that there were (1) a functioning spousal system with a clear boundary differentiating it from other subsystems, (2) a parental subsystem with clear executive functions and authority, and (3) a sibling subsystem free from enmeshment with both the parent and the spousal subsystems.[24]

Minuchin utilized three main strategies to accomplish his goals: challenging the system, challenging the family structure, and challenging the family reality. These strategies all involved helping the family alter its view of the symptom bearer and his or her relationship to the rest of the family. Most families initially view the bearer of a symptom as "the problem." Minuchin assisted families to perceive that the individual was responding to stress in the system as a whole.[25]

In working to change family structure, Minuchin used a number of creative techniques. Among them were joining, reframing, enactment, boundary making, intensity, and unbalancing.

Joining, as described earlier in reference to JoEllen Madsen's work with the Peterson family, involves developing a trusting relationship between therapist and family as work is getting underway. Minuchin viewed therapist and family as forming a new system, which must develop its own rules of interaction.

Reframing is a technique to assist families to look at problems in new ways. Viewing a "problem child" as a symptom bearer for the family as a whole is one example. Reframing will be explored in more detail in a later chapter.

Enactment is a technique used by structural therapists in which family members are instructed to demonstrate their habitual patterns of interaction right in the office. Sometimes the therapist precipitates a disagreement to get the family started, instructing the members to work out the disagreement exactly as they would at home. Unexpected family coalitions (covert subsystems) may then be revealed.

Boundary making is a type of enactment in which a therapist encourages members of one subsystem to interact but blocks participation of members of another subsystem. For example, parents may be encouraged to argue with each other about an issue; if the children attempt to break into the argument, the therapist prevents them. Another kind of boundary making involves manipulation of physical proximity. For example, the therapist may ask a child who has taken a chair between his or her parents to change seats with one of them. When spouses are seated side by side, their subsystem boundary is highlighted.

Sometimes therapists want to increase the intensity of a session, to manifest certain family interactions that family members have been ignoring. An example might be the ongoing interruption of one member by another. The therapist increases intensity by commenting directly on the interaction to be highlighted, deliberately magnifying it so it becomes part of the family's field of consciousness.

Unbalancing the system is a technique in which the therapist intentionally interferes with the system's "steady state" and precipitates a disequilibrium because that steady state is not healthy for the family. As an example, the therapist may take sides with one spouse against another. The intent is not to attack any one person but to challenge the rules of the system as a whole. To be effective, the therapist must help family members understand that, although he or she may be against the *system* as it stands, the purpose of the intervention is to help each person within the system.[26]

Contributions of the Milan School

In Europe, family therapy began to gain acceptance around the same time but it took on a somewhat different form. One of the most famous models was developed in Milan, Italy, by a group of four people: two women—Selvini Palazzoli and Guiliana Prata— and two men—Gianfranco Cecchin and Luigi Boscolo. They became famous among family practitioners in the United States after the 1978 publication of their book, *Paradox and Counterparadox.*

Therapists practicing according to the Milan model were much less directive than most of their American counterparts. They were interested in the development of problems over time, and they specifically inquired about each family member's internal beliefs and feelings. In this way, these therapists were not unlike Satir. The Milan group also developed a sophisticated technique known as "circular questioning" that was intended to reveal ways in which problem behaviors were maintained by the family system as a whole. For example, family member A might be asked how the behavior of family member B affected family member C, and then how C's behavior affected A and B. Through elegant questioning alone, these therapists believed, unhealthy systems could be gently nudged out of balance. And once a system had been disturbed, these therapists did not assume responsibility for reconstructing a new steady state. Rather, they believed that families, if asked the right questions, could figure out what they wanted themselves and could develop a new balance on their own.[27]

The Milan model was systems-based. Therapists in this school believed themselves to be closer to Bateson's theoretical approaches than

American schools were, in that therapists maintained a position of neutrality and collaborated in teams almost as if they were engaged in a research project. A primary therapist worked with a family before a one-way mirror, with a team behind the mirror providing ongoing consultation. The therapist frequently left the office to brainstorm with the team. The team then created elaborate written messages for the family to take home and study.

The Milan group's move toward helping families explore their own problems and potential solutions, as opposed to imposing forceful interventions, was the harbinger of what is now known as the postmodern era in family therapy, characterized by constructivism.

Constructivism

By the end of the 1970s, family therapy had come into its own, and the very acceptance of the field allowed members to reexamine basic assumptions and techniques. One line of the critique that ensued became known as "constructivism." According to constructivism, reality is only a mental construction of the observer. Therefore, family therapists must be aware that what they think they perceive in the therapy process is only a product of their assumptions.

Constructivists discarded many former assumptions of systems-based family therapists, such as the hypothesis that certain family structures or patterns of relationships induce members to bear symptoms. Instead, they focused on an exploration of meaning with family members with the aim of understanding people's assumptions about their own problems. Together, family and therapist searched for the meaning of a given situation, and in the process the family was encouraged to tell its own "story." Gradually, through conversation with an accepting, attentive therapist, a new, more hopeful story might emerge.[28]

Some constructivists allow families to develop their own stories entirely, but Australian therapist Michael White developed a new twist. He actively guided families toward a story in which their presenting problem was externalized, or viewed as *causing* the family's problem rather than, say, serving to stabilize a stressed family system. For example, in a case of a 6-year-old boy with encopresis, White helped externalize the boy's problem by giving the soiling behavior a name of its own, "Sneaky Poo." Then, through extensive use of questions designed to help map the influence of the problem on the boy's life and family relationships, White helped the child develop a story in which he was able to defeat Sneaky Poo's "tricks." The approach resulted in cessation of the symptom.[29]

An influential constructivist model, known initially as "brief therapy" and later as "solution-focused therapy," has been developed by Steve de Shazer, Insoo Berg, and colleagues in Milwaukee, Wisconsin. In the solution-focused approach to family work, people who come for help are first encouraged to tell their story. Then they are asked to identify exceptions to their problems, solutions that have worked in the past. People thus are assisted to disentangle from their problems and are encouraged to develop a more empowering story. One technique of doing so is to have clients imagine a miracle in which their problems are already solved. The therapist asks the clients specifically what happened for the miracle to take place and then helps the clients develop a step-by-step practical solution based on their own ideas. The solution-focused model is short term and pragmatic. It has grown in popularity throughout the 1980s and 1990s, partly as a result of economic advantage in a growing managed-care environment.

Feminist Critique of Family Therapy

Another challenge to systems-based family therapy came from feminists. Feminists pointed out that while all parts of a system may interact, with each part affecting every other, still, the impact of various parts is not equal. They pointed out that sexism in the wider culture makes males more powerful than females in their families; this can and has resulted in horrifying physical and sexual abuse of women and girls, often by their significant others. Feminists pointed out that family therapists generally either overlooked the power differential between males and females in the family or minimized it, to the detriment of the females. Feminists feared that without direct intervention to modify the misuse of power by men in families and to empower women, women in therapy were being poorly served.

The feminist challenge came as a surprise to family therapists, who had believed themselves progressive. But Bateson had indeed claimed that universal control in a system was impossible, since all elements influence one another. This viewpoint was enthusiastically embraced by most family therapists because, if all parts of a system influence a problem, no one person has to be blamed. However, feminists pointed out that battered women should not be held responsible for their battery. Research demonstrated that approximately 95% of batterers were male, providing sobering evidence for the need for a new perspective. From the feminist point of view, holding women equally responsible for the abuse they received was only a new way of "blaming the victim."[30]

Systems-based family therapists responded to the feminist critique with considerable soul searching. Moreover, in addition to considering gender, therapists began to recognize that other major societal factors affect family relationships as well, such as ethnicity, race, class, age, and homophobia. Fortunately, however, nothing in general systems theory itself precludes assessment of influences from the wider society in the process of conducting family therapy. To the contrary, Bertalanffy, who originally developed systems theory, did so as a way of attempting to understand relationships among systems, subsystems, and suprasystems that extended as wide as the universe itself.

Although many theorists who originally adapted general systems theory to family therapy (like Bateson and Jackson) may have overlooked systems effects external to the family, systems theory itself can be an excellent tool for remedying this oversight. The systems approach provides an elegant framework to assess the interactive effects of myriad systems. Satir, for example, perhaps because she was a woman, always considered gender effects in her work. Minuchin, who conducted most of his work with families from the slums, certainly considered the effects of poverty on family organization and disorganization.

Family therapy today includes practitioners who describe themselves as systems-based and those who do not. The constructivist and feminist critiques have helped mature the field. For example, even therapists who consider their work firmly systems-based now assess the impact of symptoms on families as well as families on symptoms. A child's bed-wetting behavior, for example, strongly affects family relationships whether its origin pertains to family stress or not. More attention is paid to meanings families attach to their problems. Many therapists are far less active and directive than the pioneers were, and they pay more attention to the family's point of view. It is now recognized that influences from outside the family system can generate a "symptom": for example, school phobia in a child *may* be a response to stress within the family system, and it *may* be a mechanism that helps strengthen the spousal subsystem so the family survives intact. However, school phobia may also be a fearful response to academic failure at school or even a response to behaviors of other children. The family therapist's role is to conduct thorough assessments, in consultation with family members, to help determine which of these or many other processes may be at work.

Many of the contributions of the pioneers in family therapy have stood the test of time and still guide the field today. Families usually do provide the means for their members' survival and comprise their offspring's initial world. Within the world of the family, each member develops behaviors that will enhance survival, even when those behaviors may seem inexplicable without careful assessment. The challenge for family therapists today is to make use of all the frames available for viewing human behavior, perhaps even to conceive some more, and to put them into the service of helping create happier, healthier human beings.

CHAPTER 13

An Exercise in Reframing

The Peterson family came in for their third appointment right on time. Family members did not look as relaxed or happy as they had when they arrived the week before, however. Molly's face in particular looked almost grim, and she opened the session without any prompting.

"I'm very angry with Charlotte," she began. "She's just moped around all week. She hasn't done her summer school homework, and if this keeps up, she'll just have to repeat her entire junior year of high school."

"That's not fair, Mother!" Charlotte yelled in an unusually loud voice, using a formal term for Molly for the first time in session. "If you just didn't bug me so much, I'd get things done!"

"Molly is pretty hard on Charlotte," Henry broke in. "She's a nut on education. I can't blame my daughter for goofing off. Her mother needs to understand that school just isn't everything for everybody."

"Dad doesn't think I need to be grounded anymore, and I don't either," Charlotte broke in once more. "It isn't fair. My whole summer is being ruined."

"Molly and Henry, I take it you disagree on the importance of Charlotte's being grounded this summer, and also about the importance of her completing summer school," said JoEllen, summarizing what she had heard.

"That's right," Molly spoke up. "Charlotte has been impossible all week. She hasn't been getting her schoolwork done and Henry won't back me up when I tell her to study."

"I'm so mad at Mother I could scream," Charlotte broke in, her voice loud and angry. "I hate going to summer school. I've never had to go before. Mother doesn't trust me. I'd get my work done if only she'd just let me have a little fun once in a while."

"Sounds to me like you are coming between your parents again, Charlotte," reflected JoEllen.

"What?" The girl sputtered, startled.

"Remember how we talked about a process called triangulation last week?"

"Sure. The love triangle stuff in the novels."

"That is one kind of triangulation. Yours is another. Do you see how you may be getting triangulated right now in your own family?"

"Not really," Charlotte replied.

"Your parents left here very angry with each other last week. Yet it sounds to me as if they've been disagreeing over your behavior this week, not theirs. Would you agree?"

"Well . . ." Charlotte looked confused. She fell silent.

"Molly," JoEllen said turning to the mother, "your homework this week was to observe examples of triangulation at home. Have you noticed any?"

"Sure," Molly replied, "Henry uses it all the time. I don't know if he uses Charlotte, as I think you just suggested, but he constantly puts other women between himself and me."

"Have you and Henry discussed that, Molly?"

"No. The message from the team was just to observe and gather information." Molly's tone sounded a little defensive.

"Are you willing to talk about it here tonight?"

"Sure," she stated firmly.

"Just a minute," Henry broke in. "You said I'd get my chance to talk this week, JoEllen." His voice tone was light, almost teasing, but the expression on his face was clearly annoyed. "I've been observing this triangulation too. Molly uses it all the time against me with the kids."

"OK, it *is* your turn, Henry," JoEllen responded in kind, her tone slightly teasing. "But tell that directly to Molly," she coached, more seriously.

"No problem," said Henry, and he launched into a lecture with an almost triumphant air. "Molly, you use triangulation against me with the kids all the time, and I don't think it's fair. You get the kids on your side, especially Josh. You used to get George on your side too. I may do this triangulation thing sometimes with grown women, but that's different. You do it with the kids, and I have to *live* with them. You don't have to live with the other women in my life."

Molly snapped back. "What do you mean I don't have to live with the other women in your life! You bring them right into our household. You expect me to be friendly to them, even cook dinners for them."

"I invite people home so that they can become *our* friends, *both* our friends! And some of the folks I invite home are men! I can't help it if more women than men are interested in getting to know us!"

"You know perfectly well why women are more interested. You flirt with them."

"So what? And anyway, they know I put you first; I tell every woman I bring home that you are my wife, and my primary relationship. I tell them up front that I am never going to leave you."

"Yes, but do you think these women believe it, that you are never going to leave me?"

"Of course they do," Henry replied. "And you yourself have said how much fun we all have together."

"Sure we have fun with our friends, I admit it. But most of your best friends are women, and sometimes your friendships become affairs. I hate that. I am humiliated and embarrassed. And I don't think you set a good example for the children." Molly's voice sounded notably different from the week before. She revealed her anger and her hurt clearly and directly.

"The affairs I have are only occasional," Henry replied in an even, reasoning manner, "and you know they never last more than a year or so. That's how affairs are, like I've told you over and over. Each one is like skiing off the top of a mountain. You know you're going to end every run at the bottom sometime, but you sure enjoy the trip on the way down. And you know you can go back up the mountain again for another one."

"But what about US?" bellowed Molly. "What about our *MARRIAGE?* You are my *HUSBAND!*"

"Marriage is different—it's for the duration. I couldn't live with anybody but you, Molly; you know that because I've told you at least a hundred times. I want you to be my wife, and I want to live with you always." Henry's voice was ardent, smooth. Powerfully convincing.

"Well," Molly wavered.

Henry continued persuasively, with a debonair smile. "You're my primary relationship, Molly. Nobody could ever take your place."

His wife smiled at him shyly, pride apparent upon her features.

"But you know you can't give me what an affair can—no wife can or ever could—I have to have the romance and the excitement too. As long as I can get that extra energy in my life I can stay with you forever."

Molly's tender smile shrank, her face clouded suddenly with a look of confusion.

Charlotte entered the conversation then, siding with her father. "Dad doesn't mean to hurt Mom," she said seriously to JoEllen. "I've heard Dad tell the lady he's dating now that he'll never leave Mom. He's a very honest person; he really wants to stay married to my mother. He just likes a lot of other women too."

"Charlotte, will you do me a favor?" asked JoEllen.

"Sure," said Charlotte. Her agreeable tone mirrored her father's.

"Will you change seats with your mother?"

Charlotte looked surprised. So did Molly.

"Change seats?" the girl repeated.

"Look where you're sitting," responded JoEllen. "Right between your mother and father. It seems to me as if you protect your parents from each other."

Charlotte looked startled. "Huh?" she said.

"You said last week that you kept your father's latest affair a secret from your mother, apparently for quite some time."

"Yes, I did. I didn't want to hurt poor Mom."

"That's what I mean. You protect your parents from each other. You protect your mother from being upset by not telling her. You protect your father so that he doesn't have to deal with a wife who is upset."

"I guess I didn't look at it that way," said Charlotte.

"I want to pull you out of the middle, Charlotte. Change seats with your mother."

Charlotte and Molly changed seats. Charlotte then looked toward JoEllen from her new chair and grinned. She tossed her long hair out of her eyes.

"How do you feel now?" asked JoEllen.

"Better," said Charlotte.

"And how are you feeling, Molly?"

"Upset. I'm very upset."

"What specifically is upsetting you?"

"That my own daughter kept a secret from me. I should have expected it, though. She usually sides with her father. He usually sides with her, like this week, saying her homework isn't important."

"So you are angry at Charlotte."

"Yes, I sure am."

"Are you aware that being angry with your daughter may get in the way of your feeling angry with your husband?"

"You mean if I'm angry at Charlotte I may not get as mad at Henry?"

"That's right. Charlotte's being triangulated, to use that fancy term again. She's being pulled between you two."

"But she kept an important secret from her own mother!"

"Sure she did, and she may have gained something from it, too. She may have gained more attention from her father, for example, at your expense. That could make you angry at your daughter for good reason. But let's look at things in a different way. How do you feel toward Henry when he has an affair?"

"Furious. Absolutely furious."

"And in your most furious moments in the past over your husband's affairs, haven't you said you've thought about leaving him?"

"I certainly have!"

"Couldn't it be, then, that Charlotte kept that secret with Henry to try and help save your marriage, to do what she could to keep the family together?"

JoEllen thus reframed Charlotte's behavior for the mother. Reframing is a technique in family counseling in which the therapist shifts the meaning of a behavior originally perceived as negative toward one that is more positive.

Molly looked thoughtful. "I suppose you could look at it that way," she said slowly. She looked over at her daughter, who appeared surprised and pleased. This was a new and interesting idea for both of them.

"Really, Mom," Charlotte said. "I did the best I could, but sometimes it's hard for me to know just what I ought to do."

"That's OK, Charlotte," said Molly with a sigh. "I should probably be angry at your father, not you. His affairs are not your fault."

"Tell Henry how you feel," coached JoEllen.

"I'm mad at my husband," Molly said, directing her words to JoEllen.

"Molly," JoEllen intervened, "Henry is sitting right beside you now. You can talk to him directly."

"What's the use? He won't listen."

"How do you know?"

"I've told him I'm angry—hurt and angry—a thousand times. Henry doesn't care. He won't change. He's said so." Molly's eyes remained directed toward JoEllen, almost pleading.

"This time things may be different. Look at Henry directly, Molly. Talk to him."

Molly glanced at Henry, who met her eyes briefly. Then the woman looked down and said in an angry, frustrated tone, "You make me mad, very mad, you, you . . ." she struggled for words.

JoEllen intervened again. "Molly," she coached, use 'I feel' statements. 'I feel angry when you—.' Take responsibility for your own feelings, and take care to avoid name-calling."

Counselors often teach their clients to use "I feel" statements, because they are usually less threatening to their receivers. A statement such as "I feel angry when you have an affair" elicits a less defensive response, for example, than "you dirty rotten adulterer."

Molly looked at Henry again. This time her look was long, measured. She seemed to be gathering strength for a major assault. The woman squared her small shoulders and lifted her animated, delicate features toward her husband's smooth visage. Her dark eyes burned with intensity.

"HENRY, WHEN YOU HAVE AN AFFAIR I FEEL HUMILIATED AND ANGRY AND I NO LONGER WANT TO BE YOUR WIFE!" The words, the tone, the facial expression were absolutely congruent.

Whew, thought JoEllen, Molly sure can express herself directly when she wants to. She looked toward Henry to find out how he was responding. Henry finally let his anger show, and he used a clever tactic of distraction.

"Look," he said, "I came here this evening prepared to discuss triangulation from my point of view. Look here, Molly. How come you always take sides with Josh and our older son, George, against me?"

"We're talking about your affairs with other women," said Molly, bravely sticking to the subject. "Besides, who do I have to talk to except the kids when you're gone all the time?"

"You know you shouldn't talk to the kids about things that aren't their business!"

"Look who's talking!" Molly retorted. "Who told Charlotte you were having an affair? Is that her business?"

"She's old enough to know!"

The telephone rang, bringing the exchange to an uneasy halt. JoEllen listened intently for a moment.

"OK, Kurt," she said. Then she rose to her feet and moved so that she stood directly in front of the parents, separating them from their children.

"The team says Henry's affairs are an important issue you two must resolve yourselves, without triangulating the children," JoEllen said. "Do you understand how you have been triangulating your children?"

"That's just what I was saying!" exclaimed Henry, looking up at JoEllen appealingly. "Molly uses Josh against me. She doesn't back me up when I discipline the brat and she tells him not to listen to me."

"Remember the time when Josh was doing poorly in school, Henry, before he went into counseling?" continued JoEllen.

"Remember? Of course I remember!" the man almost shouted. "The kid didn't do his work at school or at home. He had a real problem."

"And have you noticed that after Josh went into counseling, and his behavior improved, Charlotte got into trouble?"

"Of course I noticed!" Henry sounded exasperated.

"That was also around the time you told your daughter about your affair, was it not?"

Henry looked startled. Slowly, he nodded.

"Your children have both been triangulated by one or the other of you," JoEllen said sternly. "The particulars aren't important right now. What is important is that your children have been under enormous stress not of their own making. I believe they've been trying to help save your marriage." JoEllen spoke these words slowly and deliberately, her standing height adding emphasis.

"What do you mean?" asked Molly.

"When Charlotte shoplifts or flunks out of school or refuses to do her summer school assignments," the therapist continued, "her behavior forces you and Henry to talk to each other, to communicate, to try to figure out what to do as a parental team. Is that not so?"

Slowly, Molly nodded.

"Then," continued JoEllen, "your anger gets directed mostly at Charlotte. You could say that your daughter is sacrificing herself to save your marriage. Her misbehavior also distracts you from remembering how mad you are at your spouse. Josh made a similar sacrifice earlier in the year, I believe."

Silence ensued. Then, weakly, from Henry: "That's nuts."

Molly said, "It makes sense to me."

Josh spoke for the first time that evening. "Wow," he said. "I'm a hero! So's Charlotte!"

More silence followed as the various members of the family took in the meaning of JoEllen's words, each in his or her own way. Then the telephone rang.

"Come on back for your end-of session consultation, JoEllen. Let's quit a little early today," said Kurt. "This is a good place to stop, with the family off balance and paying attention. The team will reinforce the message."

JoEllen excused herself and went behind the mirror. From the observation room the family could be seen sitting silently. Henry and Molly both had stunned expressions on their faces. Though seated side by side, their bodies did not touch. Molly's hands were folded in her lap, and Henry's were placed upon his knees. The fingers of his right hand drummed against his knee cap.

Charlotte and Josh looked tired but pleased. Josh began to wiggle and make silly grins into the mirror.

"Oh come on, Josh," Charlotte reprimanded. "This is serious." The boy got out of his chair and began dancing around the room. He sat down only at his mother's direct request.

The message the team sent the family that evening was as follows: "The team wants to congratulate the Peterson family on its will to survive. Despite difficulties that might have separated many a family, you have found the means to stay together. We congratulate Charlotte and Josh for the creative ways you two have developed to help hold your parents' marriage together.

We encourage all of you to identify other ways that Charlotte, Josh, and perhaps even George have sacrificed themselves to keep this family together. We encourage the children to continue their good work to help save Molly and Henry's marriage."

CHAPTER 14

Reframing as a Therapeutic Tool

Reframing, as illustrated in the previous session with the Peterson family, is a way of influencing perception. It involves a conceptual leap so that behavior that is first seen from one frame of reference is suddenly seen from another. The same behavior then takes on new meaning. The reframing process requires a creative leap. Not every person or family can manage such a leap but, if accomplished, dramatic behavioral change can follow.

JoEllen Madsen engaged in reframing frequently with the Peterson family. In the second session, for example, the trainee reframed Molly's jealousy and insecurity as "good friends" rather than weaknesses. They were "friends" because they informed Molly that energy that should be going into her marriage was being diverted elsewhere. Later, JoEllen reframed Charlotte's "little secret" from her mother as an attempt to save the parents' marriage. Charlotte's shoplifting and poor school performance and Josh's earlier troubles in school were reframed in the same way. The consultation team behind the mirror then further reframed the children's misbehavior as "good work" to reinforce JoEllen's message.

Reframing is a powerful tool employed by family therapists (and other therapists as well). The term *reframe* is a metaphor, coined by Gregory Bateson, the famous anthropologist who conducted communication research in Palo Alto, California (discussed in Chapter 12). Bateson used the picture frame as a metaphor to convey a sense of bounding items in communication, to highlight them just as a picture frame focuses attention on the work of art within its borders.[31] A therapist may reflect back a particular set of data (behavior, information, and so on) a client provides, highlighting it by the very act of attention and thus "framing" it. The therapist may then "reframe" the same data for the client by shifting the emphasis or meaning of some part or parts.

Ideally, "reframing" shifts the meaning of data in a positive way for the client, allowing the person to generate new behaviors that may lead to problem resolution. According to Watzlawick, Weakland, and Fisch, reframing changes "the conceptual and/or emotional setting or viewpoint in relation to which a situation is experienced and places it in another frame which fits the 'facts' of the same concrete situation equally well or even better, and thereby changes its entire meaning."[32] Another illustrative definition of reframing is "the deliberate manipulation of information that clients use to ascribe meaning to thoughts, feelings, behaviors, or situations."[33]

Family therapists frequently reframe fighting between a marital couple as a sign of intense commitment to one another. For example, fighting behavior is not an insurmountable problem, it is merely the process the couple uses right now to demonstrate commitment. In the case of the Petersons, the consultation team in the first session defined Henry and Molly's fighting behavior as a demonstration of their "passion" for one another. Fighting interpreted as a process of achieving or maintaining commitment places this experience in a relatively nonthreatening light. As Kersey and Protinsky note, "the therapist offers a reframe which prompts a 'Well, now that you put it *that* way,' response from clients."[34] This frees up emotional energy toward generating alternative processes to strengthen commitment.

Wayne Jones reflects that sensory information must be interpreted by each person before being stored in the brain as memory. The person's past experience will form the basis of how he or she interprets sensory data, which is then classified and organized for memory storage. Whether a person's initial interpretation persists will depend at least to some extent on feedback from significant others, so that an individual's reality is always a mental construction to some degree. It is this penchant of humankind's to interpret raw sensory data and check it against the reality of others that allows reframes to work. The therapist joins in the client's social reality and influences interpretation of raw sensory data.[35]

Jones points out that the objective "truth" of suggested reframes is less important than the power new meanings can have to generate new problem-solving behaviors. Reframing is intended to change the way a client classifies a problem, refocusing from the problematic aspects of symptomatic behaviors to the positive.

Similarly, LaClave and Brack describe reframing as a "second-order change" whereby the therapist facilitates "first-order change" (changing one's problem-solving strategies) by providing a radically different means of viewing the problem for the client. These authors believe that "at the core of reframing is the simple belief that one can find a more adaptive, and less painful, means of viewing the world."[36]

As LaClave and Brack note, the therapist is challenged to look beyond the immediate dysfunction of a symptom to discover its hidden benefits. These benefits can then potentially be utilized to promote change. They suggest that reframing merely shifts the focus of a client's attention from "problem" to "process," which often allows less resistance to problem resolution because the client will usually be able to imagine experimenting with different processes to achieve an already desired goal.

Looking for hidden benefits in a symptom usually viewed as "bad" (such as marital fighting or children's misbehavior) and prescribing more of the same may be viewed as a type of paradoxical intervention. *Paradoxical interventions* are suggestions that the therapist actually *wants* family members to resist, so that their undesirable behavior will change. Reframing is only one technique among many that can be used in a paradoxical manner.

Paradoxical interventions are especially effective in inducing resistant families to change. These are the families who disagree with the therapist's interpretations, deny making progress, or do not do their homework assignments, for example. The therapist then encourages the very problem behavior that brought the family into treatment—in effect, "prescribes the symptom." If the family is to continue resisting the therapist, it must change.

In the case of the Petersons, the consultation team's message to the family after the third therapy session included a reframe that was also a paradoxical intervention. The "symptom" bringing the family to therapy, the children's misbehavior, was reframed as "good work" in that it helped hold the parents' marriage together. Family survival being a worthy goal, the children were then encouraged to do more of the same.

The team, of course, did not want the children actually to follow such a suggestion. The intent, instead, was to provoke them to rebel.

Given the team's instructions, Charlotte and Josh would be unable to misbehave without remembering the function the team ascribed to their misbehavior. The children would then probably resist the team's suggestion and insist instead that their parents fight their own battles. Hopefully, at the same time, the parents would begin to work on solving their marital problems themselves.

Some therapists have expressed ethical concerns regarding paradoxical techniques, since they seem to manipulate clients into behaving in new ways without their full understanding of what is happening. However, most reframing activities—even those that involve paradoxical interventions—simply reveal a different part of the "truth" to the client, a truth already somewhere in the client's reality. The part of truth revealed may previously have rested in the client's unconscious, or it may have penetrated to the conscious to some degree but remain unacknowledged.

The following case synopsis helps illustrate how reframing can reveal a different part of "truth." A highly educated professional sought counseling because of a problem she described as "uncontrollable obsessive thought." The client described this type of thought as "neurotic" and "sick," and as a result she felt helpless, angry, and out of control. The therapist soon learned that the client had recently suffered the loss of a lover; the obsessive thoughts related to that loss.

The therapist discussed the grief process with the client and reframed her "obsessive" thinking as normal under the circumstances, even necessary for grief resolution. Such a reframe contained nothing deceitful, and it was probably much closer to the truth than the client's own self-deprecating labels. A focus on the "problem" of compulsive thought, which brought the client to therapy, was thus shifted to the "process" of grieving necessary to resolve loss.

The therapist then "prescribed the symptom" as a means of relieving it. The client was urged to take ample time to work the grief through properly. She and the therapist determined certain hours of the day when thoughts about grief and loss were to be pursued religiously. The client was instructed to "obsess" during the designated hours, whether the desire was present or not. If obsessive thoughts intruded at other times, the client was to put them aside until the next designated hour. In this way, she learned to control the timing of her symptom, which made her feel less helpless. Shortly thereafter, the client reported having difficulty filling her designated hours with feelings of grief and loss; she began to forget to carry out her assignment. The presenting problem was resolved.

Perhaps the best use of reframing and other potentially paradoxical interventions is to help reveal what the therapist genuinely believes to be the process maintaining the presenting problem. Careful assessment, of course, is required for effective interventions to be designed. Some therapists view the shift in focus from problem to process in reframing as "a reversal of the usual figure and ground" in human perception.[37]

A figure-ground reversal is reminiscent of a common illustration pertaining to Gestalt psychology that is frequently presented in introductory psychology texts. This illustration outlines the profiles of two people facing one another. Viewed from one perspective, the two profiles practically leap off the page. Between them, however, is outlined a vase. The vase (ground) remains hidden as long as attention is riveted on the profiles (figure). Viewed from another perspective, however, the profiles disappear (ground) and the vase outlined between them leaps into focus (figure). The observer can choose which image to focus on as "figure," and the other then automatically becomes "ground."

The therapist in the preceding example of the grieving client assisted the rejected woman to recognize the normality and health of her symptom. "Healthy grieving process" could become "figure" in the client's mind. Thus freed of self-deprecation, she could studiously pursue a controlled schedule of grieving. Any potentially pathological aspects of her obsessive thoughts could fade into "ground" for this client.

Reframes do not always work as intended, of course. Like any other technique in counseling, reframing should be used with care and only after appropriate groundwork has been laid. (Paradoxical techniques are *always* inappropriate for suicidal or homicidal clients. The slightest chance that such a client might follow that paradoxical suggestion is too much chance indeed.)

James Coyne points out that the metaphor of the picture frame "becomes problematic when it is taken to suggest that frames are well defined and static, rather than ambiguous, dynamic, and, very often, precarious."[38] In other words, frames (or reframes) may work in some situations but not others, and they may not always "take" the way the therapist intended. Consider the following example.

Husband: It wasn't until she started working that we began having problems. I blame everything on her decision to go back to work.

Wife: It's all his fault. He never listens to me or concerns himself with what I need. Then he yells all the time.

Therapist: So, Joe, you blame your wife, and Diane, you say it's Joe's fault. Maybe you're both right about some things. And because you're both right we can start working on something together, now, to help your marriage.

Husband: What do you mean, we're both right? She can't be right. I'm not at fault and I'm not blaming anyone. You just don't understand.[39]

From this example, it is obvious that information may be reframed by a therapist to ascribe new meaning to client thoughts or behaviors. But only sometimes does the reframe achieve its therapeutically intended results (problem amelioration or resolution). Sometimes reframes are rejected, misunderstood, or accepted by only part of the system to which they are offered. In the Peterson case, for example, JoEllen Madsen's reframes seem to have been accepted by Molly and the children, but not by Henry.

Therapists who wish to utilize the technique of reframing will find it wise to move slowly, to study each respective client system carefully before attempting reframes as part of the therapeutic intervention. Reframes that work with one client system won't necessarily work with another. When done effectively, reframing is not a gimmick or a slick trick to throw out indiscriminately. As Jones writes,

> *before serious farmers begin to plant the seeds for a new crop, they first become well acquainted with the soil. . . . Therapists, like farmers, before giving any serious consideration to planting new frames, must first become well acquainted with the unique nature of their client-families and the tried-and-true frames that already organize their lives. This enables therapists to speak the language of the family.*[40]

The successful therapist learns how the client views the world before attempting to reframe a part of it. Kersey and Protinsky use the terms *pacing* and *joining* to describe how the therapist lets the client know he or she understands the client's world.[41] First, the therapist *listens* to the client carefully. Then, in pacing, the therapist reflects back to the client exact content provided by the client, using language (vocabulary, concepts, and so on) familiar to the client. The meaning of current experience is reflected back to the client as the client has described it. In this way, the therapist begins to build rapport (join) with the client and enables the client to feel understood. Later, the therapist can lead the client toward new perspectives and perceptions.

In reality, an important goal of any therapy is to help clients gain new perspectives and perceptions, to broaden their view of the world. In that sense, reframing can be understood as simply another technique in communication related to the wider goal of learning. Reframing can, however, alter clients' perceptions of the world in dramatic ways, leading to relatively immediate behavioral changes.

In utilizing reframing, then, the therapist must take time to understand the client's worldview, "pace" it back to the client, and then "join" it so that the client feels safe and understood. Any use of reframing will have to accept the client's beliefs about the world, at the same time that they are broadened. Milton Erickson, a hypnotherapist famous for his work in reframing, once stated, "You never ask the patient to falsify his own understanding; instead you give him other understandings that nullify, that contradict, that absorb and hold his focus, so that he cannot give all his attention to what is distressing him."[42]

Returning to the Peterson case to illustrate these concepts, JoEllen Madsen and the consultation team took time to understand and "join" their clients' worldview by exploring the family's presenting problem in detail. The therapists accepted and explored Molly's resistance to therapy as well, utilizing the resistance by asking her to talk about the reasons she didn't believe that the family needed to be in therapy after all. Only when Molly was encouraged to talk about her family's strengths did the team learn about the meaning of "fun" for this client. Learning about "fun" led to information about Henry's sexual affairs and Molly's struggles to cope. Then a hypothesis about how the children's misbehavior might relate to marital distress could be developed, leading to therapeutic reframing. The misbehavior was reframed as a process of "good work" being performed to save the parents' marriage.

The reframing of the children's behavior shifted the previous "ground" to "figure." In other words, the reframe shifted the family's attention from the "problem" of the children's misbehavior to the "process" it was maintaining. The process was positive: helping maintain the parents' marriage, and thus survival of the family as a whole.

Even if accepted as positive in function, however, the parents could not consciously allow such a process to continue. What self-respecting parents could consciously want their children to continue to fail in school, to shoplift, and so on to help save their marriage? Henry and Molly would be forced to pay attention to their own relationship, if only to prove the team wrong.

CHAPTER 15

❀

An Early Termination

Henry brought a tape recorder to the next session. "Hell," he said to JoEllen as he walked into the training office with a grand air, "if you're going to make videos of these meetings, I'm going to tape them too. I want to make sure I don't get misquoted later."

The man sat down, pressed the "record" button on his little machine, and placed it carefully on the floor in front of him. Then he stretched his long legs and arms luxuriously, as if he didn't have a care in the world. The two actions didn't seem to fit but JoEllen merely responded, "No problem."

"Good," Henry said. "I don't have time to drive all the way down here to look at your videotapes, JoEllen. But we've been arguing about what's been said in session at home."

"You've been arguing?"

"You'd better believe we've been arguing. This counseling is making things worse than ever."

JoEllen responded in a teasing tone. "Well, Henry, you know how the saying goes. Sometimes things have to get worse before they can get better."

"The hell with that. My wife's trying to control me again. She doesn't remember what she's said down here—that she really likes the fun we have with all our friends at home. She denies agreeing it's OK for me to have special relationships."

"By special relationships, do you mean affairs, Henry?" asked JoEllen.

"Of course I mean affairs," Henry retorted, "but Molly knows darned well I'm not going to leave her. That's what counts."

Molly spoke up. "Henry makes me so mad. I don't deny saying that I enjoy having fun with our friends. But I have never willingly agreed to his having affairs. I simply can't stop him. He gets furious at me when I try. And now that we've learned what his affairs are doing to the children—"

"My affairs have nothing to do with the kids!" Henry retorted.

"What about your homework for last week, Henry," JoEllen interjected calmly. "Remember, the team congratulated your family on its will to survive. Your children were congratulated on their good work to help hold your marriage with Molly together. Did you do the homework that the team assigned then?"

"What homework?" Henry said crossly.

"If I remember correctly, the team asked you to think about other ways the children may be sacrificing themselves to save your marriage, besides shoplifting and flunking out of school."

"That's ridiculous," said Henry. "I won't do homework like that because it's crazy."

"It's not crazy, Henry," said Molly loudly, "and you know it. I'm very angry at you because of your affairs with other women. I probably only stay in this marriage for the sake of the family. Most of our friends know about your other women and feel sorry for me. It's embarrassing. I hate living this way, pretending everything is OK between you and me when it isn't."

"You see, JoEllen," said Henry, "Molly's trying to control me again, just like I said. This has nothing to do with the kids. She just doesn't want me to have any friends."

"Friends, or sexual partners?" asked JoEllen.

"Molly doesn't want me to have either," said Henry.

"Henry, that's not true!" said Molly.

"Before we get into a whole different argument, about whether friends are OK and if so, what kind," JoEllen said sternly, "I want to hear from Charlotte and Josh about the homework assignment for this week."

"OK," said Molly.

"That's ridiculous," sputtered Henry.

"Henry, is it OK with you if the children talk with me about the homework?" JoEllen inquired. "I don't want to put them in the position of having to take sides with you or Molly. If you refuse to discuss the team's assignment for this week, the children may feel they have to refuse also."

"It's OK with me if the kids talk about the homework," Henry said in a resigned tone. "That doesn't mean I'm going to agree with what they say."

"Fair enough," said JoEllen. The trainee then turned to Charlotte. "Charlotte, I want to begin with you. What did you think about the homework assignment for this week? And did you do it?"

Charlotte's facial expression was apprehensive. She looked at each of her parents in turn. She was no longer sitting between them, but she clearly didn't want to say anything that might upset either one.

"Charlotte, your father has said it's OK if you express yourself, even if he disagrees with what you say."

"Sure, he says that but I don't think he means it."

"Henry, will you tell Charlotte directly that it's OK for her to tell us what she thinks?"

Henry gave a long, theatrical sigh, rolled his handsome blue eyes very much as Charlotte had done in a previous session, and bowed gallantly to JoEllen from his seat. He turned then to his daughter.

"It's OK, Charlotte," he said. "Remember, I probably won't agree with you, but go ahead."

Charlotte grinned at her father then and shook her head fondly. A light of compassion beyond her years shone in her intelligent blue eyes.

"Whew, this is hard," she said. "I know you won't like this, Dad. But I thought that the homework did make sense and I came up with other ways that Josh and I try to keep you and Mom from fighting with each other."

"Good for you, Charlotte," said JoEllen when Henry remained silent, the corners of his mouth turning down. "Can you give us an example?"

"Well—when Josh used to get to classes late at school every day. He knew that made Mom very mad at him. But when Mom got mad at Josh, she didn't get mad at Dad so much, because Dad agreed with her then."

"Sounds like a reasonable example, Charlotte."

"And then, I think my going dancing with Daddy might be another example. It made Mom jealous. That made her mad at me, not so much at Dad."

"You could be right about that, too, Charlotte. Anything else?"

"Well—my not doing my work at school this year and now this summer. That makes Mom really upset with me. She hardly says anything to Dad about the other women then because she wants him on her side to get me to do my homework."

"What have you concluded from all this, Charlotte?"

"Well . . . ," the sensitive young girl's shoulders hunched forward so that her long blond hair formed a waterfall over her eyes, nose, and mouth. She spoke softly from behind protective tresses. "I didn't go dancing with Daddy this week, and I'm not going to go again. And I decided I want to graduate from high school. Flunking out seems like a stupid way to help Mom and Dad stay married. It makes them mad at me anyway. So I decided to do my summer school homework this week."

"Good for you, Charlotte! I suspect that took a lot of courage. Do you plan to continue doing your summer school work?"

"I think so. At least for now. It takes the heat off *me*. But Mom and Dad have been arguing with each other all week."

"Are they coming any closer to working out their problems?"

"Do you mean about Dad and other women?"

"Well, that seems to be the biggest problem between your parents right now."

"No. Dad has been pretty mad at Mom for trying to control him."

"How hopeful are you that things may get better between your parents, Charlotte?"

There was a long sigh. "Not very."

"What about divorce? Are you worried that your parents may get a divorce?"

More silence ensued. At last, Charlotte whispered, "I don't know. They might."

"Do you mind if I ask your brother, Josh, what he thinks?"

"Go ahead. Ask him."

JoEllen turned her attention to Josh, leaving Charlotte hidden behind her golden mane.

"Josh, you've been listening carefully, I know. Did you do this week's homework?"

"I sure did!" the boy replied with a grin. "It was fun."

"What did you learn?" asked JoEllen.

"Well, I remembered that every time I did a sloppy job on the lawn, Dad got mad at me, so he didn't get quite as mad at Mom when she complained he was out late too much. It didn't always work, though, because sometimes Mom and Dad got even madder at each other. They fought over whether the job I did was good enough."

"But they still got mad about *you* and what *you* were doing, not at what your Dad was doing with other women."

"Well, yeah . . . and Mom and Dad *both* got real mad at Charlotte when she didn't do her work for school. Then they got along much better with each other, because they agreed about Charlotte."

"What have you decided to do about all this, Josh?"

"Well, I can see now that it's easier on me to do the things I'm supposed to do. You know, mow the lawn better and do my homework and that sort of stuff. Then Mom and Dad don't get mad at me. The problem is, though, they fight with each other more."

"Are you hopeful that your parents might learn to get along better, or are you afraid they might get a divorce, like your sister Charlotte worries they might?"

Now it was Josh's turn to be silent for a moment. He looked very serious. "I'm afraid Mom and Dad might get a divorce," he responded finally.

"Oh Josh! Charlotte!" Molly broke in. "You two don't need to worry about anything like that! Your father and I have been married for over 22 years. We aren't about to get divorced now!"

Both children looked at their mother, their expressions hopeful.

The telephone shrilled loudly just then, startling everyone in the room. Given the intensity of the session, JoEllen and all of the Petersons had completely forgotten about the team behind the mirror. The trainee picked up the receiver. It was Kurt, of course.

"JoEllen," Kurt remarked, "the team wants to know from Molly if a change in the children's behavior will be enough for her. Will she be satisfied with her situation if the children's behavior continues to improve as they say it will?"

The trainee hung up the telephone and posed the team's questions directly to Molly. Molly didn't answer at once. Then she responded clearly and decisively.

"I'll be very happy if Josh and Charlotte behave better, both at school and at home. But I have to say no, that won't be enough for me. I want my husband to stop having affairs."

"Wait a minute!" Henry said. "JoEllen, listen to me!"

"Henry, I suggest that you talk directly to Molly," JoEllen responded calmly.

"Molly, you're not being fair!" Henry almost shouted at his spouse. "We came here on account of Charlotte's behavior. If that kid's saying she'll do her school work now, that's all we came for."

"Wait a minute, Henry," said Molly in an unusually firm tone. "If JoEllen and that team back there think the kids misbehave on account of the relationship between you and me, what's to keep them from doing something crazy again next week? You heard both Charlotte and Josh say they are afraid we're going to get a divorce!"

"The kids can just leave what's going on in our marriage to us, Molly, the way they should have in the first place!"

"But I don't want you to have affairs, Henry!"

"That's beside the point. We've made it for 22 years this way. We can make it for 22 more."

"What if I told you I'd file for divorce?" said Molly.

"I know you too well," said Henry. "You need me, Molly. You wouldn't have any friends if it weren't for me. You won't get a divorce, even though you threaten sometimes. You know that as well as I do."

Molly looked down toward the floor, her face flushed and her expression confused, chastened. Henry sat back with a triumphant air. JoEllen spoke then.

"Henry," she said, "I have to tell you that it's not as easy as you think. If your wife continues to feel put down and betrayed, she's likely to consider divorce whether she pursues it right now or not. Then these two very intelligent children of yours will probably produce some more creative distractions to help save your marriage, as they've been doing in the past."

"Hell, no," Henry said. "We won't tolerate that kind of stuff anymore."

"Won't tolerate it?"

"We'll just tell the kids to mind their own business, not Molly's and mine."

"That makes sense, Henry, but how effective do you think that would be in reality?"

"I don't know," Henry said. "And anyway, it doesn't matter. I refuse to let Molly control me. You just don't understand. My way works best for this family. As Molly said, we have more fun together than any family I know. My wife will stay with me. I don't doubt that for a minute."

"Molly, what do you have to say?" said JoEllen.

Molly's face crumbled into tears. "What choice do I have?" she cried. "I love Henry. I'm his wife. I can't stop what he does with other women. I've tried for years. And I have to stay with him for the sake of the kids."

The telephone rang.

"JoEllen," Kurt said, "you're beginning to do marital therapy. Your contract so far is only to work on Charlotte's behavior. If you're going to begin marital work, you need an explicit agreement, and Henry will have to put his affairs aside at least for the duration."

"What if he won't?" JoEllen asked logically.

"We'll take this one step at a time," said Kurt. "First, you need to find out whether this couple *wants* marriage counseling."

JoEllen hung up the telephone. She knew Kurt was right; the focus of therapy was taking a turn that needed to be acknowledged. A new contract was necessary.

Molly was still crying softly. Henry looked annoyed. Both children sat looking down at their hands, the expressions on their faces uniformly sad. JoEllen let Molly cry herself out, offering her a box of Kleenex as her sobs subsided. Then she began.

"Molly and Henry, the team has called my attention to the fact that we've shifted our discussion to your marriage. Our initial contract was to work on Charlotte's behavior. Your daughter's behavior seems to be considerably improved now. How do you feel about taking some time to work on your marriage?"

"I would like to do that very much," said Molly sincerely. "I'm so tired of having to pretend I'm happy."

"I don't mind marriage counseling," said Henry. "I just don't like the way she tries to control me, like she was doing right now by crying. Molly tries to get her way by making me feel guilty."

"Do you two both want to remain in your marriage? That's important for marital counseling to succeed."

"Of course I do!" said Molly. "I want what's best for the kids, and I love my husband."

"I've always told Molly she's my primary relationship. She's the person I want to spend my life with. Of course I want to remain in my marriage," said Henry.

"OK, then I would say you two are excellent candidates for marital therapy."

The telephone rang immediately. Kurt's voice tone was sharp. "Don't forget the requirement about affairs, JoEllen."

"Yes, but I don't think he'll—at least not—"

"Henry's giving up his affair for the duration is a requirement," said Kurt. "Otherwise we're wasting our time." He hung up abruptly.

JoEllen experienced a flash of anger. She disagreed, and strongly. Here were two people who said they were committed to each other. Henry and Molly both said they wanted counseling to improve their marriage. JoEllen thought that counseling might help the couple. It had already helped Charlotte to change her behavior. But Kurt was insistent, and he was not only JoEllen's consultation team leader but the director of the Family Therapy Training Institute.

The trainee sat still for a moment, looking perplexed and upset. Was this a time to rebel? She considered leaving the therapy room to talk with the team. Suddenly she decided to do just that.

"Excuse me a moment, all of you," JoEllen said in a grim tone "I need to consult with the team." And she got up and left the office.

"What's up, JoEllen?" Kurt inquired as the trainee entered the tiny observation room.

"Kurt, I think that when two people agree to counseling and both say they want to stay married, that's enough for a start."

"JoEllen, we well may have more than that here. Henry may well agree to give up his affair for the duration. You haven't even asked him yet."

"Yes, but I know he won't."

"Is this reminding you of your own former marriage, JoEllen?"

"Of course it is. But there are children to consider here as well. I think the marriage should be given every chance."

Kevin Lord spoke up then. Kevin was a Lutheran minister, enrolled at the institute because members of his church frequently asked him for family counseling.

"I agree with JoEllen," Kevin said. "This woman has been willing to live with her husband's infidelity for 22 years. I think it's best she continue to sacrifice herself for the family for another few years, at least until the children are grown. After all, the wedding vows say 'for better or for worse.'"

Sandra, the high school guidance counselor, said, "I'm not so sure. Kids aren't that dumb. They know when their parents aren't happy and they feel pretty guilty if their mother sacrifices herself for their sake, especially if she tells them that's what she's doing."

"Listen, all of you," said Kurt. "You're responding according to your own personal values and experience. We're here to learn a systems approach to marriage and family therapy. Right?"

"Right," said JoEllen. "But what about Molly? What about the kids? Isn't it important to do everything we can to work on this marriage, given that Henry is willing?"

"JoEllen, of course it's important to work on this marriage," responded Kurt. "But there's a problem right now, and a big one."

"You mean Henry's affair."

"Of course."

"But maybe Henry'd give it up during counseling!"

"He might. Anything is possible. But it isn't likely."

"Isn't taking a chance better than nothing?"

"Not always. Marital counseling takes an enormous investment of energy on the part of both couple and counselor. When it fails, a couple may never again be willing to enter counseling under any circumstances. You want to be very sure you don't set things up to fail."

JoEllen took a deep breath. She examined Kurt's serious face, took in his earnest tone, and sighed.

"So you want me to go back in there and talk to Henry, I suppose," the trainee said after a few moments. "You want me to try to persuade this man to put his affair aside for the duration."

"That's right. And why?"

JoEllen smiled ruefully, remembering she'd had a similar discussion before in this very same spot. "Because otherwise energy that should be invested in problem solving within the family system gets poured into the extramarital relationship with the person who's been triangulated," she parroted, in a singsong voice.

"Right," said Kurt, unable to suppress a grin at JoEllen's attempt at humor despite her disagreement. Then he continued seriously. "And also, in that way, you strongly increase the odds that the marital counseling will be successful."

"I guess so," said JoEllen, not quite convinced.

"If worse comes to worst," continued Kurt thoughtfully, "and Henry absolutely refuses to give up his affair, there's a possibility that we may still see this family again, you know."

"What makes you think so?" JoEllen asked.

"For one thing, we can offer to work with any of the members of the family individually. That's a choice each person can make. For another, what we are maneuvering to do here in systems terms is to unbalance the homeostasis or steady state of this family as a whole."

"We *want* to unbalance the family system?"

"Of course. We want to precipitate a crisis, because the family's current steady state is not healthy. Its current equilibrium literally must be destroyed if a new and better way of life is to be created."

"So you *want* Molly and Henry to split up?"

"That may be necessary if the family is to have a chance to rebuild a healthy pattern of relationships. Other types of crises could occur too, of course. One of the kids could run away, for example. Whatever the crisis, if it's serious enough, there's a good chance this family will return for counseling."

"Yes, but on the other hand, Molly and Henry might get divorced instead."

"That is a serious risk," admitted Kurt.

JoEllen turned to observe the family as they waited in the training office. Molly's eyes remained tearful. She made occasional dabs at them with a Kleenex. She did not look at Henry. Henry fiddled with his tape recorder, not looking at anyone. Josh made increasingly ridiculous faces into the mirror, playing the clown again, and Charlotte smoothed her long hair with jerky, nervous motions.

"Look carefully," instructed Kurt. "Notice the lack of supportive behaviors here. This is a family under stress, but nobody comforts anybody else. They each withdraw into their own world."

"Or else get mad at each other," contributed John, the psychologist. "Did you see the expression on Henry's face when Molly first began to cry? He was annoyed as hell."

"He sure was," said JoEllen.

"Well, you'd better get back into the office and wind things up for today," said Kurt. "We're getting close to the end of the hour."

JoEllen walked back into the training office and sat down in her chair with a long sigh.

"Henry," the trainee began, "I don't know quite how to say this, but I guess it has to be said. The consultation team feels that marital therapy cannot succeed unless you are willing to give up your affair, at least for the duration of counseling."

"The team wants me to give up my affair?" Henry sounded incredulous.

"Yes, they do. The team feels that energy that needs to go into problem solving in your marriage is being siphoned off into the extramarital relationship."

"Hell, I *get* my energy from my extramarital relationship. I'm willing to go into counseling with Molly, but I won't give up my affair with Marlene." This was the first time a name had been mentioned. The hurt on Molly's face hardened into anger.

"Henry, what I mean to say is that the team will not work with you and Molly as a couple unless you agree to give up your current affair, with Marlene or anyone else."

"That's a requirement for marriage counseling?"

"Yes, I'm afraid so. At least it is here at the institute."

"Well then, the hell with it," said Henry. "The answer is no."

Molly spoke then, setting her anger aside to plead with him. "Please, Henry, we need to work on our marriage."

"Forget it," said Henry. "Nobody's going to control me."

JoEllen began to plead then. "Henry, Molly, I want very much for you two to remain in counseling. I don't think we need the children with us any longer unless they want to come, but I think you two can work out a much happier life for yourselves. Henry, the team's requirement is only for the duration of counseling, after which you can make your own decision. Isn't your marriage worth that much investment of time and energy?"

"Sure it is," Henry replied, "but I give my marriage plenty of time and energy as it is. You still don't understand. I get most of my energy from my friends. Without them, I wouldn't have anything to invest in this marriage. I won't give up my freedom, and that's all there is to it."

"Then I'm afraid we can't proceed with marital counseling."

"No problem," said Henry, clamping his jaw.

"Well," said JoEllen, "if that's your decision, Henry, we have no choice but to accept it."

"But wait a minute!" said Molly. "Henry and I need counseling *now.* He might be willing to give up his affairs later. Can't we at least try counseling together for a few sessions?"

"Molly, the team insists that Henry give up his affair *before* beginning marriage counseling."

"I don't understand why," said Molly.

"It's difficult, I know. But the team believes counseling cannot succeed with an active affair claiming so much of your husband's attention—and yours as well, of course. A lot of your own energy probably gets expended in being mad at this Marlene."

"Well then," said Henry, "forget it."

"You definitely won't agree to the team's terms, Henry?" JoEllen responded.

"No way," the man replied.

"Then," said the trainee, "I'm afraid marriage counseling isn't an option." She sighed again, paused and continued. "However, each and every one of you is welcome to return for counseling individually. I urge any of you to do that. Especially you, Molly, or you, Henry."

The children squirmed uneasily. Henry shook his head. Molly spoke.

"I'm very disappointed we can't come back for marriage counseling. But I don't see any need for individual counseling, for any of us. Charlotte is her old self again, and Josh is doing fine too. I don't need individual counseling—I need a husband who *cares* about me."

"Well, coming back separately is anyone's choice, at any time. We'll leave it at that for now," said JoEllen. "I need to go consult with the team. I'll bring you their written message in a few minutes."

The message the team delivered to the Petersons was as follows: "The team congratulates the Peterson family for making such good progress. Charlotte and Josh are now separating themselves out from Molly and Henry's marital difficulties and are doing the work necessary to grow into self-directed young adults. However, we encourage both Charlotte and Josh to continue to think about how more creative behavior on their part may help preserve Molly and Henry's marriage in the future.

"Molly and Henry, we welcome working with you as individuals if you so desire, and we also welcome working with you as a couple if Henry is willing to meet the conditions of our contract. We think the two of you demonstrate the passion and desire that is necessary, but not sufficient, to make a good marriage.

"We wish the entire Peterson family well."

CHAPTER 16

❀

A Conference among Institute Supervisors

Supervisors at the Family Therapy Training Institute regularly met together for about two hours every week to discuss their students' progress. There were five supervisors in all: Dr. Kurt Knaak, the director of the institute, clinical social worker, and JoEllen Madsen's evening consultation team leader; Dr. Madeleine Sweet, clinical psychologist and JoEllen's noon discussion group leader; Dr. Donald Miller, educational psychologist; Dr. Maria Sanchez, clinical social worker; and Ms. Sara Weiner, also a clinical social worker. These five were all clinical members of the American Association for Marriage and Family Therapy (AAMFT), and were AAMFT-Approved Supervisors as well. Kurt Knaak and Maria Sanchez also served on the faculty of the Graduate School of Social Work at a nearby university. Madeleine Sweet, Donald Miller, and Sara Weiner were employed full-time by the social service agency that developed the institute and achieved its AAMFT accreditation. Each of these supervisors was a highly trained, experienced therapist and educator.

Each week the team of supervisors at the institute routinely "staffed" several students, ensuring that the progress of each trainee was monitored and assessed on a regular basis. Supervisors also sometimes requested staffings of additional trainees at these meetings, on an as-needed basis.

As institute director, Kurt Knaak chaired the supervisors' meetings. At the beginning of each one, he read the names of the students scheduled for routine review and then asked if there were any requests for additions. Today, there were no requests to add other students to the list. Kurt, however, surprised everyone by adding a name himself, JoEllen Madsen. The other supervisors were curious, as JoEllen had been reviewed recently according to the regular schedule; her work seemed to be going reasonably well. When the students on the regular agenda had all been discussed, Kurt brought up his concerns regarding JoEllen.

"We staffed this student only about a month ago," he began, "as I'm sure you all recall. At the time, I thought JoEllen's work on my consultation team was developing quite nicely. This week, however, she seems to have regressed. She was resistant to the team's instructions a few nights ago, to put it mildly. She walked out of the therapy room and came behind the mirror to challenge us on one of our interventions."

"That doesn't sound like JoEllen," responded Madeleine Sweet. "She's usually almost too compliant. Please tell us more, Kurt."

"JoEllen's still struggling with personal issues relating to her former marriage, and they are getting in the way of her work," Kurt continued. "Madeleine, I especially want you to know what happened this week, because I think you may need to deal with it further in your noon discussion group."

"What happened, exactly?" asked Madeleine.

Kurt proceeded to describe JoEllen's recent angry reaction to his intervention in her work before the mirror. He reminded the group that JoEllen, like Molly Peterson, had been married to a man who pursued extramarital affairs. (Sensitive information like this about trainees was kept confidential at the institute, shared only among supervisors for professional purposes, just as information about clients was kept confidential and shared as appropriate only during professional consultation or supervision.)

Kurt ended his narrative by quipping in his characteristic way: "We have one unhappy camper right now. JoEllen did *not* want to deny marriage counseling to this couple. I'm careful to look both ways when I cross the corridor next to the training office now, in case she's there waiting to throw rotten apples at me!" Kurt then opened the case for discussion.

"Wait a minute. From what you've described, JoEllen accepted your intervention, Kurt, even if she didn't like it, and she carried it out to the letter," Madeleine interjected. Madeleine was almost always protective of her trainees.

"That's true on the surface," responded Don Miller, "but as Kurt said, this woman is resistant. It's pretty rare for a student to walk behind the mirror to challenge a team's directive."

"Sure she's resistant, Don," Madeleine replied. "However, JoEllen had her reasons and she was open with her disagreement. She told the team what she thought right on the spot."

"Yes, but her motivation was unconscious," Don continued. "JoEllen was clearly overidentifying with her clients, Madeleine—especially Molly. JoEllen acted like she was sitting right in Molly's chair, in fact. I think she'd do anything to keep Henry around rather than lose him, from what Kurt just described. JoEllen seems to have confused Henry with her own former husband. I suspect she was probably unconsciously regretting her own divorce at that moment as well."

"I think you're right, Don," Maria Sanchez chipped in. "I think JoEllen was unconsciously trying to prevent a repeat of her own experience for these folks. And it sounds to me as if she was inappropriately projecting feelings onto Henry in the process. From what you just described, Kurt, JoEllen seems to have felt sure in advance that Henry would refuse to give up his extramarital affair in order to pursue counseling.

(*Projection* is a psychological mechanism in which one externalizes ones own thoughts and beliefs and perceives them as belonging to someone else.)

"You're right," Kurt responded. "I think JoEllen was projecting her own experience of rejection by her former husband onto Henry. So she didn't believe for a moment that Henry would give up his affair for his marriage, just as her former husband would not. So JoEllen was totally ineffective when she tried to approach this man."

"I also see issues of transference and countertransference in this case," offered Sara Weiner. "Henry, of course, seems to be transferring his fear of being controlled by his wife onto JoEllen. But JoEllen also seems to be struggling with countertransference. She obviously likes Henry very much. She's even admitted feeling attracted to him, if I remember our last staffing of JoEllen's work correctly. Maybe she's experiencing Henry much as she did her former husband, Chip—as charming and challenging, rather than as untrustworthy. So a part of her tries to make excuses for his behavior."

(*Transference* is a psychological mechanism in which a client feels emotions toward a therapist that reproduce repressed emotions from a primary relationship; *countertransference* is a parallel mechanism in which the therapist unconsciously feels emotions toward a client that reproduce repressed emotions from a primary relationship.)

"That's an interesting point," Maria Sanchez spoke up. "I wonder if JoEllen would find herself excusing the same extramarital behavior so easily in a woman? Somehow our culture teaches us that it's OK for a man to express his power sexually, so that if he succeeds in seducing someone other than his marital partner, he is within his masculine prerogative. He's only 'sowing his wild oats.' But women are treated differently. If a women exhibits the same behavior, she is called nasty things like 'slut' and 'whore.'"

"I doubt if JoEllen has made that connection—that Henry's behavior could actually be described as sexist," responded Sara. "In fact, come to think of it, JoEllen's interpreting the value of marriage in a sexist way as well."

"How do you see that, Sara?" asked Madeleine.

"Well, JoEllen seems to want to rescue Molly by 'saving' her marriage, just as JoEllen apparently wished someone would save hers a few years back. But why? Probably because a sexist society teaches women that they aren't valuable unless they are married. But it seems to me that Molly's marriage brings her a lot of pain, just as JoEllen's did at one time. The most effective way to 'rescue' Molly might be to assist her to dissolve her marriage, rather than to save it."

"That might be true, Sara," responded Madeleine, "but that option is hard to perceive as desirable in this culture. Women usually do gain status through marriage and lose it through divorce."

Everyone in the room sat quietly for a few moments. Of the five, only three of the institute supervisors were currently married: Don, Maria, and Sara. Sara had been married relatively recently, for a second time. Neither Kurt nor Madeleine had ever been married. Kurt was in his early thirties and was thus likely to experience marriage sometime in the future, but Madeleine was well into middle age and thus not so likely. Each reflected for a moment on his or her own personal situation. Then Madeleine broke the silence in a rare personal comment to her professional colleagues.

"I suppose being married isn't only a matter of status for women. As a single woman myself, I think I've probably had to cope with a lot more loneliness than most married people. Still, I know from my work that unhappily married people often experience a great deal of loneliness too. And they have a lot of other problems that I'm never faced with. I enjoy being free to make all of my own personal and financial decisions, for example."

Sara spoke then. "Being free of the conflicts of my first marriage felt like a blessing to me when that marriage finally ended in divorce. But I chose to try again because, I suppose, overall I like living with a partner. I like the companionship. I think life is more fulfilling when another person is a part of it on an everyday basis."

"Hey, I'm not so sure of that!" said Kurt, the bachelor. "Speak for yourself, Sara! When I listen to the hassles married folk go through in my work at the institute, I'm not sure I'll ever want to take the plunge myself!"

"That's just what I was getting at before," Sara responded seriously, "when I said the best way to rescue Molly now might be to help her dissolve this particular marriage. Maybe we need to work with JoEllen so she can appreciate that, even though the status of divorcee certainly isn't desirable in this society."

"The societal dimension introduces another important element to consider, Sara," responded Kurt. "Social norms may be pressing Molly toward remaining in her marriage, even though the marriage isn't serving her personally very well right now."

"Hey," Maria spoke up loudly then. "I believe strongly that societal norms *need* to support marriage! Otherwise, too many people would take marriage too lightly. We all know how difficult it is for couples to remain together nowadays. I must admit I admire Molly's commitment and loyalty, even though she's clearly a very unhappy woman."

"So where do we go with this case?" Don Miller, who had been sitting quietly for some time, interjected suddenly. He pointed at his watch. "We're getting close to the end of the hour."

"That's true," responded Kurt, glancing at his own watch. "Let's sum things up with respect to JoEllen Madsen's current work with the Petersons. What important concerns have we identified this afternoon?"

Don responded: "We know that this trainee is being affected by unconscious psychological processes such as projection of feelings, transference, and countertransference, especially with respect to Henry; and overidentification, especially with respect to Molly."

"And," added Maria, "JoEllen is probably also responding according to sexist cultural norms, so that she unconsciously underplays the importance of Henry's affairs in the marriage."

"She may also overvalue marriage due to cultural norms," contributed Sara.

"And she may find it difficult to objectively explore dissolving the marriage with Molly due to her own experience with loneliness after divorce," added Madeleine.

"Good summary," said Kurt. "Now, how can we assist JoEllen to carry on with the work at hand?"

"Well," Don replied, "We don't really know if any of the Petersons will return, so her work with this family may be over. However, JoEllen still needs to be aware of her unconscious processes, because they're sure to get in the way when she works with other families as well."

Madeleine spoke up then. "I intend to work with JoEllen on unconscious processes and how they may affect her work when I meet with her next in discussion group. But there's something else we need to talk about here."

"Yes?" Kurt sounded surprised and interested.

"Let's be honest, folks," Madeleine stated bluntly. "Who among us hasn't continued to work with a married couple after an affair's been revealed, even when theory suggests that continuing is questionable?"

Sara spoke up. "Well," she said, "I'll bet we all have at one time or another."

"Right," continued Madeleine. "Probably all of us have taken on cases that might be questionable from a theoretical standpoint. And we may not have taken them on for reasons we fully understood at the time, either. I know that's been true for me. And at times, I've done successful work in circumstances such as these."

"That's interesting," responded Sara. "Now that you mention it, last year I took on a case of marital counseling with a couple whose circumstances closely paralleled mine with my former husband. The man was deeply involved in an extramarital relationship that, while not sexual, was emotionally intense."

"How did that case turn out?" asked Madeleine.

"It was a tough situation to work with, but eventually the man reinvested his energies in his wife," said Sara. "So I'm not one who would *categorically* refuse marriage counseling when a third party is involved. In fact, in that particular case, I actually brought the third party right into my office along with the couple. That was pretty scary for all of us, but it helped resolve the triangulation. The 'other woman' realized she was being used and bowed out."

"Now there's an interesting piece of work!" said Kurt. "We could probably spend the rest of the hour discussing it, but we don't have time today. Right now, we need to decide what do with respect to JoEllen. Madeleine, you've made a point, but how does it pertain to this trainee?"

"What I'm trying to say," responded Madeleine, "is that I'm aware that unconscious issues are getting in the way of JoEllen's clinical work. But I want to remind all of us that some of these same issues also help make this student a determined, energetic, highly motivated therapist-in-training. Most of us have done effective therapy even when propelled by unconscious issues of our own. Sometimes we've even succeeded, when theoretical principles would predict failure."

"Ah, yes," Kurt replied. He frowned for a moment. "Embarrassing, isn't it." Then he grinned and continued, "Madeleine, you're being overprotective as usual. But in this case I agree. I've seen JoEllen Madsen conduct some pretty sophisticated marital therapy, and I personally hope the Peterson family returns to benefit from more of it. Maybe then this trainee won't be quite so mad at me."

Shortly thereafter, the meeting adjourned.

CHAPTER 17

Consultation and Ethical Considerations

"JoEllen, do you have a case you want to present today? I see you've brought along a videotape."

Thus Madeleine Sweet began the regular Monday noon "rounds" with her discussion group students. She hoped, of course, that the videotape would involve the Peterson case.

JoEllen groaned and rolled her eyes. "I do and I don't, Madeleine. I've brought a case I think I ought to present, but I don't really want to talk about it at all."

"Would you mind running that by again, JoEllen?"

"I feel ridiculous," blurted the trainee in a frustrated tone of voice. "We've been through this so many times before."

"This?"

"Yes, 'this.' Meaning that issues from my former marriage and divorce are affecting the way I look at things. I had a serious disagreement with Kurt last week. I can understand Kurt's point, but I still disagree with his decision. But I think he's probably right, from a purely objective, theoretical point of view."

"So you hate to talk about a disagreement you had with Kurt when you're already pretty sure he's right and you're wrong."

"Something like that."

"OK," said Madeleine. "I expect your experience will raise good questions for all of us. Are you willing to discuss the situation, even though the issues involved may be uncomfortable for you to talk about?"

"I am, or at least I know I should be, so yes, I guess I'm willing."

"I've rarely heard you sound so enthusiastic!" Madeleine teased. "However, I'm going to take you at your word. How much time will you need?"

"Probably about half an hour."

When JoEllen's turn came, the trainee fast-forwarded her videotape to the first telephone call from the team, when Kurt asked her to ask Molly whether a change in the children's behavior would satisfy her. JoEllen played the tape through from there until the time she left the office to get the final message from the team. Her consultation behind the mirror, of course, was not recorded. JoEllen sat back with a frown on her face, awaiting a response from her fellow trainees.

Rose spoke first. "It's clear to me that you wanted to work with Molly and Henry in marriage therapy, even if Henry wouldn't agree to give up his affair with the other woman, Marlene."

"That was clear to me too, JoEllen," said Bob. "You were actually in the process of contracting to do marital work when the telephone rang a second time. Did Kurt tell you to come behind the mirror?"

"No. He said I had to get Henry to agree to give up his affair before I could do marriage counseling; otherwise I was wasting everyone's time. I disagreed with Kurt so much that I went into the observation room to argue with him."

"And what did you use as your argument, Molly?" asked Madeleine.

"Well, it seems to me that if both marital partners request therapy, and both say clearly that they want to remain married to each other, that that's enough commitment to begin."

"I strongly agree," said Harry. "As a clergyman, I've counseled members of my parish in situations like this. Sometimes because of the counseling, the unfaithful partner has agreed to give up the affair."

"Yes," Gretchen spoke up with her usual wry humor, "but in what percent of the cases, Harry?"

"Well," the minister replied, "it isn't very often, I have to admit, but don't we have to appreciate every small success?"

Madeleine spoke. "JoEllen, you said earlier that your former marriage and divorce colored your view of this issue. You also said Kurt was probably right theoretically, but you implied you thought you were probably right in a different way. Tell us what you mean."

"I know why cutting off extramarital affairs during marriage counseling is important," the trainee replied. "It frees up energy for problem solving between the spouses. You all know I wish I had exerted more energy to try to stop my former husband from having affairs, rather than investing most of it to suppress my own jealousy and insecurity."

"Right," several voices responded.

"OK, putting that aside, remember that Chip *left* me when he was forced to make a choice between the other woman and me."

"We remember."

"That's *not* the outcome I wanted."

"Of course not," sympathetic voices murmured.

"What if I had had children? Doesn't that complicate the picture? If Henry leaves Molly, she suffers as I did, because she loves him; but even more, two other littler people suffer. I'm not sure it's ethical not to do everything possible to try to save that marriage."

"So you think that sometimes ethical considerations warrant putting theory aside."

"Yes. And in fact, I can even imagine systems theory *supporting* marital counseling in the case of an affair. The therapist's presence always has an impact on the system, according to the theory. I would think that input from a marriage therapist could theoretically contribute to the termination of an affair *during* counseling, just as Harry suggested."

"Do you think that's realistic?" Gretchen asked.

"I don't know. But I can't forget Molly's face when I said I wouldn't work with her and her husband. She hasn't been able to change Henry by herself. She's desperate for help. She thought we were her allies. And we let her down."

"Yes," said Harry, "and it was clear to me you dreaded having to tell Molly you couldn't work with her and Henry. When you walked back into the training office after your talk with the team, you looked pretty discouraged. You even sighed out loud. I must say, though, that I'd have felt the same way."

"Wait a minute," said Madeleine. "When JoEllen walked back into the training office looking so discouraged, she didn't have to tell Molly anything yet. She only needed to ask Henry if he'd agree to give up his affair while in counseling. And JoEllen, it looked to me as if you had decided what Henry's answer would be in advance."

"I had," said JoEllen. "I just knew he wouldn't agree."

"How could you know that?"

"Well, he had said as much before to Molly and me . . ."

"And also, your former husband, Chip, wouldn't agree." Madeleine's voice was stern.

"Well, yes, that too."

"JoEllen, I think you were right when you said your experience with Chip clouded your perception. Henry *didn't* agree, to be sure, but you didn't come across as persuasive at all in this session. You apparently gave up in advance," Madeleine spoke, gently but firmly.

JoEllen looked downcast. "Well, yes, I suppose I didn't try very hard to persuade Henry," she said. "I didn't believe it was possible."

"You didn't believe it was possible because you were projecting the rejection you experienced with Chip onto Henry."

"I suppose that's true," the trainee replied with a long sigh. Her face looked even more downcast. The room fell silent. The trainee's features began to rearrange themselves into a vacant expression.

"JoEllen, are you experiencing being criticized as a child again?"

"Huh?"

"It looks as if we've lost you."

"Er, ah," said JoEllen. "Ah—well—I guess you're right, I got lost in the past somewhere. I'm coming back. Hold on." The trainee's lips curved into an embarrassed smile. She continued. "You're right, I wasn't very persuasive with Henry. I honestly don't think, though, that anything I could have said would have made any difference."

Rose stepped in with her usual gentle support. "Henry looks pretty darned stubborn to me in this videotape," she said. "I'm glad *I'm* not working with that family, JoEllen!" JoEllen nodded her thanks.

"There are two different issues here," said Madeleine. "The first is the way JoEllen actually approached Henry and why. The second is whether the desired result *could* have been achieved had she approached Henry differently, say in a confident and convincing manner."

"I can see that," responded the trainee.

"Since we can't really know what would have happened had JoEllen approached Henry differently," continued Madeleine, "let's return to the issue of whether or not it makes sense to work with a couple if one is having an affair."

Harry spoke up then. "Maybe it's my training in the church, Madeleine, but I find myself agreeing with JoEllen. If a couple asks for help to save their marriage, no matter what the circumstances, I think we should offer whatever help we can. I can say some pretty strong things about an affair during counseling."

"That's not a bad argument," said Madeleine. "As JoEllen pointed out, even systems theory doesn't provide an absolute answer to this question. For example, from a systems perspective, a therapist brings something new into any marital situation. That something will prompt changes in other parts of the system."

"You mean I'm not nuts?" JoEllen blurted, a huge grin transforming her face.

"No, JoEllen, you're not nuts," said Madeleine. "There have been special situations where I have decided to work with a couple even though one of them is involved in an extramarital affair. However, from my practical experience, the prognosis is very, very poor. The amount of leverage I can exert as a therapist usually isn't nearly enough to counter the influence of the person who's being triangulated. I find myself accepting fewer and fewer of these cases. In fact, I haven't accepted any for a long time."

"That reminds me of something else Kurt said that bothers me," JoEllen spoke again. "He said that an important purpose of refusing counseling in a situation like the Petersons' is to help *precipitate* a crisis. Aren't there ethical considerations involved in hastening a couple's movement toward divorce?"

"Wait a minute," said Bob, the nurse. Bob was a no-nonsense person. "Precipitating a crisis is not necessarily the same as hastening a couple's divorce. It could hasten the rebuilding of a better marriage, instead."

"How do you think that could happen, Bob?" asked Madeleine.

"Well, it just makes sense. A family in trouble limps along without change as long as it can. That's the nature of a system, maintaining its steady state, its ongoing balance. But when a family has a crisis, that family suddenly has to do something radically different."

"That's just what Kurt explained," admitted JoEllen. "Still, he also admitted that divorce could be the result. And Kurt's right, because that's exactly what happened to me."

"How was the outcome with Chip different when you engaged in counseling with your first therapist, JoEllen? The one who agreed to work with you despite your husband's affair?"

JoEllen let out a long sigh. "It wasn't any different, to be honest. We broke up during counseling that time too."

"That's what I thought," said Madeleine. "Do you think your marriage may have lasted longer, though, because of that first counseling experience?"

"I believe the marriage did last longer. The therapist helped us resolve various smaller disputes so that we could hang in there."

"Now that you have the luxury of hindsight, do you think that was good, hanging in there longer?"

JoEllen hesitated. Madeleine waited.

"Well," JoEllen said thoughtfully after a few moments, "at the time, I thought the counseling was helping us. But I suppose it also helped me stay in a very painful situation longer than I would have otherwise."

"How did the counseling help you to do that?"

"Well, being in counseling gave me more hope that Chip might give up his affair. Also, when other things made me very mad, like Chip's not helping out much with earning a living, or doing chores at home, the counselor helped us work out compromises."

"Do you think that the marriage counseling experience with Chip was valuable in the long run, then?" Madeleine repeated her former question.

JoEllen hesitated. "The counselor provided me with a supportive experience for which I was very grateful," she said. "In fact, I went back for individual therapy a few months before my divorce."

"How about the marriage counseling part, when Chip was involved in his affair. Was that a good experience for you too?" Madeleine persisted.

Slowly, JoEllen shook her head. "As I think about the marriage counseling part now, those were probably the worst months of my life. I was drowning slowly, losing my self-esteem bit by bit, gradually losing ground inch by inch. It was an agonizing process, really. I kept hearing that my husband thought I was boring and not particularly attractive physically. It hurt—a lot."

"Would you choose to go through that experience again?"

"I'm not sure I could stop myself. I wanted to save my marriage very much. But in hindsight, I think it might have been better to get on with the rest of my life more quickly."

"You see," Madeleine continued her line of reasoning, "sometimes counselors may actually do a disservice to their clients by helping them stabilize a bad situation. Does that make sense to you, JoEllen?"

"Yes, I can see that now."

"Most people would probably rather be married," Madeleine continued. "But being single is certainly a viable way of life, as you've learned yourself from personal experience."

JoEllen nodded.

"A woman who leaves an unhappy marriage," Madeleine continued, "may have to cope with a certain loss of social status in this society, but at least she is subjected to much less emotional stress on a daily basis. She no longer has to drown in pain day by day coping with a husband she cannot trust. Eventually, she'll be able to reinvest her energies in more satisfying pursuits."

JoEllen nodded again, thoughtfully. Silence ensued for a few moments.

"There's another factor to consider in a decision like this, too, about whether to accept a couple for counseling when one of them is having an affair," Madeleine continued thoughtfully.

"What's that?" asked JoEllen.

"If a spouse is willing to give up an affair to work on a marriage, a favorable outcome for the marriage is simply much more likely. A person who won't give up an affair for marriage counseling is clearly demonstrating an unwillingness to invest much effort toward saving the marriage. Words to the contrary may be sincere, but actions make important statements as well. One committed spouse and one good counselor cannot save a marriage."

"That certainly fits my experience," said JoEllen.

"There's something else as well," said the discussion leader. "Can anybody in this group think of another reason marriage counseling is more likely to succeed if a wandering spouse agrees to put aside an affair before beginning marriage counseling?"

Gretchen responded immediately. "It seems to me that when an affair is active, the therapist is in danger of being viewed as the ally of the injured party. Remember, JoEllen, how you said a few minutes ago that Molly viewed you and the team as potential allies?"

"Yes, of course."

"How long do you think Henry would have been willing to take part in marital therapy if he also viewed you as Molly's ally, not his?"

"I don't know, but that's a very good question."

"Think about it." Madeleine took the floor again. "Gretchen has just made the very point I hoped someone would make. When an affair is active, the marriage therapist can't help but invest a good deal of effort trying to bring it to an end. That's sure to please one spouse and alienate the other."

"That's been a frequent experience for me in my pastoral counseling work, unfortunately," admitted Harry.

"On the other hand," continued Madeleine, "if a couple comes to counseling with the extramarital affair already 'on hold,' then they have some time and space to work on the issues that led to triangulation of a third party in the first place. The therapist can assume a much more neutral, balanced role."

JoEllen reentered the discussion. "You know, the more we talk about this, the more I think that Kurt was right last week. It does seem like a poor idea to attempt marriage counseling when an affair is going on. Still, I'm uneasy about refusing to help someone in as much pain as Molly Peterson."

"Didn't you offer Molly the option of individual counseling, JoEllen?"

"Well, yes, I did. But she wasn't interested."

"Wait and see, JoEllen. We can't be sure, but Molly may be back one of these days. The important thing is that she knows she is welcome to return."

JoEllen nodded.

"Now," said Madeleine, "have we done enough with the Peterson family for today?"

"Yes," said the trainee. "Thanks, everybody, for your feedback. It wasn't always what I wanted to hear, but I'm much more convinced now that the team made the best possible decision last week, given the options."

CHAPTER 18

A Family Crisis

About a month after the last session at the institute with JoEllen, Molly Peterson sat at her dining room table working hard on a letter. She chewed her lower lip in deep concentration. Dinner had been over for about an hour, the table was clear, and the dishes were done. Henry had gone to teach a dancing class. Both children were working quietly in the living room. Josh was assembling a model airplane with pieces strewn all over the floor, and Charlotte was curled up in a chair reading a book, an assignment for her summer school English class. It was an apparently peaceful family scene that would have warmed the heart of anyone viewing it through the big picture window facing the lovely little pond down the hill.

Molly, however, was not feeling peaceful. She had just had another fight with Henry about what time to expect him home that evening. Henry had told her it was none of her business, and Molly had told him it certainly was because she was his wife. The children had scattered. As Molly and Henry continued to fight, Charlotte and Josh had commenced their current activities with studious diligence. Henry had then left in a huff. Molly sat down with her head in her hands. Finally, she picked up a piece of paper and began to write.

> *Dear Marlene,*
>
> *I know my husband is with you tonight, not home with me where he belongs. It's time for you and me to talk about this. I want to meet with you at the East River Cafe Friday morning at 9:00* A.M. *Please let me know if*

you cannot make it. Otherwise, I will be there. I hope you will have the courtesy to be there also.

Sincerely,

Molly Peterson

Molly sat staring at the letter, not quite believing that she'd actually written it. Finally, she got up and rummaged an envelope from its slightly crumpled box under the kitchen counter. Then she picked up the telephone book and looked for Marlene's address. She found it, and wrote it on the envelope. She reached for a stamp from the basket by the telephone, licked it, and put it on the envelope. She signed the letter, folded it, and started to put it into the envelope. She halted before she completed the job. With a troubled expression on her face, she turned and spoke to her daughter.

"Charlotte, I've written a letter to Marlene. Would you read it and tell me if you think I should send it?"

"Mom," said Charlotte, "I don't want to read the letter. That's between you and Marlene."

"But I don't know if I should send it. I want your advice."

"Mo-o-o-om—" Charlotte's voice registered protest.

"All right." There was tension in Molly's tone. She spoke impatiently. "Well, I'll just have to ask your brother instead. Josh, will you read my letter, please?"

Josh's face took on a pained expression. "Remember that triangle stuff, Mom? I don't want to get stuck in the middle again."

Now Molly was angry. "Do you mean to tell me that neither of you two children will help your own mother?" she snapped.

"Mom, that's not what we mean," Charlotte whined in the voice of a much younger child.

"Well," said Molly loudly, "Then I want you to read this letter and tell me what you think!"

Charlotte got up from her chair with an angry toss of her hair. She stomped over to the kitchen table and sat down next to her mother. Molly handed her the letter. Charlotte read it.

"Well, what do you think?" asked Molly.

Charlotte pursed her lips. "Well, if you want my opinion, Mom, I think it's OK to send it," the girl said. "I don't think it will do any good, though."

"What do you mean?" asked Molly.

"Well, talking to Marlene isn't going to make her leave Daddy alone."

"What makes you say so?"

"Well . . ." Charlotte's voice was low, almost inaudible.

"Go on," her mother ordered.

"Because Daddy chases her," Charlotte finished, her words quiet but clear.

Josh scattered the pieces of his model airplane with a swipe of his arm and headed for the bathroom.

"Thank you, Charlotte, for your information," said Molly with dignity. She rose from the table with a resolute expression on her face.

"I'm going to mail this letter right now," the woman said. "I can tell dear old Marlene a thing or two about your father that will make her think twice about what she's doing. Watch Josh for me please, Charlotte. I'll be back soon."

While Molly was gone, Charlotte reached toward the pad of paper her mother had been using to write the letter and began to disassemble it. She tore the pages out one by one, and then rumpled them up into little balls. The girl did not finish her reading assignment for summer school that evening. When she wasn't rumpling pieces of paper, she sat looking vacantly out the window. When Josh came out of the bathroom eventually he wandered toward his model plane. He picked up the tube of airplane glue and began sniffing at it absently.

Charlotte saw him and yelled, "Josh, stop that! You could hurt yourself!"

"Who cares," the boy muttered. But he stopped. Then he began kicking at parts of his model, destroying several pieces completely. Charlotte let him alone. Finally Molly came back and sent them both to bed.

For the next few days, the anxious mother waited by the telephone, expecting a call from Marlene that would decline her request. None came. So Molly drove to the East River Cafe on Friday morning. She arrived at exactly 9:00 A.M., extremely nervous and wondering if her rival would show up. She walked in and was about to ask for a table when she saw Marlene already seated in a far corner of the dining area, sipping a cup of coffee. Marlene looked up, caught Molly's eye, and waved her over.

Marlene and Molly were already acquaintances. Marlene had met Henry as her dancing instructor a couple of years previously. She was one of the women he had brought home to become a friend of the family. Recently divorced, Marlene's dime was taped to the Peterson's refrigerator. Molly had had Marlene over for dinner, along with others, on a number of occasions; that was before she knew about the affair. What had once been a cordial relationship now felt awkward, tense. Marlene broke the ice.

"Molly," she said, "I admire you for writing that note to me. I'm grateful for the opportunity to talk with you, woman to woman. I should have talked with you a long time ago."

"Well, Marlene, we're both here, so that's a start."

"I guess I owe you an apology," began Marlene. "After all, you're the one who's married to Henry. That makes me the 'other woman.' "

"Exactly," said Molly. "How could you do this to me? I thought you were my friend!"

"Molly, I think you need to know that Henry is on the prowl constantly. To watch him, I would never guess that he's a married man."

"That's not news, Marlene—that's exactly what I was going to tell *you!* You may think you're special to Henry, but you're not! He'll be through with you before the year is out, you can be sure of it! Then, there will be someone else!"

"My god, if you believe that, how can you stay with Henry?" asked Marlene in a startled tone. "How can you stay with a husband who is always having affairs?"

"Because my husband loves me best," Molly said with a smug expression. "You may not like it, Marlene, but you're just another temporary diversion for Henry. I'm the one he wants to spend his life with."

"How do you know that?" asked Marlene.

"Because we've been married to each other for 22 years, and that's what he's always told me. Besides, Henry needs me."

"Henry needs *you?* Lady, you are the needy one! Molly, I don't know how to tell you this, but Henry says very unflattering things about you."

Molly experienced a flash of anger. Her face felt suddenly hot. Her voice rasped against her will as she replied, as firmly as she could, "I suppose he probably does. But that's because he wants you as a lover. Men always tell their mistresses bad things about their wives. Henry doesn't mean anything by what he says!"

"Molly," said Marlene, "I think you need to know that Henry tells all his friends, male and female, that you are a very needy woman, that you have no friends except for him, and that he's stuck with you because he feels sorry for you."

Molly suddenly found it hard to breathe, but she kept herself under firm control. "And what do you suppose he says about you, Marlene?" She shot back between clenched teeth.

"And just what *does* Henry say about me?"

Molly's eyes filled with angry tears. "He says he gets his thrills from you right now, but that it won't last more than another year. Marlene, give him up. He's using you."

"He's using me? Do you know what he says about you?"

"Of course I do, that I'm his primary relationship. I have the best part of him for life."

"Henry tells other women something like that. He says you are his primary relationship right now. He also says he'd never have stayed with you this long if it weren't for financial necessity. He says his job doesn't pay very well and he couldn't afford child support right now if you two were divorced. Molly, he's using *you*." The two women sat and stared at each other; then Marlene spoke again. "I suppose you're right. Henry is using both of us. But I love him and I don't want to lose him."

"*You* love him!" yelped Molly. People at nearby tables turned to look. She lowered her voice.

"How can you let yourself love a man who's never going to leave his wife?"

"How can you be so sure?" said Marlene. "I'm not needy, like you are. I have friends of my own. Henry says he likes that. I can wait. Besides, I have a good job that probably pays better than yours."

Something snapped inside Molly. She stood up. "That's enough. I'm leaving," she said.

"I feel sorry for you, Molly," said the other woman. "I'm not sure what my future with Henry will be, but I'm pretty sure about yours. If Henry really loved you, he couldn't possibly treat you the way he does. Everybody I know feels the same way."

Molly turned and walked rapidly away from the table and out the door of the little cafe. As she drove home she gripped the steering wheel of her car with all her strength. She did not cry. Her face took on a resolute expression. Her whole body seemed to harden.

She walked into the house with a determined step. Charlotte, who was supposed to be taking care of Josh, was nowhere in sight. Josh, however, lay sprawled on the living room floor amid a pile of new airplane parts. Molly came upon him unexpectedly. The faces of both mother and son suddenly registered shock. Josh was holding a tube of glue near his nostrils. His hands were cupped around end of the tube, trapping the vapors near his nose, and he was inhaling deeply.

"Josh, what the hell are you doing!" yelled his mother.

"Nothing, Mom. The airplane glue just smells good," the boy gasped, and quickly lowered the tube. Molly marched over and snatched the glue from the boy's hands.

"That's enough," she snapped. "Where on earth is your sister?"

Just then Charlotte entered the house. The girl stopped short when she glimpsed her brother on the floor and her mother standing next to him holding the tube of glue.

"Josh, not again!" Charlotte cried.

"Where have you been, Charlotte!" Molly attacked her daughter.

"Mother, I just went after the mail! And Josh promised me he wouldn't sniff that stuff again!"

Molly sat down. She was suddenly extremely tired, and her anger was gone. "I had a terrible meeting with Marlene this morning," the mother said in a quiet voice, "and now you kids are letting me down like this. Josh, don't you know that sniffing glue is dangerous?"

"Sure, Mom," the boy said. "It just smells good to me. I'm not sniffing enough to hurt myself."

"I thought you weren't going to do any more crazy things like this. I'm very disappointed in you."

"I'm sorry, Mom." Josh began to cry softly. Suddenly Molly was sobbing too, and Charlotte joined in so that their three voices merged as a trio for several minutes. Finally, Molly stopped.

"This is it," she said, "this is really it. Charlotte and Josh, I have something important to tell you."

Both children looked at her with damp, streaked faces. Molly continued.

"You know your father and I have been having serious problems in our marriage. You mustn't try to solve them, like that counselor JoEllen said at the institute. That job belongs to your father and me. And since your father isn't interested, I guess it's up to me."

"What do you mean, Mom?" said Charlotte, breathlessly.

"I am moving out of this house just as soon as I can find an apartment. You children are coming with me. I know leaving your father will make you very unhappy, but I don't see any other choice."

Josh nodded soberly.

"Mom," said Charlotte, "I don't know what's taken you so long. But couldn't we stay here and make Daddy leave for a while? That's what happens with most of my friends when their parents break up."

"I don't think your father would leave this house without a court order. And I can't do that to him. He loves it here. Besides, I don't want to make Henry *too* angry because maybe he'll want us back badly enough to give up Marlene. We can find someplace else to live not too far away, so you children won't have to change schools. I'll check the housing ads in the newspaper and call a rental agency today."

CHAPTER 19

Further Complications

"Thanks a million, all of you. George and Sally, I don't know how we could have managed this move without you."

Molly's older son, George, and his wife, Sally, had just finished carrying what seemed to be hundreds of boxes up three flights of stairs to Molly's new apartment. The place was small and boasted only two bedrooms, so Josh would have to sleep on the couch in the living room. The boy was not happy about that. However, Molly had figured her budget carefully. The apartment was all she could afford, since she planned to send Henry a hefty portion of her paycheck every month. Henry earned only sporadic commissions at his sales job, not nearly enough to manage the mortgage payments on the family home. Someone had to make sure the property didn't go into foreclosure, the way Molly saw things.

"No problem, Mom!" George boomed in his hearty voice. "Sally and I are glad to help. We both think you have a lot of guts to make a move like this. And we think it's about time, really."

"I still hope I'm not making a big mistake," Molly said. "I miss your father already."

"Yeah, Mom, we know. We hope things work out for you."

"Thanks George. Now drop by and visit us sometime, when we get this place fixed up a bit."

"We'll do that soon, Mom. Bye now."

Molly, Charlotte, and Josh immediately began to sort out their new living space. Each person worked hard to create order out of chaos. Within the first week, the three were relatively comfortable. Josh had carved out a place to do his homework at a table in the living room, next to the couch where he slept. Charlotte had set up a sturdy card table in her bedroom to use as a desk for her homework assignments. Molly had claimed one end of the kitchen table as her work space. By concentrating and encouraging each other, mother and children managed to do the work required for school and to manage the small household. The little family felt as if it were engaged in a major adventure, and a certain excitement kept them going.

What also kept them going, however, was the fact that not one of them felt the change would be permanent. Perhaps that conviction helped fuel their sense of relatively good cheer. Henry called almost every evening to urge his family to return home. The man still insisted on his own terms, however; he wanted Marlene in his life as well as his wife and children. Molly continued to refuse. Henry's calls made her feel wanted, however, and she and the children felt sure that he would give up his affair once he was convinced that his family would not come back otherwise.

Proudly, Molly didn't tell Henry what Marlene had said that made her decide to leave, but the woman's words continued to echo in her ears. Molly intended to prove to Henry beyond a doubt that she was not a needy person. She would prove she could live entirely on her own. She would make friends, and she wouldn't ask Henry for a thing. She would continue to help him out financially. She would show her husband that he needed *her.* Then Henry would want her back—enough to promise to be faithful. That became Molly's driving desire and belief.

Every time Molly found herself having fun on her own, part of her willed the vision of herself back to Henry. Look at me, she said to his internalized image many a time. See? You're entirely wrong about me. I am not needy. I have friends. I can make it on my own. And the determined woman did a remarkable job succeeding in her new role. As principal breadwinner for the entire family, and sole parent to her children for all practical purposes, Molly began to carve out a successful new life for herself.

Henry, however, continued to pursue his affair with Marlene. In fact, Henry and Marlene began to be seen together as a couple regularly. Molly knew that irrefutably, through reports from her older son George, who sometimes went dancing at the same night clubs frequented by his father. Hearing George's stories depressed Molly sometimes and angered her at others. Charlotte and Josh tried to comfort her.

One Friday evening, a month or so after the move, Molly felt reckless. She gathered up her courage and decided to go out dancing at the very place she believed Henry might be. There he was, capering about the dance floor with Marlene. Molly, dressed in her finest, attracted other partners, so that she felt almost giddy swirling and dipping among the crowd. She hoped fervently that Henry would notice how much fun she was having. He did. Before long, her husband cut in to take her as his partner.

"You look great, Molly," Henry said. "You should do this more often!"

"Thanks, Henry!" Molly said. And the two twirled and dipped expertly as only two people can who have danced together for decades. Then Henry was gone, back to Marlene. He asked Molly to dance one or two more times that evening, his manner gallant and debonair. Each time Molly was thrilled and hopeful, but then Henry was gone again. Other partners kept Molly busy, but her heart was elsewhere, and she went home early. Again, the children tried to comfort her as best they could.

As the weeks passed, the initial excitement of change settled into the routine pattern of daily living: get up in the morning, make breakfast, pack lunch, go to school, come home, shop, cook, make dinner, clean, do homework or correct papers or develop lesson plans, go to sleep. The children began to complain about their cramped living quarters and the fact they had to carry homemade lunches to school because Molly didn't have much money. Most of the time, though, Charlotte and Josh worked hard to make do, and their school performance was exemplary. Molly felt very proud of both children. She herself, however, was gradually growing discouraged about her own situation. Henry wasn't calling nearly as often any more, and he wasn't asking her to come back to him.

Evenings were lonely for Molly, especially on the weekends. So she was delighted when her son George and his wife Sally invited her, Charlotte, and Josh over for dinner one Saturday evening. When she arrived she found a pleasant surprise awaiting. George had asked another guest to dinner as well! The guest was a neighbor of George and Sally's, Herbert Stone, a man probably a dozen years Molly's senior. Herbert had been widowed for several years, and his children were grown and married. He took an immediate, strong interest in Molly.

Perhaps the inevitable happened then. Herbert learned from Molly about the events that had led to her separation from Henry, and he felt great sympathy for her. He himself was lonely, and Molly was a very attractive woman. A considerate man, Herbert worked his way into Molly's heart initially by taking her and the children on outings together. Herbert had plenty of experience with children. He had raised a son and a daughter alone through their teenage years, and he was a proud grandfather now. Josh took to the man immediately. Charlotte did not, although Herbert made great efforts.

Before long, Molly and Herbert began seeing each other regularly. Eventually, they became lovers. Molly was thrilled. She began to wonder what life might be like as Herbert's wife. It was clear to her that that was exactly what Herbert had in mind. He had begun talking about marriage early in their relationship. There was a problem, however—or rather, there were two of them. First and foremost, Molly still missed Henry. A big part of her still longed to be with her husband. Second, Charlotte made it clear that nobody was going to take the place of her father. She was rude to Herbert, and her schoolwork began to reflect her anger. Of the three Peterson children, Charlotte had been the one that Henry had treated with consistent care and affection. Charlotte felt close to him, and she didn't give up hope that her father would ask his family to return.

One day the young girl called Henry on the telephone.

"Daddy," she said, "Don't you know you're going to lose Mom and all of us kids if you don't do something fast?"

"What do you mean, Charlotte?"

And in that way, Henry learned that he had a serious rival. He became upset. He didn't want to lose his way of life, which required a wife to allow him to maintain his freedom from commitment to the other women whose company he enjoyed. He also needed a second income. Henry didn't consciously view his relationship to Molly in that calculating a manner, but that was the way things were, and part of him knew it very well.

Henry called Molly the day after his conversation with Charlotte, to complain.

"Molly," he said, "I have no intention of marrying anybody but you. You know that. You know I don't get emotionally involved with the other women I go out with. You shouldn't get emotionally involved with other men, either. I've been waiting for you to decide to come home. You're the one who left, and you know you're welcome back here any time. I want you to give up this Herbert and come home to me. Now."

Despite her involvement with Herbert, Molly was initially overjoyed to hear these words from Henry. This was the kind of thing she had wanted to hear from her husband for so long! But soon Molly asked Henry an important question.

"Henry, are you willing to give up your affairs?" Molly carefully used the dread word in the plural because she knew that after Marlene, there would be more, unless Henry agreed to change his lifestyle.

"Hell, no," roared Henry! "Molly, that's not necessary and you know it! You and I have managed our marriage very well for 22 years, affairs or no. You know I only need an occasional fling, and you also know you come first with me. I want you as my primary relationship. And besides, Charlotte says she wants to come back home."

"Henry, you know I'm involved with another man now."

"Yes, of course I know. Charlotte told me. But you need to stop what you're doing, because you're doing it wrong. Charlotte says you're so involved with this guy you're thinking of marrying him. That's ridiculous. When I have affairs, I don't let myself get emotionally involved like that."

"Henry, I don't care how you conduct your affairs. I won't agree to come home unless you agree to give them up entirely, for good."

"That's ridiculous. Besides, Charlotte wants you to come home too. She doesn't like this Herbert of yours and she says she isn't happy living at your apartment any more."

"Henry, I'm sorry about Charlotte, but some things take time. Charlotte just needs to get to know Herbert a little better."

"I don't think time will do it for our Charlotte, Molly. That's not what she told me. Our daughter has told me that she can't stand Herbert. How about letting the kid come home? Charlotte can live here with me."

"By herself? Certainly not, Henry," Molly said. "You wouldn't get her to bed on time, and you wouldn't feed her properly."

"Well, I think you'd better talk to Charlotte about that. I've told her she's welcome home any time. She says she wants to come right now."

"Henry, don't expect to see any of us unless you give up your affair with Marlene."

"Molly, I want you to come home now. Just forget about Marlene."

"I'm sorry, Henry, I can't. I'll come home if you'll give her up."

"No way, Molly."

"Then I guess there's no reason for us to talk right now, Henry. Good bye." And Molly hung up.

Molly had sounded firm on the telephone, but after she hung up, she burst into tears. Henry had said he wanted her back! How wonderful! But still he refused to give up his affair with Marlene! How terrible! And now Charlotte wanted to go home! How could Charlotte say something like that to her father? Didn't the girl love her mother any more?

Molly cried for a long time. She was aware that she was furious at Charlotte and felt betrayed. Still, as a mother, Molly wanted what was best for her daughter. Would it be better for Charlotte to go live with Henry now? Or should Molly give up Herbert, so that Charlotte would be a little happier living at the apartment, and might do better in school? That idea made Molly feel very lonely again.

A few hours later, confused and miserable, Molly Peterson picked up the telephone and called the Family Therapy Training Institute.

CHAPTER 20

Molly Returns for Counseling

JoEllen Madsen telephoned the institute to get her schedule for the evening's appointments ahead of time, as she had learned to do early in her training. It was helpful to know in advance who was coming and when.

"Molly Peterson at 7:00," JoEllen repeated when Kelly read the name. "Kelly, are you the one who made the appointment for Molly?"

"Yes," the receptionist replied, "and I remember her from before. Didn't she come in about six months ago with her husband and children?"

"Yes," said JoEllen. "Did Molly say she was coming by herself this evening?"

"She did," replied the receptionist. "Mrs. Peterson said she was separated from her husband now and needed to talk with you alone."

"Did she say what she wanted to talk about, specifically?"

"Not exactly," said Kelly. "When I asked, she just said it was a family problem."

"Molly's a pretty private person," JoEllen responded. "Well, I'll be glad to see her again. Thank you, Kelly."

JoEllen hung up the telephone, a thoughtful expression on her face. I guess Kurt was right on this one, she said to herself. The Peterson family must have had a crisis after all.

Later that evening, when JoEllen met Molly in the waiting room, the two women greeted each other warmly.

"I think you have a lot of courage, Molly!" JoEllen said in a teasing tone as she led her client along the gracious atrium toward the training office. "You scheduled your appointment at the same time as before, so we'll be working in the training office again. There will be a consultation team behind the mirror. Did you know that?"

"Not really, but that's OK," Molly said. "Believe me, I can use all the help I can get."

The first several minutes of the session were spent in signing the necessary permission forms to use the video equipment and the one-way mirror and in taking down Molly's new address and telephone number. Then Molly brought JoEllen up to date with respect to the major events in her life. She described the talk with Marlene that had precipitated her decision to leave Henry, reinforced by Josh's glue-sniffing incident. She described moving to the small, third-floor apartment, and then her involvement with her son George's neighbor, Herbert. Finally Molly told JoEllen about Charlotte's telephone call to Henry.

"I just don't understand how my daughter could do this to me, her own mother, after all we've been through together!" Molly's tone was hurt and angry.

"What do you think Charlotte had in mind, Molly?" the trainee asked gently.

"Charlotte wants me to break up with Herbert and go back to her father, even though Henry is still seeing Marlene!"

"Is that what Charlotte said, Molly?"

"No, that's not what she *said.* What Charlotte actually said was that she wants me to break up with Herbert. She told me she could never stand to have Herbert as her father. But poor Herbert is wonderful to Charlotte, and to me too, so I just can't figure out where she's coming from. I think we could all be so happy together."

"How serious do you feel about Herbert, Molly?"

"Very serious," replied the woman. "In many ways I like Herbert a lot better than Henry."

"For example?"

"For example, Herbert's absolutely faithful to me. He says he has no intention of ever being otherwise. I believe him, too. Herbert was married for 19 years before his wife died of a stroke. He says neither one of them ever had an affair during their marriage."

"That's an admirable record!" responded JoEllen. "It speaks clearly of Herbert's values."

"Yes, I think so," said Molly. "And Herbert is great with the kids, too. Or at least he's very considerate and spends a lot of time with them, a lot more than Henry ever did. It's just that Charlotte doesn't appreciate him. In fact, she's plain rude to Herbert. I'm embarrassed by her behavior and very disappointed. Charlotte's usually such a good kid."

"Molly, you've talked so far this evening about your sense of dissatisfaction with Charlotte, your new relationship with Herbert, and your husband's request that you go back to him. What do you want to talk about first?"

"Charlotte. My dissatisfaction with Charlotte. I'm so mad at her I don't know what to do. I'm not sure what makes me more angry—her ratting to her father about Herbert and me or her wanting to live with Henry all of a sudden. I just don't get it. Here I've finally started to feel happy again, and my daughter spoils everything for me."

The telephone rang.

"JoEllen," said Kurt, "be sure Molly understands that you empathize with her before you get into the probable purpose of Charlotte's behavior. Otherwise, her relationship with her daughter could continue to deteriorate. That wouldn't be in the best interest of either one of them."

"Right," said JoEllen. She knew what Kurt meant by "the probable purpose." Charlotte was very likely producing more creative behaviors aimed at saving her parents' marriage. Molly, in the flush of her new relationship with Herbert, might not appreciate such a purpose at this time, whether it was conscious or not.

The trainee smiled at her client when she hung up the phone. JoEllen knew that Molly knew that the team had given her instructions. JoEllen acknowledged the team's input with gentle humor.

"Yep, Molly," she bantered to gain some time, "the team is definitely alive and well."

"What did they say, JoEllen?" asked Molly.

The trainee's mind whirled. As usual, the team could give her a suggestion, but not the specifics as to how to carry it out.

"The team feels for you, Molly," JoEllen replied after a few moments. "I empathize with what you're going through too. It must be terribly frustrating to develop an encouraging new relationship with an attentive man, only to have your own daughter try to sabotage it."

"That's it exactly!" said Molly. "Charlotte *is* trying to sabotage my relationship with Herbert. My own daughter, who knows how much I have suffered with her father!"

"That would make most people in your situation very angry."

"I am *furious,*" declared Molly. "Absolutely *furious!*" Her eyebrows drew close together, and her lips curved down deeply in a frown. She thrust out her lower jaw.

Even considering the circumstances, JoEllen was surprised at Molly's intensity. The woman looked suddenly like a very angry child. Her face was stormy, her lower lip thrust forward in a pout.

On a sudden hunch, the trainee asked, "Molly, did anything like this ever happen to you when you were growing up?"

Molly's look changed to one of surprise. "What?" she said.

"You said once or twice that your father was not an easy man to live with, Molly," JoEllen continued thoughtfully. "Did your mother ever seriously think about leaving him when *you* were young?"

"Of course she did," Molly replied. "But Mother always said she had to stay on account of the children."

"Was there ever a time your mother came close to leaving your father anyway?"

"Maybe once," the woman replied slowly. "I haven't thought about this in years, but I remember there was a man who took an interest in my mother once. He was a grocer in town, and I think he liked Mom a lot. I remember seeing the two of them talking together a number of times in the store. Once I saw him touching her on the shoulder."

"How did you feel about that, Molly?"

Molly grimaced. "I didn't like it. I wanted mother to come home and leave that man alone."

"Do you think anything like that could be happening with Charlotte?"

Molly grimaced again. "I never thought about anything like that, but do you suppose Charlotte feels about Herbert the way I felt about that grocer?" she responded.

"Perhaps," said JoEllen. "How *did* you feel about the grocer, Molly?"

"Why, I didn't really feel much at all. I didn't know him very well. I suppose he was a good enough man but . . ."

"But he wasn't your mother's husband. He wasn't your father."

"That's it, I guess. My mother belonged at home, with me and Daddy. At least that's how I saw things when I was a child, no matter how mean Daddy got at times." Molly stopped, pulled herself out of her memories with effort, and said, "I suppose that's the problem with Charlotte, isn't it."

"I think so, Molly," JoEllen said gently. "Charlotte probably feels disoriented and upset right now. She wants her old family back. Things are starting to get really scary for her. You might never go back home. Then where will she belong? With whom?"

"Oh dear, said Molly. "So Charlotte's trying to pull Henry and me back together, the way things used to be."

"That's the only way she knows," said JoEllen. "That's been her entire world so far, except for the past few months."

"The poor kid. And it isn't going to work."

"It isn't going to work? Molly, do you mean you are thinking seriously of leaving Henry for good?"

"Yes. I've been thinking about divorce."

"Hm. Tell me more about that."

"I don't really want to get a divorce, JoEllen, but what choice do I have?" Molly cried suddenly in a voice full of pain. "I can't just go back to Henry after all this—I can't pretend all these months haven't happened! Henry's never going to change—he's told me so himself a hundred times!" At this point, Molly began to cry.

"But I don't really *want* to leave Henry!" she sobbed. "Not really. What I want is for Henry to want me enough to leave Marlene. Henry's been my husband for so long I can't imagine living without him. Not really. Why, we practically grew up together! He's the father of my children!"

"Yes, of course," JoEllen murmured sympathetically, remembering her own struggle at a time like this. She realized suddenly that she had had it relatively easy. There had been no children to consider in her relationship with Chip.

Molly's sobs subsided gradually. JoEllen handed her a box of Kleenex.

"What do you think would be best for you now, Molly?" the trainee asked after a suitable interval as Molly wiped her eyes.

Molly sighed a long sigh. "I guess I have to recognize that Henry doesn't really love me. I guess maybe Marlene was right. If Henry did love me, he couldn't possibly treat me this way."

"Sometimes people tell us things we don't want to hear," said JoEllen softly, "so we don't recognize the truth in their words until later. But remember, people do love in different ways. I suspect Henry does love you very much in his own way."

"Well, I'm getting tired of Henry's way," Molly replied sharply.

JoEllen continued. "Maybe the question is, is Henry's way of loving right for *you?*"

For a moment, Molly brightened, thinking about Henry's possibly loving her after all. Then she shook her head.

"No," she said sadly, "Henry may love me in his own way. I'd certainly like to think so. But he pays much more attention to Marlene. The night I went over to the club hoping to see him, I'll bet Henry danced with Marlene ten times to every once he danced with me. And even if he gets tired of Marlene soon, somebody else will come along."

"So being Henry's primary relationship, as he puts it, is not enough for you." JoEllen carefully used the words she remembered Henry using to describe his relationship with Molly.

"No, it isn't. Besides, Herbert says that 'primary relationship' idea is crazy. He says a man who loves his wife doesn't seek out sexual affairs with other women."

"Well, again, we don't know what love means to Henry. What's important to think about tonight is what is right for you, Molly. You are the one who is trying to make a decision. And what you seem to be saying is that while you still have a lot of feeling for Henry, you are no longer willing to stay with him under his conditions."

"That's right," Molly said. Her voice sounded firm. Then she hesitated. "But what about the children? My mother stayed with my father on account of my brother and me. Do you think maybe I should stay with Henry on account of Charlotte and Josh?"

"That's an important question," said JoEllen. "Many a woman has stayed in an unsatisfactory marriage on account of the children. Charlotte and Josh are going to react if you decide to leave Henry for good, there's no doubt about it. Charlotte may already be reacting just to the *fear* that you may leave her father for good."

The telephone rang.

"JoEllen," said Kurt, "ask Molly how she thinks the children would be helped if she stayed with Henry on their account. Ask her to be specific. And then ask her how she thinks they might be hurt."

JoEllen hung up and repeated the team's instructions almost word for word to her client.

Molly looked surprised. "Of course I can tell you ways the children would be helped if I stayed with their father. They could go back and live in our old house, for one thing, which is much more comfortable than the apartment. The kids would each have their own bedroom again, and a decent place to do their homework. And of course they'd get to see their father more often. But the team wants me to list how the kids might be *hurt* if I stayed with Henry? I never thought about that."

"Well, now is the time!" said JoEllen.

"Hm," said Molly. "I'm stumped. Except, of course, I've wondered what kind of example we're setting for the kids."

"That's a definite consideration. One way children learn how to behave toward one another as adults is through observing their parents."

"Then, too, Charlotte and Josh certainly experience a lot of stress when Henry and I are together, because we get so mad at each other all the time," Molly continued.

"That's another consideration. As I recall, the reason you came to therapy in the first place was Charlotte's behavior in response to that stress."

"So if I go back to Henry, Charlotte might begin goofing off at school again or maybe even shoplifting."

"Those are possibilities, if your marriage remains in trouble."

"But Charlotte's *already* starting to goof off again at school, and I haven't gone back to Henry!"

"You may not be living with Henry, but he's still your husband. You're still very much involved with him emotionally."

"So whether I go back to Henry or live apart from him, Charlotte will probably misbehave? Where does that leave me? I'm damned if I do and damned if I don't!" Molly's voice took on a whining, indignant sort of tone.

"My gosh, what a terrible dilemma! That doesn't sound fair at all!" And JoEllen began to laugh merrily. Molly looked surprised, and then she grinned along with the trainee. If JoEllen could laugh, then things couldn't be quite as bad as they seemed!

"You mean things aren't so bad after all?" the mother asked the trainee almost shyly. "I was beginning to feel like there was nothing I could do for me that would also be right for my kids."

"You know," responded JoEllen, still grinning a little, "sometimes when we look only at what is going wrong, and then at what *might* go wrong, we get so bogged down that everything looks completely hopeless and unfair. But that's not the way life really is, thank heavens. Change is always possible, and we do have choices."

"Do you think there are any good choices in my situation?" asked Molly.

"Every decision has certain costs, of course," responded JoEllen, serious now. "But your children are intelligent and capable human beings, Molly. You can talk with Charlotte and Josh about your dilemmas and the choices you have to make. If your children understand what is happening, they can control their behavior much more consciously. They're growing up now; they already understand more than we know."

"I suppose you're right," said Molly.

"Talking with the children, of course, is not the same as asking them to take sides. These are decisions you must make yourself, or with Henry."

"Yes, I can understand that," said Molly.

"Good," said the trainee. "Now—what *do* you want to do about your relationship with Henry at this point?"

"I'm not sure. But being in limbo is hard. I think I want to come to some kind of decision about the marriage."

"What do you see as your options?"

"Going home, or getting a divorce. And I don't like either one."

"Can you think of any other options?"

"Well, I could postpone making any decision for a while. I could just hang in limbo with Henry for a little while longer."

"You could do that. But remember, staying in limbo is a decision too. And no decision is cost-free."

"I suppose not knowing what's going to happen is pretty hard on the kids."

"Uncertainty is part of the cost of limbo, for everyone, not just the kids."

"If I thought just living apart longer would make any difference . . ."

"Do you think it might?"

"No. I almost think Henry prefers to live this way. He has the run of the house, and no kids to worry about. Henry hasn't even been calling very much lately, except right after Charlotte talked with him a couple days ago."

"Hm," said JoEllen. "What do you make of that, Molly?"

"I don't think Henry misses me very much, actually," Molly said sadly. She sat quietly then, taking in the import of her own words.

A resolute expression came over her face then. "The more you and I talk, JoEllen, the more I think it's time I made the decision to leave Henry for good. I've hung in there waiting for him now for six solid months. He hasn't changed his tune one bit. Marlene's still the lady he spends his time with."

"That makes sense to me, Molly," said JoEllen. "In some ways, I think you've been wanting to say that all evening."

"You're right," said Molly. "I can't really explore a future with Herbert unless I've wrapped things up with Henry."

"It's important to take things one step at a time."

"But I feel so guilty," Molly continued, the edges of her mouth turning down again.

"*You* feel guilty, when it's Henry who's been having affairs and who explicitly refuses to give them up?" JoEllen's voice registered her surprise.

"Yes," said Molly seriously. "I've always been told that a good wife does whatever is necessary to make her marriage work. The marriage is her responsibility, no matter what the husband may be doing."

"Many women get messages like that from society as a whole," reflected JoEllen. "Do you know where your messages come from specifically?"

"My mother, I suppose," said Molly. "And the church I went to when I was a child."

"How much do you believe these messages?"

"Well, of course I don't believe them the way I used to. My mother eventually left my father, as I've told you before. But for her, it took several major physical beatings. My brother had already died, probably from internal injuries, and I had left for college."

The telephone rang.

"Ask Molly more about her idea that the woman alone is responsible for the success of her marriage," said Kurt. "You may be onto something important. Molly said earlier that she and her two kids are crowded into a small apartment, while her husband has the run of the family home. That doesn't make sense to the team. I wonder if it has anything to do with this 'women at fault' belief."

"I'll check it out, Kurt," said JoEllen.

Molly looked at JoEllen with a questioning expression.

"Molly," the trainee said, "you said a few moments ago that your mother believed the woman was solely responsible for the success of her marriage. From what you've told me, it sounds as if your mother endured years of physical abuse before deciding to leave your father. Is that correct?"

"Yes," said Molly. "The beatings were terrible. I remember bruises and black eyes and swellings on her face."

"And your father beat the children too?"

"He beat my brother, Ben, a lot. I wasn't as brave as Ben. I never talked back and I ran and hid when Dad started drinking."

"What did your brother do?"

"Ben tried to protect my mother, and that's when he got in trouble. I have a terrible feeling that injuries Dad caused may have led to Ben's death. They had a terrible fight a few days before my brother died."

"And still, your mother stayed."

"Yes."

"What do you think about that now?"

"I think now that Mom should have left Dad long before she did. I wish I hadn't been such a brat about that grocer. Maybe Mom would have left my father years before if only I had encouraged her."

"When you remember how you felt as a child, can you understand why you wanted your mother to stay?"

"I think so. I was so scared back then, but I couldn't imagine living without my father. I didn't understand what choices we had."

"That's right, you didn't, and your mother probably didn't either. She probably kept hoping things would get better with your father, just as most abused wives do."

"Yes, she sure hoped. She hoped for years."

"Now, as I understand it, when your parents' marriage broke up, your mother left and your father stayed in the house where you grew up?"

"Yes, of course. Mom's the one who walked out."

"Well, sometimes women can get a court order and have the man evicted instead."

"Good heavens, JoEllen," Molly said. "Mother would never have done anything like that. She felt too guilty. She just took the few clothes she had and sneaked away in the middle of the night. She left everything to my father."

"What do you think about that today?"

"Well, things sure weren't easy for my Mom after that. I couldn't help her much, because I was putting myself through college at the time.

Mom had to take any work she could get. Finally, she met another man, and they got married. She's been much happier since then."

"Did your mother deserve to suffer all those years?"

"Of course not," said JoEllen. "That's just the way she was. Mom always took the weight of the world on her shoulders. And as I say, to some degree she thought *she* had failed when her marriage with my father didn't work out. I think she thought she deserved to suffer."

"What do you think, Molly? Do you think your mother is the one who failed, and that she deserved to suffer?" JoEllen pursued.

"Of course not," said Molly. "My father acted like a brute. He wasn't really a brute; I think he meant well. But he couldn't control himself when he was drinking. My Mom certainly wasn't perfect, but she sure didn't deserve the beatings Dad gave her."

"If you could go back and do things over again, would you want your mother to be able to keep her house and make your father leave?"

"Sure I would. I never thought about it, though, at the time. I just wanted my mother safe. I wrote to her several times from college, urging her to leave. Anything was better than living with my father, even the street."

"So you wanted your mother to leave!"

"Oh yes, eventually I sure did. I think Ben's death changed something in me. I decided I wanted to get out of that place as soon as I could. I was a sophomore in high school when Ben died. I left home the day after my high school graduation."

"Molly, do you have any idea why I'm asking you all of these questions about your mother and how things were when you were growing up?"

"Ah . . . well . . . no, not really."

"The team told me a while back that they thought it was odd that you are living in a little apartment with your two kids, while your husband has the run of the family home. Do you see any parallels between yourself and your mother here?"

"Certainly not! My father was physically abusive to my mother so that she practically had to flee for her life! My husband never hits anybody, ever!"

"Molly, many therapists would describe the way Henry treats you as emotionally abusive."

"Oh no. Henry's not emotionally abusive. He hurts my feelings sometimes, sure, but living with him is absolutely *nothing* compared to what it was like living with my father."

"Life did sound much worse with your father," acknowledged JoEllen. "But still, you have suffered quite a bit in your marriage, Molly. Whatever term you use, abusive or not, isn't important. What's important is that you have endured a good deal of pain for a long, long time."

Molly took a deep breath and nodded slowly. "That's true," she said.

"I think you learned how to endure so much pain from your mother. You both have great strength, for which you can be very proud," continued JoEllen.

Molly smiled a little, nodding again.

"The flip side of that endurance, however, is that you may have a tendency to suffer too long in a bad situation, when it might be better to change the situation instead."

"Hm," said Molly, not looking or sounding convinced. Instead, her eyes seemed to glaze. She stared off into the distance.

The telephone rang.

"JoEllen," said Kurt, "I think your ideas are good but you're losing Molly. Too much, too fast. Why not just ask how she and Henry made the decision regarding who would leave the house?"

"OK," said JoEllen.

She turned to her client. "Molly, how *did* you and Henry decide who would stay in your house, and who would have to move out?"

"Oh," said Molly, "I did. That was my decision. I knew Henry wouldn't move away. I didn't even ask him."

"What about the children?"

"Well, of course the kids wanted to stay in the house. Charlotte even suggested that I ask Henry to leave; she said that's what happens with her friends who have family problems—they stay in their own house while the father goes. But I explained we couldn't do things that way."

"Why was that, Molly?"

"I knew Henry would never leave the house!"

"What about a court order?"

"Oh, I couldn't do that to my husband."

"Hm. Is Henry helping you out financially, Molly?"

"Well, he's paying part of the mortgage on the house."

"I mean, is Henry paying you any child support, or part of the rent on your apartment?"

"Oh, no. I have to help Henry financially or he couldn't afford to stay in our house. He doesn't earn very much money from his sales job any more."

"You mean, not only are you living in an inadequate apartment to make Henry more comfortable, but you are also sending him money?"

"Yes," said Molly. "I want Henry to know I still love him."

The telephone rang.

"I want you to ask Molly how she justifies harming the children to help her husband." Kurt's voice was no-nonsense.

JoEllen hung up the phone and turned to Molly. "I don't know how else to put this, Molly, so here goes. The team wants to know how you justify harming your children in order to help your husband."

"What do you mean, harm my children?" Molly was clearly offended.

JoEllen responded as gently as she could. "Molly, you said earlier, in making a list of reasons for going back with Henry, that the children would then have a more comfortable home in which to live, including bedrooms of their own and a place to do their homework."

"That's right." Molly looked confused. She wasn't making connections that seemed obvious to the trainee.

JoEllen tried again. "You could probably live in that house with the children right now, Molly. *Without* Henry. It might require a court order, but living at home would be much better for Charlotte and Josh. You know how children need stability."

"Yes, but Henry would never leave the house," Molly insisted again stubbornly. "I know my husband. He'd let us all come home to live with him, but he'd never leave."

"You could still at least *ask* him, don't you think? You said you hadn't done that yet. Don't you think it would be better for the children to enjoy the security of their own home?"

"Sure, but as I said, Henry wouldn't agree."

"Molly, remember that you said your mother left her home to your father, possibly because nobody realized there might be a choice?"

"Uh huh."

"Well, here it is a generation later. You have the luxury of hindsight. Didn't you say it would probably have been better for your mother if she could have stayed in her own home?"

"Yes. But Mom probably felt better just leaving at the time. It was simpler, and she didn't feel as guilty that way."

"Do you think she was still acting as if the failure of her marriage were her own fault, perhaps believing she should suffer for it?"

"I suppose so."

"Is that the way you feel now, Molly? Do you feel so guilty about considering divorce that you won't ask for what is best for yourself and your children?"

"Well, as I said earlier, what I've gone through with Henry is nowhere near as bad as what my mother went through with my father."

"So maybe you haven't suffered enough?"

"I guess not."

"Molly, do you hear what you're saying?"

"I guess so." Molly, however, did not look as if she understood what she was saying. She looked confused and somewhat upset at being pursued so hard by JoEllen.

The telephone rang. The trainee felt grateful. She didn't know what else to say or do at that point.

"JoEllen, you are starting to work much harder on Molly's behalf than she is. You know that doesn't work. Try something different. Try bringing some humor into this. See if you can't get Molly to laugh at herself."

That was a tall order! JoEllen hung up the telephone with a touch of exasperation. Now what was she to do? Suddenly, the trainee decided to be honest with her client.

"Help! Molly, I'm stuck!" JoEllen burst out.

Molly looked startled. Certainly the members of the team were surprised.

"I'm so frustrated!" the trainee continued in the same agitated tone. "In fact, I feel like I could tear my hair out!" And at that, JoEllen amazed everyone by grabbing hunks of her hair and making exaggerated yanking motions.

"What—!" gasped Molly, and she started to grin.

JoEllen continued, waving her arms in grand gestures, "Molly, I just can't understand how you look at things, so I'm going to give this another go. OK, I agree, you *are* guilty as a woman and a wife. You are fully responsible for breaking up your marriage. You should probably do penance daily!"

"Huh?" said Molly.

"I hope you are taking care of Henry's laundry for him! And doing his food shopping, and cooking his meals! That's the responsibility of every good wife worth her salt! Let's see, there must be more—shouldn't you also be taking care of your husband's car payments?"

Molly stared at JoEllen for a long moment, and then laughed out loud.

"Car payments!" she exclaimed. "Why that man's plain too cheap to buy a car that takes payments!"

"Well, what about Henry's laundry then! And his ironing! I certainly hope you are taking proper care of your husband's laundry and his ironing!"

"Good lord, JoEllen!" Molly continued to laugh but her voice took on an indignant tone. "You've gone nuts! How can you possibly say I ought to be doing all those things for Henry, when he's been cheating on me for most of our marriage! Henry should have to take care of himself now. If he wants somebody to do his laundry, why, he'll just have to ask his darling Marlene!"

"Oh!" exclaimed JoEllen, a little disconcerted. "You don't say!"

"In fact," continued Molly, "Maybe it *is* time I asked Henry for that house. Our poor kids shouldn't have to live away from their own home. Henry's the one who's been running around—he's the one who ought to have to find a new place for himself."

"Oh, do you really think so?" gasped JoEllen.

"In fact," said Molly, "I've made up my mind. I'm going to file for divorce."

"Divorce," repeated JoEllen. "You mentioned that earlier, Molly. How serious are you?"

"Very serious," Molly replied. "I'm very serious, JoEllen."

The telephone rang.

"Come on back for a final consultation," said Kurt. "This is a good place to quit, and our time's up anyway."

The message to Molly from the team that evening read as follows: "Molly, the team urges you to go slowly. After all, leaving a spouse formally is a very serious step, and you can never anticipate exactly what will happen. You have said in session tonight that you don't believe Henry will leave your family home voluntarily. If you get a court order, he may become very upset with you. Consider carefully before making such an important decision.

"We admire your courage and look forward to working with you in the future. Bring the children next week if you wish."

The team, of course, was deliberately taking on the role of expressing Molly's own feelings of fear and hesitation, and providing permission for her to pay attention to them. Such inevitable feelings identified and acknowledged, Molly would then be able to recognize and acknowledge others. She consulted an attorney regarding a divorce only a few days later.

CHAPTER 21

Henry Receives a Summons

Henry Peterson stared at the Summons and Petition for Divorce clasped in his hands. One of the documents included a court date for a preliminary hearing. He held his hands poised at some distance from his face, as if the papers they gripped were offensive to him. Near Henry stood the bearer of these unwanted documents, shifting awkwardly from foot to foot, sympathy written all over his features. Molly, in her characteristic way, had made delivery of the summons and petition as easy as possible for her husband, sending them via a mutual friend, not the county sheriff. The laws of her state permitted either method. The intent of the papers, though, was the same: divorce. Henry, despite the events of the past several months, received the summons with shock and disbelief.

Along with the official documents, Molly sent a short, personal letter:

Dear Henry,

After all our years together it seems impossible that I am filing for divorce. However, as we both know, our marriage is over for all practical purposes. We may as well legalize what has become reality.

For the sake of the children, I intend to ask for custody, child support, and occupancy of the house until Josh has completed high school. While I doubt you will contest custody, I expect that a legal requirement to provide child support and to leave the house will be upsetting to you. However, Charlotte and Josh both need stability right now. They miss their home badly and are tired of penny-pinching. I will not be sending you any more money for mortgage payments.

I hope we can handle our settlement by mutual agreement so that we won't have to waste our assets on unnecessary legal fees.

Sincerely,

Molly

"This is ridiculous," Henry sputtered to his fidgeting friend over and over. "This is completely ridiculous. Molly knows she can come home any time she wants. She's welcome to bring the kids with her. She just doesn't get it. She doesn't realize what she's got and now she thinks she's going to throw it away."

"Henry," said his friend after listening to the man fume bitterly for ten minutes or so, "I'm awfully sorry this has happened but I'm afraid there's nothing I can do. I have to go now. Will you sign the receipt as proof of delivery?"

"Sign a receipt?!" exclaimed Henry. "I'm not signing any receipt. I don't want a divorce!"

"Please, Henry," said his friend. "The receipt is only to prove you have received the papers. It doesn't say anything about agreeing to a divorce. If you don't sign it, I'll have to give everything back to Molly and I expect she'll have the sheriff deliver this stuff the next time."

"Oh, hell," said Henry. He stamped out of the room dramatically, and his friend feared he might not return. But Henry did return, an old ballpoint pen clenched in his fist. "I'll sign the stupid receipt, damn it. But Molly'd better not think I'm agreeing to this divorce."

Mission accomplished, Henry's uneasy friend exited quickly, looking as if he needed fresh air in a hurry.

That evening, Henry called Molly. In a manner unusual for a man who was characteristically either exceedingly charming or pointedly silent, Henry began shouting almost before his wife picked up the telephone. Henry told Molly in no uncertain terms that divorce was not acceptable to him. He insisted that Molly didn't understand: she came first in his life, no matter what he did with anybody else, and he expected her to give up her foolishness and come home forthwith.

When Henry had calmed down somewhat, Molly asked her husband a single question—would he stop seeing Marlene?

Silence ensued for a few moments. Then, in an enticing tone, Henry replied softly, "You know you'll always be my primary relationship, Molly."

"That's not good enough," Molly replied, and she hung up.

Henry called back the next evening. "What about counseling?" he asked. "Why don't we go back together to see that what's-her-name down at the institute, JoAnn, JoLene—"

"JoEllen," said Molly, "and I've been seeing her recently on my own, Henry. Remember, therapists at the institute won't begin marriage counseling until both partners agree to give up their extramarital relationships. I'm not sure I'm willing to give up Herbert now, and you have never been willing to give up any of your affairs."

"Hell," said Henry, "that's a crazy requirement, especially in our case. We did fine for years until you got all emotional about Marlene. And now you're getting much too involved with that fellow Herbert. Family therapists are supposed to save marriages, aren't they? I'm going to call JoEllen down at the institute and tell her it's time she saved ours."

Henry called JoEllen the next morning. The trainee was not present at the institute at the time, so Henry left his name and phone number. Kelly called JoEllen at work to let her know about the message, and JoEllen returned Henry's call late in the afternoon. Henry was blunt on the telephone.

"My wife wants a divorce," he said. "You're a marriage counselor, JoEllen, right? I want you to do what you have to do to save our marriage."

"Henry, if Molly agrees, you are welcome to come for counseling as a couple. In fact, I strongly recommend you do so. I can't make any guarantees, of course, but couples' counseling is the best way I know to help a troubled marriage."

"Good. When can we come in?"

"First, Henry, there's that requirement I need to discuss with you."

"Oh, yeah, you mean the one about giving up extramarital relationships?

"Yes. Are you willing—at least for the duration of marriage counseling?"

"That requirement is ridiculous," said Henry. "Of course not. I've told you so before."

JoEllen then offered to work with Henry individually. To her surprise, the man agreed. The trainee tried to arrange a time to meet with Henry when the team was available for consultation, but conflicting schedules made this impossible. She had to arrange a time when she would see the man by herself.

Henry Peterson came for his session with JoEllen promptly on time. His careful dress indicated he was on a serious mission. Soon, however, it became clear that Henry had no interest in discussing individual issues of his own. The man's purpose for coming was to find out from JoEllen as much as possible about Herbert and Molly's relationship and to persuade the trainee that her conditions for marriage counseling were wrong.

Tactfully, JoEllen explained to Henry that she could not discuss Molly's relationship with Herbert for professional reasons of confidentiality. The AAMFT Code of Ethics requires the client's written permission for disclosure of private information such as this. And JoEllen continued to insist on the need to terminate the extramarital affairs—both Henry's and Molly's—before engaging in marital counseling with the two of them together. Patiently, JoEllen explained the reasons once more. But when the therapy hour was up, little had been accomplished. Henry remained correctly cordial throughout the session but left obviously upset, saying he probably wouldn't return. He was annoyed at JoEllen's refusal to talk about his wife's relationship with Herbert, and he crossly remarked that he thought it was the business of marriage counselors to save marriages, not to set conditions for counseling.

JoEllen felt ineffective as a therapist and sad as a person by the time Henry left. She recognized, however, even more strongly than before, how small the chances were of repairing such a troubled marriage. Henry clearly wanted Marlene's ongoing attentions at least as much as he wanted Molly's. JoEllen had little hope for the survival of the Peterson marriage at that point. The trainee had had enough experience by now to realize she was not the determining factor in saving marriages in danger; that honor and responsibility belonged to the respective spouses. Both had to be willing to invest fully in the effort.

Not long afterward, Molly and Henry Peterson's preliminary hearing for divorce was held. Not surprisingly, Henry was ordered by the court to vacate the family home in 30 days. Molly and the children were to move back in at that time, and Henry was to begin making regular child support payments. The payment schedule established by the family court commissioner was reasonable, but Henry was nevertheless shaken and upset. His income from sales was sporadic, and there was no other place he wanted to live besides the house he had built with his wife. Henry thought about living with Marlene, but Marlene's home harbored teenage children, of whom he was not especially fond.

Henry approached Marlene shortly after the court hearing to find out if she would be willing to send her children away to live with their father, who resided in another state with his second wife. After serious deliberation, Marlene talked with her children about Henry's request. The children were furious and told their mother they had no desire to leave home. So Marlene said no to Henry. She felt she had little choice. She invited Henry to come live with her *and* the children, if he wished; Henry declined.

A few days later, Henry called Molly again.

"What about marriage counseling," he said. "I don't want this divorce. Why don't you and the kids just move back home and we'll all live together again?"

"What about Marlene?" asked Molly.

"I'm getting a bit tired of Marlene, to tell you the truth," Henry replied blandly. "I've decided to stop seeing her for a while—it's only for the duration of counseling, anyhow. Now what about this Herbert of yours? You'll have to stop seeing him, too, you know."

"Oh my," said Molly. Her heart suddenly skipped a beat. She wasn't sure what she wanted to do. She had not expected to be in this position now, to have such a choice when she already had given up on Henry. But she still loved her husband in many ways. She had known Henry for so many years; they had experienced so much together, the good as well as the bad. However, Herbert was now also very important to Molly. Molly and Herbert were talking seriously about marriage. Molly knew that Herbert would be terribly disappointed and hurt if she left him now.

"Let me think about this for a while, Henry," Molly said.

Henry called Molly several times during the next few days, pressuring her for a decision. Finally, Molly agreed to put her relationship with Herbert on hold and to participate in marital counseling with Henry.

Neither Herbert nor Marlene took to the sidelines easily. Both argued long and hard with their respective admirers. Eventually, temporarily defeated, they stepped back. Herbert told Molly he would be waiting for her, no matter how long it took for her to return to him. Marlene told Henry he was taking a chance and she couldn't promise to be around for very long. The times were tense for all.

Henry called the Family Therapy Training Institute and made an appointment with JoEllen Madsen for marriage counseling.

CHAPTER 22

❀

Resuming Family Therapy

The team behind the mirror learned from JoEllen the next Wednesday evening that they would be working with Molly and Henry Peterson again. Marital therapy was on the agenda.

"Has Henry given up his affair?" asked Kevin. As the answer was affirmative, the clergyman trainee smiled with beneficent satisfaction. "I'm impressed," he said. "Henry's finally learning to be more responsible. Good man."

"Hmph," said John, the psychologist. "There's probably more to it than that. Henry goes after what he wants, I'm afraid, without much consideration for others."

"I wonder how Molly got him to give up Marlene?" mused Sandra, the guidance counselor.

"Careful not to jump to conclusions, everyone," warned Dr. Kurt Knaak. "We've been out of touch with this couple for months. We've worked with Molly recently, of course, but not with Henry or with the couple together. What happened when you saw Henry individually, JoEllen? Will you bring us up to date on that meeting, please?"

JoEllen provided the consultation team with a brief synopsis of her difficult encounter with Henry two weeks before. She explained that he had left the session angry and upset. JoEllen was quite surprised that the man had decided to return this evening. In fact, when she learned that Henry had made an appointment for marital therapy, she had called him back to ask about Marlene.

JoEllen went on to describe how surprised she had been with Henry's response: "No problem, JoEllen; I've put that relationship on hold." Henry had sounded amazingly casual to the trainee, considering his recent considerable protest. Henry had then volunteered the information that Molly was no longer seeing Herbert, either.

"Well," said Kurt, "it seems we are finally ready to begin the work of marital therapy."

Shortly thereafter, Molly and Henry Peterson were seated in the training office in front of the one-way mirror. JoEllen felt grateful for the unseen presence of the consultation team behind the mirror. She expected she would be rigorously challenged that evening and in need of expert assistance. She was right.

Henry's expression was cheerful as he settled into the most comfortable chair in the office. The man was neatly dressed and had obviously showered and shaved with care. Molly, on the other hand, appeared somewhat disheveled and distressed. Her usual ubiquitous smile was missing and she looked as if she hadn't slept very well the night before.

After the usual greetings, JoEllen asked who wanted to begin. Molly did.

"This is very, very hard for me," Molly began. "I was becoming used to the idea of getting a divorce. I was beginning to put my life with Henry behind me, and Herbert and I were discussing marriage. Now I've hurt Herbert to please Henry. I'm not sure I'm glad to be here this evening, even though a few months ago I would have given anything for the chance to have my husband back."

"Sometimes a person leaves a marriage as a last ditch effort to save it, Molly. Does that description fit for you?"

"Yes, it certainly does, JoEllen. Henry had stopped paying any attention to me or to what I wanted, as you know. Instead, he did whatever Marlene wanted. I felt that the only way I could ever get my husband's attention again was to leave him."

"So you took a great risk, hoping it would save your marriage."

"Yes, I did. That's the only reason I'm here tonight. My marriage always meant a great deal to me, but maybe it only *used* to matter. I'm not sure that I *want* to save it any more. Henry made no effort to get me back for several months, and now there's somebody else important in my life."

"Yet you agreed to stop seeing the other man, Herbert, in order to work on your marriage with Henry."

"Yes. But I'm not sure how long I'll be willing to work on the marriage if I have to stay away from Herbert."

"We can take that question week by week, if necessary." JoEllen paused. She looked thoughtful for a moment, and then asked Molly, "Have you asked Henry about his intentions?"

"His intentions?"

"Yes. Have you asked Henry what he hopes to accomplish in marriage counseling?"

"Why, not exactly," said Molly. "I guess I assume Henry wants to save our marriage. He says he wants me back, anyway, and that he doesn't want a divorce."

"Ask Henry specifically what he hopes to accomplish through marriage counseling. It's important to find out if you two can agree on your goals."

Molly complied. Henry replied simply that he wanted Molly to agree not to pursue a divorce and that he wanted his wife to come back home.

"Are those goals OK with you, Molly?" asked JoEllen. "Are they what you have in mind to work on here also?"

Molly frowned, and shook her head. "Not really, come to think of it," she said.

"Tell Henry what goals are important for *you,*" instructed JoEllen.

Molly spoke up then in an agitated tone. "What about the other women, Henry? If I agree to come home as your wife, what about those extramarital liaisons of yours?"

"Well, I'll take some time before having another one, you can be sure of that. I can tell you're too upset to handle my having a little affair right now, Molly."

"But what about in a year or two?"

"Why, I suppose I'll probably want another little fling by then—just a short-term thing. But it won't mean anything, you know. You're the most important person in the world to me, Molly."

"Then I won't come back to you, Henry. I'll go on with the divorce." Molly's words were straightforward and underscored the grim expression on her face.

"Don't be nuts!" roared Henry with considerable heat. "You and I have our own way of doing things in this marriage, and it's always worked for us before. It's worked for 22 years! I realize you're upset about Marlene, Molly, and maybe about some of the women who came before. But I've been thinking about this. I realize I brought Marlene and some of the others right into our home so that your territory was invaded. That was wrong of me and I apologize. I'll keep any new women I get involved with completely separate from you in the future. That's a promise."

"Henry, that's just not possible. Now that I'm involved in a relationship with another man, I know it's not possible to keep an affair separate from marriage. When you're in love with somebody new, you can't think about anything else. It's on your mind all the time."

"Molly, you just don't realize that you get much too emotionally involved with these things. You don't understand how to do it right. Even our son George knows that. George told me a little while ago that he's starting to have an affair too. He's being careful not to get emotionally involved with the other woman, just like me. That's the key, you don't get emotionally involved."

"Oh, no!" said Molly. "Oh no! Our son George is having an affair? How terrible! Does Sally know?"

"One of Sally's friends told her a few days ago, and I hear she's pretty upset. That's why George talked to me about it. He wants to do his affair right, so it doesn't get in the way of his marriage. I gave the kid some pointers."

"Imagine!" Molly addressed JoEllen in a voice filled with indignation. "Just imagine!" Outrage suddenly distorted her features. "A father tells his son that it's all right to have an extramarital affair, as long as he does it the right way! What kind of father tells his son a thing like that?!"

Henry jumped in. "JoEllen," he said, "Molly isn't listening to me! See? She never listens to me! I've told her that marriage is important to me but there are different ways to be married! Make Molly listen!"

As JoEllen tried to gather her thoughts for a reply, the telephone rang. It was Kurt, of course.

"JoEllen," he said, "we're noticing back here that Molly and Henry keep trying to put you in the middle. Have them talk directly to each other, not through you. Get them to enact how they argue at home, if you can." He hung up.

"Get them to enact." JoEllen remembered from her textbooks that enactment is a therapy technique in which couples are encouraged to try to solve a problem in session exactly the way they do it at home. The therapist can then observe firsthand their style of problem solving, what works for them and what does not.

"Molly, Henry," JoEllen instructed, "I want you to talk to each other about this issue of affairs, not to me. Go ahead. Talk about your disagreement with each other, just as you would at home."

Little encouragement was required for this angry, articulate pair. Molly began.

"Henry," she said, "you not only have hurt me personally, but you are also a very bad example to our son. Now George is having an affair just like you. The poor kid probably thinks affairs are perfectly normal, since you have them so often."

"Molly, you just don't realize that affairs *are* normal. I happen to be more honest than most men, so I tell you about them. Most men I know have affairs but don't tell their wives."

"I don't believe it," said Molly. "I don't know a lot of other women whose husbands have affairs. My friends feel sorry for me. And now poor George is following your bad example."

"Molly, there's nothing wrong with having an affair. Affairs bring new energy into our lives that can help both of us. They don't last long, and they work out fine as long as nobody gets emotionally involved."

"It's impossible not to get emotionally involved when you're having an affair, Henry."

"That's not true, Molly. You're doing it all wrong with this fellow Herbert, talking about marriage and that type of thing. I *never* talk about marriage with any of my other women, except to tell them it's not in the cards. I tell them from the beginning that you come first and that I'm never going to leave you."

"That's what you say, Henry, but who do you spend most of your time with? Who do you dance with at the clubs? Who do you talk to most?"

"That's only for a short time, when I'm in the middle of a romance. You know how I've described these things. Having a romance is like skiing down a mountain slope. You get a great rush on the way down, but you always know you're going to hit bottom. I'm all yours once the rush is over. You know that."

"Great. Terrific. I get to have a little attention once the rush is over with somebody else. How romantic. Then you develop another rush. Meantime I get to do your cooking and cleaning and take care of your kids."

"That's not fair. You just don't realize that you're always on my mind. I never forget about you."

"What I don't realize is how you can treat me so badly, Henry! 'Hell hath no wrath like a woman scorned'! I've had just about enough!" Molly spoke with an anger more intense than JoEllen had ever witnessed from the woman before.

"You have it wrong, Molly," Henry responded, bland and unruffled. "I do not get emotionally involved with the other women when I have flings. I've told you that over and over. I enjoy the rush of a good romance, but you are the only woman I want to spend my life with. I tell you that over and over, but you just never seem to understand."

Molly looked as if she wanted to respond, but she didn't. An uneasy hush settled over the room.

"What are you thinking, Molly?" asked JoEllen.

"I'm so mad I can't think," Molly replied, her vague tone of voice contrasting with the look of confusion and despair on her face.

Henry broke in then. "JoEllen," he said, "Molly just doesn't realize that no woman can possibly give a man everything he needs. It's not just Molly. No one woman can ever meet a man's total needs, so by looking for things in other women that Molly can't give me, I help both of us preserve our marriage."

"You see," said Molly to JoEllen, "Henry has an answer to everything. How can I possibly quarrel with the fact that I can't give him everything he needs?"

JoEllen found herself, like Molly, momentarily pulled into Henry's logic. His points didn't make his listener feel very good, very special, or very important, but they did follow a certain undeniable logic. JoEllen found herself feeling tired. Memories of similar go-rounds with Chip, her former husband, disoriented her. She felt herself pulled far back into time and space. Fortunately, the telephone rang.

"We certainly have had a chance to observe this couple's fighting style!" Kurt began in a hearty, humorous tone that helped JoEllen pull herself back into the present. "Henry beats Molly down with what appears to be airtight logic. His arguments slip in big chunks of blame, however. The man ought to be a lawyer! In the past, I suspect that Molly responded by taking on the placating role. But now she's beyond placating. She's trying to communicate straight, to tell Henry how she really feels; but Henry won't hear her, so she gets stuck. She retreats into confusion. Nothing gets resolved."

"Hm," responded JoEllen, still struggling to pull herself back into the present.

"If I'm correct," Kurt continued, "this discussion is probably reminding you of issues in your own marriage, JoEllen—former marriage, that is."

"That's right," said the trainee, gulping.

"Do you need to come behind the mirror for a few minutes to talk things over with the team, or can you continue out there?"

"I think I can continue," the young woman replied, trying to keep her words few given the curious ears of her clients.

"Then talk to these two good folks about their style of arguing. Forget the content for now. Pay attention to the process. Then, if you can, work in a question about which Henry would prefer: to be right all the time, or to have a meaningful relationship with Molly."

"OK, sounds good," said JoEllen, and hung up. She took a deep breath to continue clearing her head and then turned to her clients.

"Henry and Molly," the trainee began, "the team has just identified your style of arguing. Sometimes the style of arguing can be as important as the content of what people are saying. Do you want to hear what the team has to say about your style, your process?"

"Of course," Henry and Molly replied almost simultaneously, obviously interested.

"OK," said JoEllen. "I'll begin with Henry. Henry, you have a very logical way of laying out an argument and supporting your point of view." Henry smiled and nodded, clearly viewing JoEllen's words as a compliment.

"This is a very common style of communication for men," JoEllen continued, normalizing Henry's approach. "Most men pride themselves in their ability to think and communicate logically. Some therapists call this style 'super-reasonable.'" Henry continued to look pleased.

"Of course," Molly continued, "you do mix a good deal of blaming into your logic—for example, when you say 'Molly does it all wrong.'"

Henry looked a little less pleased. "Well, she does do it wrong," he grumbled.

"Women, however," JoEllen continued, "often pay more attention to feelings than to logic." She turned to Molly.

"Molly, the team believes you are like many women in that you pay close attention to feelings, your own and those of other people. You use feelings to support your arguments—for example, you say that you feel embarrassed and angry when Henry has affairs, and that's why you want him to stop having them."

Molly continued to look confused. She was uncertain that it was OK to pay attention to feelings in this way.

"Expressing feelings can be a risky business," continued the trainee. "One is vulnerable to rejection. It takes guts."

Molly nodded slowly.

"The team observes that you, Molly, have been expressing your feelings honestly today, and using them as part of your argument that Henry must stop having affairs."

Molly nodded again, looking hopeful this time. She sensed support in JoEllen's words. JoEllen turned back to Henry.

"The team has noticed that you, Henry, use your logic to refute or discredit Molly's feelings. Molly withdraws or gets confused, so that you apparently win your point."

Henry nodded, a cautious look on his face. He wasn't sure what JoEllen was getting at.

"In fact, Henry," JoEllen continued, "you seem to have won the argument you just had with Molly right here in the office. You apparently won by using techniques of logic very skillfully. Maybe you've even won most of your arguments for the past 22 years this way. What would you say about that?"

Henry smiled now. "You're right," he said with satisfaction. "I'm a very logical person, so Molly usually comes round to seeing things my way."

"And that's because Molly cares about how you feel, even though *she* may not feel the same way," said JoEllen.

"That's right," said Henry, looking pleased with himself.

"Henry," continued JoEllen, "I think you sincerely believe your own logic. But please notice that I've been using the words *seem* and *apparently* when I talk about you winning your arguments. I haven't said that I think that you *do* win them."

"What do you mean?" asked Henry, an edge in his voice.

"That's a good question," said JoEllen. "I mean that I don't think you *really* win, Henry. You win your immediate point, perhaps, but you lose the trust and affection of your spouse in the process. My proof is the divorce petition that Molly has recently filed."

Henry didn't look so pleased now. Molly appeared suddenly attentive.

"Which is more important for you, Henry," JoEllen pressed on, "to be logically correct all the time, to be right, or to have a fulfilling relationship with your wife?"

This was supposed to be a key question, one that would prompt Henry to stop and consider his deepest personal values. This query, or some variant of it, is used not infrequently by marriage therapists. It has been known to shift more than one ailing marriage back on track. This tactic was suggested by Kurt in his telephone consultation.

JoEllen may have asked the question too soon or at too fast a pace, however. At any rate, Henry didn't take it seriously. He responded glibly.

"I *have* a fulfilling relationship with my wife already," he said in a testy voice without any apparent reflection. "She just never realizes it."

JoEllen's immediate response was to feel thoroughly annoyed with Henry. She wanted to exclaim something like, "How on earth can you possibly say that, you, you . . ." when the telephone rang.

"Two things," said Kurt. "Notice the number of times Henry uses words like *always* and *never.* Also, he sees things only from his own point of view. He seems unable to empathize, to put himself in Molly's place. I wonder if we can find a reason, perhaps something in his childhood. Maybe it's time to look at circumstances in this man's family of origin."

"Thanks, I'll give it a go," the trainee replied.

The team was suggesting a major change of focus, one that would focus on Henry for a period of time. JoEllen turned to Molly first. She wanted her consent.

"Molly," began JoEllen, "how are you feeling right now?"

"Exhausted," said the woman, and she looked it.

"How do you feel about Henry's answer to my last question?" asked JoEllen.

"The one about would he rather be right, or have a fulfilling relationship?"

"Yes," said JoEllen.

"Disappointed and mad. I don't think our relationship is fulfilling at all, and I'm tired of Henry's insisting on winning all our arguments. He doesn't seem to care how *I* feel. Everything has to be his way or no way."

"Molly, I think you have an important point there. The team just mentioned something like that on the telephone. They asked me to talk to Henry about his background to see if there may be a reason that can help us understand. Is it OK with you if I talk with Henry alone for a while?"

"Sure, go ahead."

"OK. Feel free to speak up if you want to." JoEllen turned back to Henry.

"Henry, the message I received from the team is primarily for you. The team wonders if you notice how often you say *always* and *never*."

"No, but so what?" the man replied.

"These words are often a 'red flag,' meaning that what they assert shouldn't be taken too literally," JoEllen answered. "That's because in the real world, it's pretty rare that anything happens 'always' or 'never.' You just said, for example, that Molly never realizes that you two have a fulfilling relationship. Think about it. How true is that statement really?"

"Why, it's completely true!" said Henry. "Molly just said that she doesn't think our relationship is fulfilling! You heard her!"

"What do you think, Molly?" asked JoEllen, turning to the wife. "Would you say your relationship with Henry is *never* fulfilling?"

"If I thought my relationship with Henry was never fulfilling," the woman replied quietly, "I wouldn't be here this evening." Molly sighed then. A very lonely look crossed her sensitive features.

"Sometimes I feel so close to my husband," she mused out loud. "Sometimes I feel that Henry is so close to me too. But then, suddenly, he's gone—off with some other woman, physically or mentally. It feels sometimes like he tosses a bucket of ice at me just when I start to feel close to him."

Henry looked down. For the first time during the session he looked uncomfortable, almost sad.

JoEllen allowed a pause. Imperceptibly, the atmosphere began to alter from one of anger to one more like melancholy.

"What are you feeling now, Henry?" the trainee asked softly after a few quiet moments.

Henry sighed, looking down at his big hands. "I don't know," he replied. He sighed again, and his shoulders slumped slightly.

"Henry, did you hear Molly say that sometimes, when she is feeling closest to you, you seem to throw a bucket of ice in her direction?"

"Of course I heard her," the man said. His face looked even sadder.

"Would you agree?" JoEllen continued.

"I suppose so," the man said in a low tone. He made no explanation, no excuse.

"You agree?" JoEllen sounded surprised.

Henry looked up briefly, then back down at his hands. "I've been aware of this for a long time. Molly and I talk about it every once in a while. I can't seem to help it."

"Are you aware of any reason?"

Henry sighed. "Maybe, maybe not."

"Was there anything in your past, maybe in your childhood, that hurt you very much? That might have made you afraid to trust or get close to people?"

Henry shivered slightly then. When he spoke next, his voice was different in quality: soft, vulnerable.

"They always say these things have to do with your parents," he said. "I suppose that could be true for me."

"Tell us what you think, Henry," JoEllen prompted.

"Well—" the man began. He looked up, frowned, and stopped.

"Go on . . ."

Henry gazed down again at his hands and then away at something out of sight. When he began to speak once more, his voice was almost inaudible.

"One night when I was 13, my mother locked me out of the house. I couldn't believe it."

Henry continued to stare into space. After a few moments, JoEllen prompted, "You couldn't believe . . ."

"No," said Henry. "Until that day, I thought I was important to my mother. I thought she needed me. But she locked me out of the house. I had a key but she deliberately bolted the door from the inside. She did it on purpose. I knocked as hard as I could but my mother wouldn't open the door for me."

"What do you think was going on, Henry?"

"*He* was there. My father." Henry's mouth continued to move but no sound could be heard except for a slight whimpering noise. If JoEllen was correct, there were tears forming in the corners of Henry's eyes.

"How did you feel about your father being there with your mother that night, Henry?" JoEllen asked after allowing several long moments of silence, during which tears rolled down the man's cheeks.

"Terrible," Henry replied, almost choking as he spoke. "Betrayed," he said slightly louder. "My mother wanted to be with him instead of me."

"What had your mother told you before, to make you feel so betrayed?"

Henry was silent for a few moments. Then he spoke softly again: "My mother had always said she loved me more than him. She'd said so as far back as I can remember. I believed her."

"But then, when she wouldn't let you in the door that night, you didn't know if you could believe your mother any more."

"For sure, I knew I *couldn't* believe her any more. Not after that. I had to stay outside all night and it was very cold. There was no place else for me to go. My mother wouldn't let me in, even though I practically pounded the door apart. In the morning, mother wouldn't even look at me. After that, I didn't trust *any* female again. At least not completely."

"Your mother's locking you out was so deep a shock you felt you couldn't trust any woman again."

"You're damned right!" Henry's voice reverberated throughout the office, blasting over the intercom into the observation room so that team members covered their ears. "My mother had told me for years that *I* was the man in her life, not my father. And I stuck by her. I took care of her!"

"What made you think your mother needed your care when you were a young boy, Henry?"

"She was so lonely, so awfully lonely. My father left her alone for as long as I can remember. My brother and I even think now that our stepsister is probably actually our half-sister, though we've never told anyone. She *looks* like us. And our father was carrying on with her mother years before our parents got divorced."

"So your mother depended on you to be there for her, Henry, because your father left her to have relationships with other women."

"You've got it," Henry said. A touch of pride crept into his voice. "My mother and I were *thick*. I was her favorite. I had an older brother, but I was my mother's favorite."

"It sounds like you loved your mother very much," said JoEllen.

"Well, like I said, I loved her when I was a young boy, but then I changed my mind. Dad was hardly ever home, and I was the one she depended on. But then she locked *me* out. I can never forgive my mother for that." Henry's voice took on a shrill, angry sound. As the man continued, his voice shifted into a low growl.

"I felt so bad then," he said, "that I swore I would never let any female hurt me like that again. Ever. And I haven't."

"So you can't let yourself get too close to Molly," JoEllen reflected Henry's sentiments.

"That's for sure. I won't let any woman get me by the balls, not even my wife." Henry's language was uncharacteristically crude.

"You are afraid that if you let yourself love any woman too much, she might let you down terribly, like your mother did."

"You've got it, JoEllen."

"And that includes Molly, your wife."

"Yeah, *especially* Molly," Henry declared. His voice loud and strong. But then he let out a long sigh, and when the man began to speak again, his voice was low, almost sorrowful. "I can let myself get just so close to my wife. Sometimes I can get very close, but then that's enough. That's all I can take. Something snaps and I have to get away from her."

"Is that the time you seek out a new affair, Henry? When you start to feel too close to Molly?"

"I suppose so," the man responded. "Then if Molly and I get into a tiff later, so what? There's some place else for me to go."

"How sad for both of you," replied JoEllen. Her facial expression mirrored her words. She took a deep breath and let it out slowly. Then the telephone rang.

"There you have it," said Kurt. "This man isn't having affairs for the logical reasons he thinks he is, but to mask his childhood pain. You'll have to confront him about that, JoEllen. Or better, have Molly do it, if possible. Have these two continue their enactment, only this time guide Henry toward communicating his feelings to Molly rather than trying to win his point logically. Once you've done that, come back here for the team's final consultation and message. Our time's running out for tonight."

"OK," said JoEllen, as she put down the receiver. "Molly," the trainee began, turning to the woman who had been sitting quietly for some time now. "What do you think about the things Henry has just said?"

"Henry has told me this story before, but I didn't realize it related so directly to his pursuit of affairs until tonight."

"Anything else?" responded JoEllen, inviting more.

"Henry doesn't have affairs because I can't fulfill all his needs, does he? He has them because he's afraid to get close to me—to anyone."

"That may well be," JoEllen replied. "But why not ask Henry?"

Molly turned to Henry. "Henry, which is it? Are you just afraid to get close, or is it that one woman can't meet all your needs, like you've always told me?"

Looking very sad, almost lost in time, Henry responded. "What's the difference? I trusted my mother, and she let me down. She didn't fulfill my needs and she wasn't trustworthy. A man has to take care of himself, that's for sure."

"How does that make you feel, Henry?" asked JoEllen softly.

"Sad," the man replied. "Depressed."

"And maybe a little scared?"

"Yes, to trust women," Henry responded.

"But what about me?" blurted Molly. "Don't you think you can trust me after all these years, Henry?"

"You just don't understand, Molly," her husband replied. "If you did, you'd realize it's nothing personal."

JoEllen intervened. "Henry, do you understand now that feelings are just as valid and important as logic when it comes to resolving problems between two people?"

"What?" The man replied.

"Remember the story you just told, Henry. You were badly hurt as a boy, so now you avoid close relationships to protect yourself from feeling so badly hurt again. That may help explain why you pursue affairs."

"Well . . . maybe partly . . . ," the man replied doubtfully.

"How about telling Molly something like this: 'When I begin to feel very close to you, Molly, I get scared.' "

Somewhat to JoEllen's surprise, Henry complied verbatim, his tone sincere.

Molly responded, with deep feeling, "It makes me so sad to hear you say that, Henry! Maybe our marriage really can't be put back together again. I need to feel close to you if I'm to be your wife."

"But most of the time we *are* close, Molly! Sometimes we're *too* close!"

"Yes, and then you go out and have another affair."

"Please understand me, Molly. I don't mean to hurt you when I have affairs. It's just that I *have* to have them. It's nothing personal. Please don't leave me. You're the only woman I want to spend the rest of my life with." Henry was almost pleading.

Molly sat silent.

After a few long moments, JoEllen spoke. "Remember, Henry, that earlier in this session I said your arguments in favor of affairs sounded very logical? That you seemed to win your arguments with Molly by your skillful use of logic?"

"Sure I do," Henry said, sitting up straighter in his chair.

"Do you see now that your desire for affairs is not really based on logic, but rather on childhood pain that has not yet been healed?"

Unexpectedly, Henry looked angry then. "Having affairs is perfectly logical in my situation!" he boomed out in a strong voice. "It's how I take care of myself. I had a very bad experience and I figured out a logical way to keep it from ever happening again. It's worked, too."

"Perhaps," JoEllen responded. "But I'm not sure your wife agrees. That, of course, is why we're all here tonight."

"Hmph," said Henry.

"I certainly *don't* agree," said Molly.

The telephone rang again.

"JoEllen," Kurt said this time, "we're near the end of the hour, so we need to wind things up for the evening. But the team wants you to ask Molly and Henry if they would be willing to ask Henry's mother to come to a session next week. Ask about Henry's father, too. It's time to consider an intergenerational approach with this case."

JoEllen had become so involved in her clients' intense discussion that such an idea hadn't occurred to her, yet it made sense. The trainee felt a certain excitement, and apprehension as well. The institute encouraged intergenerational counseling that included grandparents, but JoEllen had not done any yet. The trainee turned to her clients and told them of the team's suggestion.

"My father can't come," said Henry immediately. "He died several years ago. I don't know about my mother. I certainly wouldn't want to talk with her about what we were discussing here tonight, though."

"Henry," said JoEllen, "you sound worried. Tell me, what is the worst that could happen if your mother came to a session with you?"

Henry frowned. "I've never talked with Mother about what we discussed tonight, you know."

"What do you think might happen if we talked with her about it, Henry?"

"Well, she might get upset. My mother gets upset easily."

"Henry, what would be so terrible about your mother getting upset?"

"Well . . ."

Molly spoke up then. "Henry, it seems to me that if the relationship between you and me is affected so strongly by your memories of things that happened with your mother, we need to ask for her input. I think this office would be the best place to do it, too."

"I don't want to talk with my mother about anything like we talked about tonight, " said Henry, clamping his jaw tight.

"Henry, let's face it," Molly replied. "Our marriage is on the rocks. I'm not willing to put off a divorce much longer, the way things are going. I think the team is right. I think we need to ask your mother to come and talk with us. Wouldn't you rather do that here than trying to talk to her at home?"

"Well, that's for sure," Henry said. Then, in a resigned tone: "OK, I'll ask Mother. That doesn't mean she'll come."

"Good for you, Henry!" said JoEllen. "That takes guts. Now I need to leave you two for a few moments. It's time for me to go behind the mirror to talk with the team."

Then Molly spoke again quickly and loudly, surprising everyone. "What about George? Shouldn't George come too? I'm more than upset to learn that my son is having an affair. Poor Sally."

"Do you think George would be willing to give up his affair to come into counseling?" asked JoEllen.

"No way," said his father.

The telephone rang. "JoEllen," said Kurt, "one thing at a time. Let your clients know this might be a possibility in the future; but right now, to help *their* marriage, the person we need to talk with is Henry's mother."

"OK," said JoEllen. "What do you think about recommending that the kids seek counseling for themselves right away, though?"

"Of course," said Kurt.

JoEllen explained to Molly and Henry the gist of Kurt's message and then excused herself to go behind the mirror for the routine end-of-session consultation.

The message from the team to Molly and Henry Peterson that evening read as follows: "Henry and Molly, the team continues to admire your passion for each other. This passion has been strong enough to hold you together as a couple for all these years even though you have experienced a great deal of pain in your marriage.

"Henry, your task for this week is to appreciate the importance of logic in your life. We want you to observe the ways in which you use logic to protect your own feelings, and to downplay Molly's feelings. We don't want you to change anything—just observe and think about whether this is logical.

"Molly, your task for this week is to appreciate the importance of feelings in your life. We want you to observe the ways in which you use feelings to make meaningful decisions, at the same time that you tend to devalue your feelings because they are not based on logic. We don't want you to change anything—just observe and pay attention to how you feel."

The team believed that by telling Henry and Molly that they didn't need to change anything, only to observe, there was a better chance they would actually do their homework. And if they observed carefully, they would almost be unable *not* to change.

CHAPTER 23

❀

Intergenerational Family Therapy

The team behind the mirror gathered with unusual alacrity the next week. The opportunity to observe and work with interactions between parents and grandparents was not common at the institute, although the practice was certainly encouraged. The trainees were looking forward to an especially interesting evening. Each trainee was glad that he or she would not be on display in the training office and felt a certain admiration for JoEllen, who was to be the first of their group to undertake such an effort. The big question now was, Would Henry Peterson actually bring his mother to the institute this evening? Even JoEllen didn't know for sure yet. All she knew was that her appointment with the couple still stood; no one had cancelled it during the preceding week.

JoEllen nervously walked around the training office arranging the chairs one more time. She grinned and waved at her colleagues behind the mirror. She tugged and twisted at strands of her long dark hair in an exaggerated manner and pretended to bite at her fingernails to let them know how nervous she was feeling. And then the phone rang. It was Kelly, the receptionist.

"The Petersons are here, JoEllen."

"Oh good. How many of them?"

"Three adults. Mr. and Mrs. Peterson and an older lady."

"Thank you, Kelly! That's the right number!"

JoEllen grinned into the mirror, nodding once or twice to let the team know the grandmother was coming. Then she disappeared to collect her clients.

The trainee greeted Molly and Henry warmly in the waiting room, and then turned to meet the newcomer, a slender, petite woman with striking silver hair.

"JoEllen, this is my mother, Elsbeth Peterson," said Henry.

"I'm very glad to meet you, Mrs. Peterson," said the trainee. "Shall I call you Mrs. Peterson or Elsbeth?"

"Why, thank you for asking, JoEllen. Most people call me Elsbeth."

"Fine. Elsbeth, I want to thank you for coming tonight. Is this the first time you've been to the institute?"

"It certainly is," Elsbeth replied. "I would never have come to a place like this except for my son."

"Well, it's very nice of you to come. I think you'll be helpful to Henry and Molly. Let's go on up to the office. Follow me, please."

And JoEllen led the family once again up the long staircase past the lovely little atrium. The "small talk" this architectural innovation facilitated helped JoEllen begin to establish a relationship with Elsbeth Peterson before the little group even reached the training office. The graceful trees and colorful flowers within the atrium provided ample fodder for conversation.

Once in the training office, Elsbeth seated herself facing away from the big one-way mirror. Henry seated himself across from his mother, facing the mirror. Henry was one of the few people who seemed to remember the team behind the mirror, and he sometimes actually addressed his comments to them. Molly sat between Henry and Elsbeth, facing the office door. JoEllen noticed with satisfaction that the mother had not chosen a chair that would physically separate her son from his wife.

JoEllen then explained the special equipment to Elsbeth and received her written consent to be observed and videotaped.

"Oh dear," the woman said, "I'm not sure I like this at all, but Henry warned me. I suppose if it will help my son . . ." She sighed and signed the necessary forms.

"Now we're ready to start," JoEllen said when all the written work was taken care of. "Where do you want to begin this evening?"

Henry looked uncomfortable. "I thought you'd get us started, JoEllen," he said.

"Well," the trainee replied, feeling awkward. She had never conducted an intergenerational interview before, at least not with two different generations of adults. "Well . . . I guess it would be helpful for me to know . . . ah . . . what you told your mother, Henry, so that she was willing to come in with you tonight."

"I just told Mother that Molly and I were in counseling and that she might be able to help us save our marriage if she came."

"I see," said JoEllen. "Did you tell Elsbeth specifically how she might help?"

"Oh no," said Henry. "Besides, I'm not even sure she remembers that night."

"What night?" asked Elsbeth immediately.

JoEllen turned to Henry's mother. "Elsbeth, I want to thank you again for coming in this evening. Before we get into anything specific, though, I wonder if you would tell us how you would describe Henry and Molly's marriage."

"Oh," said the mother. "I've always thought it was a good marriage. Molly and I have always had a good relationship, too. Henry and Molly lived with me for a couple of years after they got married, you know, because they were trying to save money to build a house."

"That's right," said JoEllen. "I remember now that these two lived with you for a while after they got married. So you probably have a pretty good idea about what their relationship is like."

"Oh, I think they have a good relationship, all things considered. They've had a good marriage," said Elsbeth. "I know of course that Molly has left Henry and is filing for divorce now. I'm very sorry about that. I'd like it much better if Molly stayed with my son, and that's why I'm here tonight. If there's anything I can do to help . . ."

"There may be, Elsbeth," said JoEllen, "and that's why you've been asked to come here tonight. Some of the things we need to talk about may be difficult for you, though. Is that OK with you?"

"Well, I won't know that until I hear what you want to talk about, now will I?" The mother's tone was teasing and brought a sense of relief into the room.

JoEllen laughed. "I guess not," she said, smiling broadly. The trainee turned to Henry.

"Henry, what does your mother know about your relationships with other women?"

Henry grinned. "Well, Mother's aware that I have affairs, if that's what you mean."

"OK. That *is* what I mean. Have you told Elsbeth the reason Molly left you a few months ago?"

Elsbeth answered for her son. "Yes, I am aware that Henry has been having an affair with a woman named Marlene. I told him not to. I told him it wasn't fair to Molly. I can't blame Molly for leaving Henry, I just wish she wouldn't. There aren't many women who could put up with Henry's ways for so long."

JoEllen was surprised. It sounded as if this mother knew a great deal about her son's affairs.

"It sounds as if you are aware that Henry has hurt Molly in this way more than once," she said.

"I am," replied the mother. "I'm not surprised about my son's affairs, either." Elsbeth's voice took on a bitter tone. "Henry's father did before him. My son's just following his father's bad example."

"Did Henry's father have a series of affairs too?"

"Well, in his father's case, it was only one. But that one went on for years—from the time Henry was five or six until his older brother Jacob graduated from high school. Henry was about 15 when his father finally left for good."

"How did you manage to survive in such a situation, Elsbeth?"

"Well, financially, my former husband was always good to us. I never had to leave the children to go to work outside my home, even after the divorce. But I must have cried my eyes out for nearly ten years straight."

"Sounds very hard."

"It was. Sometimes I feel guilty because I know I leaned on my two sons, especially Henry. For some reason, I always felt closer to Henry than to Jacob. Maybe because he was the baby."

Now the conversation was leading in a direction that could work naturally toward the night of Henry's disillusionment. JoEllen, however, pursued this possibility only indirectly.

"Henry," she inquired, "Did you realize that your mother felt closer to you than to your older brother?"

"Of course I did," the man retorted. "I told you that last week, JoEllen." Henry, usually gallant, was clearly too nervous to protect anyone else tonight.

JoEllen turned back to the mother. "You said that you felt closer to Henry than to his older brother Jacob, Elsbeth. Can you tell me more about that?"

"Well, Jacob was always the responsible student, studying in his room with the door closed most of the time. I suppose he took after his father in that way. His father studied for years to be a priest, long before I met him, and he was quite the serious scholar."

"Do you mean that Jacob wasn't very available emotionally?"

"You could say that. Jacob was more aloof. Henry was a wonderful comic when he was a little boy. He was always laughing and joking around. I suppose that helped me keep my mind off my troubles."

"Did you know that, Henry?" asked JoEllen. "That your were a wonderful comic as a boy?"

"Me? A comic?" the man retorted. "I sure don't remember much about that."

"Now Henry," Molly interjected. "You have a great sense of humor. I love the jokes you tell during our good times, and during parties at home."

"A sense of humor is a real gift," JoEllen reflected, "and it's important to remember your talents and the good times you can have, especially in times that aren't so good."

"That's right," said Molly. "But JoEllen, can I ask Mother about what she thinks happened that night now?"

JoEllen was surprised at Molly's request, and she worried it might be too soon. She hesitated.

"What night?" asked Elsbeth for the second time.

JoEllen hesitated again. The telephone rang.

"JoEllen," said Kurt, "you've had at least two good chances to bring up the night when Henry was locked out, and you haven't done it. What's holding you back?"

JoEllen wasn't really sure what was stopping her. She thought for a moment. "I suppose I'm afraid it's too soon, and that we'll lose Henry," she said finally.

"You mean you're afraid Henry might walk out on you during a fight with his mother?" responded Kurt.

"Maybe," JoEllen said.

"And maybe you're afraid you'll get yelled at yourself during this fight, maybe overwhelmed by a big cruel stepmother?"

Kurt's last comment brought a grin to JoEllen's face. She *was* feeling smaller and more vulnerable with an older "mother figure" in the office. There was no doubt about it. She recognized that complication consciously now.

"So you're saying it's time to go ahead?" the trainee asked Kurt.

"The team thinks so, JoEllen. Clients aren't usually either as fragile or as overwhelming as we fear they are sometimes, and this incident may need a fair amount of time to work through. Remember, we're all here to assist if you need us." Kurt hung up the telephone.

JoEllen sat for a moment. She saw Elsbeth looking at her inquiringly. JoEllen gave the older woman an embarrassed grin. "That's the team behind the mirror," she said. "You remember I told you they call in suggestions sometimes."

Elsbeth gave JoEllen a motherly sort of smile in return. "You seem to be a little nervous tonight, my dear," she said soothingly. "Don't worry. I can talk with my son about just about anything."

"Thanks, Elsbeth," the trainee responded with a humble smile. She realized her client was taking care of her in this situation, not the other way around.

"Now," Elsbeth continued in a no-nonsense tone, "what is this night that Molly just asked about?"

"Well, we may as well talk about it now," JoEllen responded. "I was afraid it might be too soon, but I guess we should go ahead. Henry, will you describe that evening to your mother as best you remember it? The one in which you couldn't get into the house?"

Henry nodded and cleared his throat. His face became anxious, drawn.

"My goodness," Elsbeth said. "Obviously this is something difficult for you to talk about, son!"

"It is," Henry replied. "But I'm sure you'll remember that night too, Mother." And he began to tell the story as he remembered it. His voice took on a low monotone, he focused his eyes on the floor, and his face revealed little expression. Henry ended his narrative with "and I had no place else to go. I had to stay outside all night and it was very cold." He *didn't* say "How could you do this to me, Mother," but the question was clearly implied.

Elsbeth Peterson no longer looked quite so calm, soothing, or motherly by the time Henry had finished. She was angry, in fact.

"How *could* you remember that evening like that, Henry? How *could* you, son?"

"Because that's the way it was, Mother!" Henry said, with strong emotion.

"But that's not the way it was!" Elsbeth cried out. "Not at *all!*"

"Tell us how you remember that night, Elsbeth," suggested JoEllen.

Elsbeth shifted in her chair, breathed deeply, and looked hard at her son. Then she moved her eyes to JoEllen and spoke in a stern tone.

"Henry's got some of the story straight, I suppose," she said, "but it wasn't at all the way it sounds the way he tells it."

"Tell us how you remember the evening," JoEllen prompted once more.

"This incident happened at a time when my husband, Douglas, and I were separated. We separated several times during our marriage. As I said, Douglas began having an affair when the children were still young, and sometimes I got so mad at him I made him leave. The other woman's name was Harriet. He eventually married her."

"How difficult for you," murmured JoEllen.

"Yes, it was difficult for me—very difficult. I loved Douglas, and I kept hoping he'd forget Harriet and come back to me."

"What happened that night, as you remember it?" JoEllen probed again.

"Well, I suppose I do feel a little guilty toward Henry," Elsbeth said sadly, digressing herself now from the immediate topic at hand. "Henry was my mainstay whenever his father was gone. He tried his best to make up for Doug's absence. Henry would come home right after school every day to make sure I wasn't lonely."

"Sounds like a pretty responsible kid."

"He was. But of course, Henry wasn't my husband. I still hoped my husband would come back."

"Of course," JoEllen murmured.

"After Douglas had been gone a particularly long time one year, I suppose I began to give up on him. I began to call Henry things like 'my little man,' and 'my little hero.' He was about 13 then. Henry spent almost all of his free time at home, keeping me company. I was happy to have him around so much and told him so often."

Elsbeth looked over at Henry with a sorrowful expression on her face. Henry glanced up at his mother briefly, quickly looking back down again toward his knees. The large adam's apple in his throat moved up and down as if he were trying to speak, but he uttered no sound. The man was listening intently.

"Go on, Elsbeth," JoEllen prompted softly.

"That's about it," the mother said. "Then one day I got a call from Henry's father saying he wanted to come back. I was overjoyed. I wanted to be alone with Douglas that night so he and I could make up under the best possible circumstances. So I *told* Henry his father was coming home that evening."

"You told him."

Henry looked up, a startled expression on his face.

"Yes, I *told* Henry, JoEllen. Of course I told him. And his brother Jacob. I arranged to have both boys stay with my sister who lived down the block. I knew I needed all the privacy I could get."

"Did the boys agree to stay with your sister, as you remember things, Elsbeth?"

"Of course they agreed. Well, they had to agree, I suppose—I was their mother! My sister had the boys over for supper, too, if I remember correctly, so that I could be alone when their father arrived after work that day."

JoEllen looked over at Henry. "What do you think of all this, Henry?" she asked.

"I don't believe it!" Henry exclaimed in a loud voice. "I don't remember anything about going over to my aunt's house that night, Mother!"

"Maybe you don't remember, son," said Elsbeth, "but you did. And I remember exactly when you came home, because the timing was so terrible for your father and me. It was about 10:00 at night, and we had just gone to bed. Together. I was so hopeful we could put our marriage back on track."

"What happened when Henry came home?" asked JoEllen.

"Well, so much for romance, with all that banging and carrying on outside the door!" replied Elsbeth. Suddenly, she laughed. "That boy was insistent, let me tell you! But I didn't answer because I knew it was Henry and I wanted him to go back to my sister's house. As I said before, my sister lived right down the block. And Douglas and I needed to be together alone that night. I had to make a choice, and I did."

"So you let Henry continue to knock, without answering."

"Yes," his mother said. "I suppose it was wrong, but believe me, Henry had a place to stay that night, and it had all been arranged ahead of time. I was very angry at that kid for bothering his father and me, to tell you the truth."

"You didn't care about me!" Henry yelled. "You wanted my father instead of me!"

There it was, the classic Oedipal drama: the boy wants to do away with his father and marry his mother. JoEllen wondered if she should pursue this theme in a family counseling session. It would have been perfect for individual therapy with Henry—but now? Under these circumstances?

"Henry, we'll talk about that in a few moments," JoEllen said firmly, surprising herself with her own quick resolution. "First, I want to find out what happened between your mother and father that night. Elsbeth . . . ?"

"Well, despite all Henry's pounding and carrying on, Doug and I got back together," Elsbeth replied. "At least for a while."

"For how long?"

"For about a year. Then we split apart again. We got back together once more after that. Eventually, Douglas filed for divorce."

"So it sounds as if Henry had to give up his close relationship with you for some time after that evening, the one when he was locked out of the house."

"That's true," said the mother. "Come to think of it, I bawled the poor kid out the next morning for disturbing his father and me. Douglas was around for nearly a year after that, so I don't really think Henry and I ever talked about what happened again. To tell you the truth, I didn't realize Henry still remembered any of it. I don't suppose we were ever as close after that, though."

"You're damned right we weren't," sputtered Henry.

"Henry, I'm sorry," said his mother. "I didn't mean to hurt you. I really didn't."

Henry raised one hand, clenched it into a fist and then let it fall into his lap. "You just don't realize how these things feel, Mother," he said.

The telephone rang. "Did you notice Henry's use of the present tense right then, JoEllen?"

"Yes," the trainee replied.

"There's a lot of pain still active surrounding this incident. And did you pick up on the Oedipal themes?"

"I sure did," said JoEllen.

"They're related, of course. Take some time to talk with Henry about that."

JoEllen hung up the phone and turned to Henry.

"Henry, I just heard you tell your mother that she didn't realize how these things feel," the trainee said. "Do you mean how it feels to be passed over for your father?"

"Damned right," muttered Henry.

"Just how do these things feel for you, Henry?"

Henry glared at JoEllen and then at his mother. "Molly's the expert on feelings, not me!" he growled.

"You're not getting off the hook that easy, Henry Peterson!" JoEllen's tone was joking but she was serious at the same time. "Please tell us how you feel."

"Lousy, if you must know," Henry replied.

"Does it make a difference that your mother arranged for you to stay with her sister that night?"

"Am I supposed to believe that?" growled Henry.

"Henry! Of course I arranged for you to stay with my sister!" gasped Elsbeth. "You can ask Jacob if you want. He'll probably remember—he was older. What mother would put her two young sons out on the street?"

"Henry, I have a notion that you'd feel lousy whether you believed your mother or not," JoEllen said.

Henry looked up. "You're probably right," he conceded sheepishly. "I guess I was pretty jealous of the bastard."

"I think you've put your finger on it, Henry," JoEllen continued. "Do you know that most boys probably feel jealous toward their fathers, even if their parents don't have problems?"

"They do? Nahhh . . . most kids are lucky enough to have fathers that aren't bastards."

"Have you ever heard of the play, *Oedipus Rex,* Henry, by Sophocles?"

"Sure. Everybody reads it in high school. Isn't that the one about the guy who kills his father and marries his mother?"

"That's the one. Many teachers assign the play because it's considered a classic. And there's good reason why it's a classic."

"It's a pretty good play from what I remember—it had lots of suspense, anyway."

"The play is well written, but it's probably become a classic because it describes a psychological tendency that many people experience."

"What's that?"

"The tendency is known as the 'Oedipus complex,' since Sophocles used it as the theme of his famous play. The idea is that boys want to kill their fathers and marry their mothers. The desire is often unconscious, but not always."

"Hmph. Well, I can vouch for that."

"So do you see, Henry, that what you experienced that night was very painful, but perfectly normal? You wanted your father to get out of your life and give your mother over to you."

"Damned right I did."

"Now suppose you had succeeded."

"Huh?"

"Suppose you had succeeded. Suppose your mother had answered the door that night, told your father to leave for good, brought you inside the house, and told you she wanted you to be hers forever."

Henry looked confused for a moment. Then he chuckled. "Good lord," he exclaimed. "Wouldn't that have been a god-damned mess!"

"Yes, it certainly *would* have been a mess, Henry!" responded JoEllen. "What kind of life would you have led then?"

"Hm. I do know a few old bachelors who have lived with their mothers their whole lives."

"Would you have wanted that for yourself?"

"Hell no," Henry said with fervor. He sat quietly for a moment. Then he spoke again. "But at least Mother could have answered the door that night to tell me to go away!"

"Talk to your mother about that, Henry."

Before Henry could open his mouth, his mother spoke.

"Henry," said Elsbeth, "I'm so sorry I hurt you that night. I'm not sure what I should have done—I did get your father back for a while, and I think that was important for our family. But I didn't mean to hurt you personally so badly."

"But you just let me stand out there like a fool, banging on the door!"

"What else could I have done?" responded Elsbeth.

"Well, you could at least have come to the door and told me to go away."

"Perhaps that's what I should have done," said Elsbeth. "I'm sorry, Henry, I really am."

"Can you understand where your mother was coming from, Henry?" asked JoEllen.

Henry was silent, pensive.

"Henry has a very hard time understanding where other people are coming from, JoEllen!" Molly intruded in a loud voice that startled everyone.

"You're not being fair, Molly!" exclaimed Henry with considerable heat. "Of course I can understand where my mother was coming from. I was just a kid then. I'm not a kid any more."

"You do understand, then, Henry." This from JoEllen.

"Of course I can understand why a woman would want her husband back," Henry stated more firmly. "Good god, what woman would settle for a 13-year-old kid in place of a full-grown man?"

"Son, I didn't mean to hurt you," repeated the mother.

"I know, Mom," said Henry. He looked up and grinned wickedly. "I guess maybe I can forgive you—at least sometime!"

"What do you know!" said JoEllen. "I think we've gotten somewhere!"

The telephone rang.

"Even though it's a little early tonight, the team thinks this is a good place to stop. Come on back behind the mirror for the final message, JoEllen."

JoEllen told the family what the team had suggested. Henry nodded with obvious relief.

"Yes," he said, "we've certainly had enough for one evening!"

"Shall we reschedule for next week?"

Henry looked over at Molly, who nodded.

"We'll be here," the man said.

"What about me?" asked Elsbeth. "Should I come again too?"

Molly spoke. "Mother, you've helped us to understand a lot tonight. I think Henry and I have to go on from here by ourselves. What do you think, JoEllen?"

"Well—perhaps. Elsbeth has helped us clarify a great deal, though. Henry, what do you think?"

Henry appeared to consider for a moment or too. "I think Mom has told me what I needed to know tonight," he said, "so I guess I agree with Molly—it's our marriage we need to work on now. Just the two of us."

JoEllen nodded, and turned to the mother. "We'll let you off the hook for the immediate future, Elsbeth," the trainee joked. "But if you decide you want to return for any reason, the door's wide open."

"Thank you, JoEllen. This has been quite an evening! I'm sure I'll be thinking about this for a long time."

"Thank *you*, Elsbeth. You've been a real help."

And at that, JoEllen rose and went behind the mirror.

The message from the team that evening was as follows: "The team wants to give Elsbeth Peterson special thanks for coming in tonight. Elsbeth, we feel the information you provided tonight was extremely important and helpful for your son and his wife.

"Henry, we urge you to go very slow in taking in what your mother has told you this evening. It is important to give yourself plenty of time to think about it logically. It is not necessary to use what you learn about yourself to improve your relationship with Molly until you are ready.

"Molly, the team wonders how the information you have learned tonight will assist you. Will it help you to understand your husband better and if so, how will that make a difference in your relationship with Henry? What will have to happen for you to be able to trust your husband again?"

CHAPTER 24

Intergenerational Marital Therapy

On the following Monday morning, Molly telephoned the institute. She said she wanted to make an appointment for a counseling session that would include herself, her husband Henry, her son George, and her daughter-in-law Sally, but she needed to talk with JoEllen about it first. Kelly took the message and promised to give it to JoEllen as soon as possible.

Kelly called JoEllen at work but had to leave another message there, since JoEllen was attending a meeting. JoEllen returned Kelly's call in the early afternoon. When the trainee learned of Molly's request, she realized she needed to contact her client quickly. The Petersons were usually seen on Wednesday evenings, and Wednesday was only two days away.

The first question in JoEllen's mind was whether Molly wanted marriage counseling for George and Sally, and if so, whether George was still involved in his affair. If so, the trainee doubted that Kurt Knaak would allow the younger couple to be served at the clinic. After all, Kurt had been adamant about Henry and Molly putting their affairs aside before they could be seen together. Wouldn't he insist that George do likewise? Besides, Molly was convinced by now that marital therapy was difficult enough *without* the complication of an ongoing affair.

JoEllen reached Molly at work late that afternoon. She learned from Molly that George was indeed still involved in his extramarital affair. Molly said that was why she wanted to talk with JoEllen before bringing her son and his wife to the institute. She was more than aware of the requirement concerning affairs!

"What did you have in mind when you called, then, Molly?" JoEllen inquired.

"It's just that this is so important to me, JoEllen," Molly replied earnestly. "I'm afraid that George is going to ruin his marriage, and I think that Sally's the best thing that's happened to my son in a long time. Couldn't George come in as *my son,* not just as Sally's husband? I'm not at all happy with his behavior, and as his mother, I want to tell him that in no uncertain terms in a place where he has to listen."

"Bringing George to a session would be no problem at all, Molly, but you seem to want Sally to come along as well."

"I want to bring both of them if possible," said Molly. "First of all, I'm not even sure George would come by himself. But Sally's asked to come; she's begged, in fact. Sally's feeling just terrible about what's going on with George, and she knows that Henry and I have been seeing you for counseling. I want to help if I can—after all, Sally's my one and only daughter-in-law."

"Molly," JoEllen said candidly, "I'd like to help also, but I'm not sure if bringing Sally and George together to our session makes sense. Looking at things from one point of view, of course, they'd be coming in as members of your family. But looking at them from another, there's the problem of George's affair. Let me call my supervisor at the clinic and I'll get back to you."

JoEllen reached Kurt at the institute that evening, where he was about to begin supervision of another training group.

"Hm," the director said after listening to JoEllen's concern. "This is an unusual request. Let me think about it for a few minutes."

"I know you're probably not going to agree to a joint session like this, Kurt," JoEllen continued after a moment or two. "After all, George is having an affair. But the issues between George and his parents do involve intergenerational themes. Does that make a difference?"

"This one is a judgement call," said Kurt. "Of course, we wouldn't want to embark on marital counseling with the younger couple under circumstances like these. But this request could be seen more as a request from the mother for assistance in communication with her son . . ."

"I suppose so—but then would it be appropriate to include Sally?"

"The request has come from Molly, as a concerned mother *and* mother-in-law," Kurt replied thoughtfully. "We could, I think, work toward facilitating communication among all four people so the younger couple had a better understanding of what the older couple has been going through—and how it might affect them as well."

"Yes, I suppose we could," said JoEllen, "but you know, Kurt, I'm not even sure I want to. I mean, there's no way issues in George and Sally's marriage won't come up . . ."

"I see we've made a convert to marital work with couples who have put aside extramarital competition!" Kurt joked.

"That's true," JoEllen said with a touch of humor in her voice.

"Still," Kurt continued, "I see no problem in devoting a session to exploring intergenerational themes with these couples. That might help impress on George the seriousness of the choice he's making. We could then offer marital therapy to the younger couple on condition that George puts his affair aside. After listening to his parents' pain, George might be more willing to accept such a condition."

"I suppose . . . ," replied JoEllen without much enthusiasm.

"You don't sound exactly eager," said Kurt, picking up on JoEllen's tone of voice.

"I'm not. It just doesn't sound like George is ready for counseling . . ."

"That may not be the most important point here, JoEllen. The most important point may just be that Molly, your client, has asked to bring in her son and daughter-in-law for a counseling session. If we focus on intergenerational concerns, not specifically on marital counseling for George and Sally, I think we can give this the go-ahead. It would be an excellent educational experience for you, you know."

JoEllen groaned. "Kurt, how can you do this to me! Two generations of troubled marriages in the same office at the same time?"

"Remember, it's all for your own good, for your best educational experience!" Kurt let out a wicked chuckle.

"Thanks a lot!" JoEllen returned in a tone that was anything but thankful. "See you Wednesday, oh fearless leader."

When Wednesday evening arrived, JoEllen wondered if both Peterson couples actually would appear. Molly and Henry came right on time, but there was no sign of George and Sally. Kelly, the receptionist, notified JoEllen when the older couple appeared.

"Let's wait a few minutes," said the trainee. "It would be better to begin with everyone present, if possible."

JoEllen reviewed her notes of the previous session, in bits and snatches, waiting nervously. The team behind the mirror speculated about whether the younger couple would come. Even Kurt was doubtful. But then the telephone rang, and Kelly told Molly that all four Petersons were present at last. Molly waved to the team through the mirror with a nod to let them know all clients had arrived and set off down the stairs.

As usual, the trainee made every effort to make her new clients, George and Sally, feel comfortable as she greeted them in the waiting room and led them to the training office. Both young people were cordial. George looked cheerful, Sally strained.

After the formalities of explaining and signing the necessary forms for use of the special equipment in the training office, JoEllen began the work of the session by addressing the younger pair. She knew she needed to develop a constructive relationship with George and Sally if the session were to be productive.

"George and Sally," the trainee began, "I want to thank you for coming in tonight. I know it takes a lot of courage to come to a counseling session. Have either of you been in counseling before?"

"Sure, I have," George said easily. "That's the reason I agreed to come tonight. Counseling was a good experience for me in high school. I met with our school psychologist, Mr. Meyers, for nearly a year. That's probably the only reason I graduated!"

"I haven't been in counseling before," said Sally, "but I was the one who asked Molly if we could come with her and Henry tonight because . . . ." The young woman stopped, looking tearful already.

JoEllen waited, and then with an encouraging smile prompted the young woman. "You wanted to come here tonight because—"

Sally tried again. "Because . . . because George . . . ," and then the young woman began to cry in earnest. Her face looked desolate, her shoulders slumped as she tried to hide her tears behind both hands.

JoEllen waited for a few moments to give Sally time and then placed a box of Kleenex by her chair. She noticed that George made no move to reach out and comfort his wife. When Sally took a Kleenex, wiped her eyes and seemed ready to talk again, JoEllen gently asked her to go on.

"Well," the young wife responded, "I think when I met George, I may have made a mistake."

"A mistake?" That was a pretty strong comment for so early in the session.

"Yes. I fell in love with George, but a lot of it was really his family. Molly and Henry felt so warm and friendly to me. Molly made me feel very welcome in her home, and Henry did too. Sometimes a lot of people gathered at their house, and Molly fed everybody supper, including me." Sally stopped.

"And?" prompted JoEllen.

"Becoming George's wife was a way for me to become part of the Peterson family."

"And now you think that was a mistake?"

"I still love the family, but it's falling apart. Molly's put the divorce on hold for a while, but sometimes she doesn't sound very hopeful."

"Yes, I know that."

"And I realize now that George wasn't ready for marriage."

"George wasn't ready?"

"George told me before we were married that his father had affairs with other women and that he might want to have them too," Sally replied sadly. "But I didn't believe him. I knew George felt very sorry for his mother and angry at his father. So I never thought he'd really do the same thing to me after we were married . . . ." The young woman stopped, tears filling her eyes again.

JoEllen pondered for a moment. The session was not supposed to be focused on marital counseling for Sally and George, she knew well. But Sally clearly was in pain and needed attention. And pain certainly was an intergenerational issue, so she decided to pursue it.

"Sally," JoEllen pursued gently, "tell me about your tears."

The young wife spoke softly then. Her words were simple. "George is having an affair. A friend told me. I've asked him and its true. He's told me he won't give it up, either."

"I see," said JoEllen. "And this is very difficult for you, Sally?"

"Difficult? Of course it's difficult! I think it's the worst thing that's ever happened to me!" Sally cried out in a strong tone, obviously surprised that JoEllen had even asked the question. The young woman began to sob again, and this time the sound was angry.

"Go ahead, Sally, cry if you need to. That's OK here. I want to talk with George for a few minutes now, though. Is that OK with you?"

Sally grabbed a Kleenex and blew her nose loudly. She nodded, looking intently over at her husband, her eyes red and wet.

"George," said JoEllen. "How do you feel as you watch your wife in pain like this?"

"Well, I don't like it, of course. I don't mean to hurt her." George's voice tone was bland, his facial expression appeasing.

"Is it true that you are having an affair?"

"Sure it is. But it isn't a problem like Sally thinks it is. I'm not planning to leave her or anything."

"Can you tell me what led to your affair, George?"

"Nothing particularly 'led' to this affair," the young man responded, annoyance in his voice. "It's just that I met this very nice other woman, and she was interested."

"What about Sally?"

"This shouldn't be a problem for Sally. Like I said, I'm not about to leave her."

"Most wives I know expect their husbands to be faithful sexually."

"Well, isn't faithfulness to the relationship itself more important?"

"Faithfulness to the relationship itself?"

"Yes. By that I mean I won't leave Sally. Sally's a good person. She's my best friend. But as you can see, she isn't . . . er . . . aah . . . exciting anymore to me the way she used to be. Let's face it—I get bored with her sometimes. This other woman has pizazz. Without the other woman bringing some excitement into my life, I might get so bored I'd have to leave Sally."

"You get bored with Sally sometimes, George. Tell me, how long have you and your wife known each other?"

"About three years. We've been married for two."

"Does the marriage feel a bit 'old hat' for you then?"

"Yes, that's it," the young man said.

"You said before, though, that you aren't planning to leave Sally. Do you mean that?"

"Of course I mean it. As I said, Sally's my best friend. I like her a lot."

"Are you telling me, George, then, that you want to be married to Sally and have an affair at the same time?"

"That's right," said George. "And there wouldn't be any problem if that stupid buddy of hers hadn't ratted on me."

"But Sally knows about the affair now, and she's obviously very hurt. Do you intend to keep on with it, as Sally said earlier?"

"Of course I do. Dad does this kind of thing all the time. Dad agrees that otherwise you'd get so bored you'd have to leave your marriage. Mom manages fine, or at least she did the whole time I was a kid."

"I'm not sure about that, George. Do you really believe your mother managed fine when your father had affairs when you were a child?"

"Sure she did."

JoEllen turned to Molly, who was staring openly at her son. "Molly," she began, "What are you feeling right now?"

"Sally may be feeling hurt," Molly exclaimed, "but I'm angry. Very angry. I want George to know that." Molly didn't take her eyes off the young man.

"Talk with George directly, Molly."

The mother required little encouragement. She jumped right in vehemently. "Son, how can you say I managed fine when you were a child? And how can you do this to your own wife? You *know* how badly I've been hurt by your father all these years!"

"Come on, Mom! It hasn't been all hurt!" George defended himself. "You've said yourself that our family has had more fun than any other family you know!"

"Sure we've had fun, George, but you *know* that's not the whole story. A good part of the time your father has left me alone in this marriage. Wondering what he was doing and with whom. Sometimes wishing I didn't know."

"Yes, Mom, but Dad's always come home, hasn't he? Dad doesn't want to leave you. That's exactly the way it is with me and Sally. I don't want to leave her, either."

"But son! What about the *hurt?* That's why I wanted you to come in here tonight. To understand how serious your behavior is. Don't you understand what I've gone through for so many years, your own mother? Don't you want to give a better life to your own wife? LISTEN to me, boy!"

"Wait a minute, Molly!" It was Henry. "Lay off the poor kid! George is right! It's perfectly possible to have a good marriage and an affair at the same time. You and I did it for years."

"*You* may have had a good marriage and an affair at the same time, Henry, but I had neither. And I'm not going to put up with it any more!" Molly's voice was hard.

"Yeah, sure, Mom," George jumped in. "If I'm not mistaken, you're having an affair too. Or wouldn't you admit that's what's going on with Herbert?"

"WHAT!" yelled Molly incredulously. "Who do you think you are, George? That's an entirely different situation! You know it is!"

"Oh yeah?" The son replied coolly with a little sneer twisting his features.

"I can't believe what you are saying," Molly declared, her face serious and her voice tone shocked and angry.

"Neither can I!" said Sally, her face and voice matching her mother-in-law's. "George, you know we fixed Molly up with Herbert because she was all alone. She had *left* your father. She had left because Henry was carrying on with someone else and he wouldn't quit. You KNOW that."

The telephone rang.

"Good work, JoEllen," said Kurt. "You've brought the intergenerational issue of affairs right out into the open. Now you need to help these folks see the parallels in their communication styles."

"OK, Kurt," she said. "Anything else?"

"These intergenerational issues may seem obvious, but I'm not sure both couples see them, especially the men. Take your time."

As JoEllen hung up, all eyes were on her.

"The team wants us to focus on intergenerational patterns," the trainee explained. "For example, George, I just noticed that you took a blaming stance with your mother. Have you noticed that your father often takes a blaming stance too?"

"I'm not blaming Mother for anything! I'm just pointing out that she can't be so high and mighty about my affair when she's having one too!"

Molly broke in. "George," she said, "when you say that, I feel very angry. I've suffered through your father's affairs for years, and this is my first. And I didn't begin it until after I left him."

"Big deal," George said. "My father didn't ask you to leave, Mom. And he wants you to come home! You're his wife! You need to be more understanding."

"Understanding of what?" fumed Molly.

"That no one woman can give a man all he needs. You can't, Sally can't. It's perfectly logical that Dad and I would find other women to meet some of our needs. It doesn't mean we don't want you as wives."

"That's right," said Henry. "You women just need to be more understanding."

At this point JoEllen entered the exchange. "I've noticed that you, Henry, and you, George, both seem to assume you have a right to fill all your needs even if it hurts your wives. What about your responsibility to meet *their* needs, such as for affection and security?"

"Meet *their* needs?" Henry looked blank for a moment. Then he brightened. "But if *I'm* happy, I bring that happiness into my marriage, so my wife is better off too."

"Are you sure about that? What about Molly's hurt? What about her anger? Do you think you have a right to overlook Molly's needs for loyalty and security, Henry?"

"Oh, I know Molly gets hurt, but that's not my problem," responded Henry. "It's her problem. She just shouldn't be so insecure, so jealous. I love her and I always will."

The telephone rang.

"Henry views Molly as insecure," said Kurt. "We may need to reframe this perception to help him confront his blaming stance. Instead, the team observes that Molly has a good deal of strength. Ask her where she got the strength to hang in with Henry all these years, despite his affairs." Kurt hung up without even waiting for JoEllen's response.

JoEllen hadn't been expecting these instructions and so she had to stop and think for a moment. Then she realized many women could never have stayed in a marriage like this one for long. Where *had* Molly learned to be so strong?

The trainee turned to Molly. "The team notices," she began, "that Henry views you as insecure. But instead, the team believes it has taken great strength for you to remain in this marriage for so long, given your husband's affairs. Where do you think your strength came from?"

Molly suddenly began to cry in deep, wrenching sobs.

"Molly, what's happening for you?" JoEllen asked after a few moments.

"Nobody's ever recognized how strong I've had to be before," Molly sobbed into her Kleenex. "But the team's right, JoEllen. I've been very strong."

"How did you learn to be so strong, Molly?" the trainee probed gently.

"Remember a few sessions back, when we were talking about my father?"

"Of course."

"I didn't think there was any connection at the time but now I'm wondering . . ."

"Wondering?"

"Yes, I wonder if living with a physically abusive father didn't teach me the skills to live with Henry. You learn not to talk about what hurts; you learn not to make them angry or you might get hurt worse."

"That is certainly a possibility. And any survival skills we learn give us satisfaction of some kind, Molly. Henry probably has helped you hone survival skills that are very important to you, given your background."

"You mean I may have stayed with Henry because I like to practice my survival skills?"

"That's possible, Molly. Both you and Henry have influenced the kind of marriage you have put together."

"But I don't want to spend my life surviving! There's got to be more to life than that!"

"Of course there is, Molly," responded the trainee. "But you have to recognize you have a choice before you can make a change."

"I'm ready for a change, then, JoEllen! What good is it to keep on being strong if your husband thinks it's OK to keep right on hurting you?"

"That's a fair question!" responded the trainee. "I think it's one you need to ask Henry, though."

Henry responded immediately without being asked. "I think this is nuts," he said. "I don't want to hurt anybody. I'm just doing what a man needs to do to live his own life." His words were strong, but his voice sounded lame.

After a short pause, Molly said, "You know, JoEllen, I'm beginning to feel less hurt and a lot more angry."

"More angry?" reflected the trainee.

"Yes! I think Henry thinks only about what *he* wants and needs and blames me if I don't give it, and now George—why, he sounds exactly like his father! After all I did for that boy, helping him cope with his dad's rejection when he was little . . ."

"Molly, sometimes a son who has been rejected has such a strong unmet need for his father's approval he'll do just about anything to get it, even as an adult."

Molly sighed. "I suppose so," she said.

Henry spoke up angrily. "I did not reject my son. All kids are a pain when they're growing up, especially boys. They need a lot of discipline. Now that George is an adult, he's starting to have more sense."

"What do you think about all this, George?" asked JoEllen turning to the son. The trainee deliberately framed her question ambiguously. Would George talk about his relationship with his father? With his mother? Would he discuss his affair? The young man had been following the dialogue in the therapy room closely.

"I do not need my father's approval," George responded immediately, sharply. "And I'm not trying to upset Mother by agreeing with Dad's affairs. It's just that nobody can make me give up Nancy. Nobody."

George had chosen to focus on his affair.

"Who is Nancy?" JoEllen asked the obvious.

"She's the other woman in my life," said George.

"His other great love," George's wife, Sally, broke in bitterly. "She's a good-looking lady and she has a fancy job. How am I supposed to compete?"

On a flash of intuition, the trainee turned to the father. "What do you think, Henry? How is Sally supposed to compete with Nancy?"

"Huh?" the man responded.

"You're an important role model for George and Sally, Henry. How do you advise Sally to compete with this other woman, Nancy?"

"Why, Sally doesn't need to compete. All she needs to do is remember she is OK herself. She shouldn't be so insecure."

"Do you remember our session last week, Henry?" replied the trainee. "The session with your mother, when we talked about your father's affair? Do you think all your mother needed to do back then was to feel less insecure?"

Henry stared at JoEllen for a few moments. Then he looked down and examined his large hands silently for some time. "Well," he said finally in a low voice, "in my mother's case it was different. My Dad ended up actually leaving my poor mother."

"So maybe not feeling insecure isn't the answer? A woman really *does* have something to worry about?"

Henry continued to look down at his hands for a few moments. Then he took a deep breath. He sat up straight and looked directly and compellingly at JoEllen, the expression in his clear blue eyes intense and dignified.

"I do things differently from my father, " Henry declared in a proud voice. "I am never going to leave Molly. I have told her that many times."

"That's admirable, in a way, I suppose," responded JoEllen dryly. "But is that good enough for your wife, Henry?"

"I don't see why not!"

"George doesn't intend to leave Sally, either," the trainee continued.

"That's right. George is my son."

"Do you believe that all Sally needs is reassurance that George won't leave her, Henry? Look at your daughter-in-law." The young woman sat sobbing deeply, trying to muffle the sounds behind her hands.

Henry's facial expression sobered slightly. "Well," he shrugged, "I suppose an affair is hard on a young girl at first. Sally hasn't had much experience with this sort of thing. But she could learn from Molly."

JoEllen shook her head in disbelief. Nothing seemed to alter Henry's point of view.

Molly spoke then. "Henry, if you think I'm willing to teach Sally how to tolerate an unfaithful husband, you're sadly mistaken. I used to be willing to do anything to make you happy, because I was afraid of losing you. But that's no longer true. I can make it on my own."

"And you have recently filed for divorce," JoEllen reminded everyone.

"That's right," said Molly.

"Well," Henry countered smoothly, "I've given up my own affair for now, right? Molly should have her way some of the time, I suppose."

"Well, that's a relief, Henry!" Molly retorted in a sharp voice that belied her words.

The telephone rang.

"This would be a good time to talk with George and Sally about marriage counseling. Explain the conditions, JoEllen," said Kurt.

"OK," the trainee replied. She turned to Sally.

"Sally," JoEllen began, "I know you requested to come in with Molly tonight because you were upset about George's affair. Are you interested in marriage counseling with your husband?"

"Oh yes, that's why I came!"

"Have you talked about this with George yet?"

The girl made a face and sighed. "No," she said. "Molly told me about the requirement regarding affairs, and I was afraid George wouldn't agree. I was hoping that coming tonight might encourage him to give it some thought."

"How about asking George now."

"Me?"

"Yes, Sally. You are the best person to ask your husband."

"Well . . . oh dear. Uh . . . OK, maybe you're right. George, would you be willing to go into marriage counseling? Maybe here at the institute with JoEllen?"

"I'm willing to go into counseling, if you want, Sally. But what about this requirement about affairs?"

Sally looked over at JoEllen. "Would you explain it to us, please?" the young wife asked.

"Of course," responded the trainee. "Sally, George—the purpose of this clinic is to provide marriage and family counseling, and our therapists want to do the very best job they can. That means we make one important requirement before we will accept a couple. Any extramarital affairs must be put aside, at least for the duration of counseling—both the sexual part and the relationship itself. We have learned that affairs get in the way of the hard work married people have to do to improve their own relationship."

"Do you mean that if I were to agree to marriage counseling with Sally, I'd have to give up my relationship with Nancy?" asked George.

"Yes," said JoEllen. "At least for the duration. It's very important to help assure the success of the counseling."

"No," said the young man.

"What do you mean, 'no'?" blurted Sally.

"I mean no, I won't give up my affair with Nancy."

A hush settled over the room.

"Now George," Henry spoke up, surprising everybody. "It wouldn't be forever. Even I've agreed to do that for your mother, at least for the counseling time, that is. You have to give Sally a chance, you know. A wife like Sally doesn't come along every day."

"Dad," said George, "you've had lots of affairs! I should be able to have at least one!"

"Things may be changing nowadays," Henry said somewhat vaguely, again surprising everyone.

"George, please," said Sally softly. "I want our marriage to work."

"I do too," said George, "but I won't give up my relationship with Nancy. That's all there is to it." His features were set and his eyes refused to meet Sally's.

"George, you have to choose," said his wife softly.

"What do you mean I have to choose, Sally?" responded George. "I don't *have* to do anything."

"George, please, do it for me," said his wife. "I've seen your mother suffer. I'm not willing to struggle for 22 years as she has. Maybe I'm not as strong as Molly. Please tell me you will give up this other woman and go into counseling with me."

"Sally—ask me for anything else! Anything! You know I *can't* give up this affair. Nancy means too much to me."

"But why, George? Don't you love me?"

"Of course I love you," but the voice tone was not convincing. George avoided Sally's eyes again.

"George," Sally said softly again, "do you love Nancy?"

"Yes," the young man replied simply.

Tears filled Sally's eyes. "You have to choose, George. It's me or her."

A hush filled the room. George looked at his father, his mother, JoEllen, his wife, the floor.

"If I have to choose," he said then, very quietly, "I choose Nancy."

Sally's tears flowed copiously then. But her words were clear enough. "This is it, then, George. I'm leaving you. Now. Tonight."

George squirmed, looking at the floor again, but he nodded. "OK Sally," he said. "That's your right, I suppose."

Sally turned to Molly. "Can I stay at your apartment with you for a few days, Molly, while I look for a new place?" The young woman struggled to bring her tears under control.

"Of course you can," said the mother. "Sally, I'm so sorry." The older woman looked like she was about to cry as well.

JoEllen spoke up then. "You're being very kind, Molly, but I wonder if it might not be better for Sally to stay somewhere else. As much as you want to help your daughter-in-law now, all of you are under a lot of stress. Sally, do you have parents or friends who live in this area?"

Sally thought for a moment. "Maybe you're right, JoEllen," she said. "I have some friends, a married couple, who live right across town. They have an extra bedroom. They'd probably let me stay with them for a couple of weeks until I can find a place of my own."

"I think that would work out better for you," said JoEllen. "I think you'd be happier in an environment with as few complications as possible right now."

Sally nodded.

JoEllen continued. "I want both you and George to know that either of you are welcome to come for counseling here as individuals. Would you like to make an appointment for next week?"

"Not right now, JoEllen. I'm too exhausted," said Sally. "Maybe later."

"That's not an uncommon response at a time like this. Sometimes in the middle of a major change, we don't have the energy to engage in serious counseling. But remember, the door's open."

"Thank you, JoEllen. I'll remember," said Sally.

"George, how about you? Do you want to return next week?" asked the trainee.

"Hell, no. If you don't mind my saying so, JoEllen, you've messed up my life quite enough already."

"George, I apologize for the difficult session tonight. But I want you to remember that individual counseling is always available for you, whether you're having an affair or not."

"Thanks," said George in a voice that implied the opposite.

JoEllen felt the sarcasm in George's tone, and took a deep breath to calm herself. She felt sad, but knew she had done the best she could under the circumstances. The trainee turned to the older couple.

"How about you two, Molly and Henry? Do you want to return next week?"

"I'm not sure," said Molly. "It seems to me from everything that's been said here tonight that it's time for me to get on with the divorce."

Henry looked troubled. "Wait, Molly," the man said. "I think we need at least one more session together."

"Will you stay away from Marlene, Henry?"

"I haven't even *talked* to Marlene for over a month! Will you stay away from Herbert?"

"I will for one more week, Henry. That's all I promise."

"Fair enough," said Henry.

"Well, it's about time for me to go behind the mirror to consult with the team," said JoEllen. "I'll be back in a few minutes."

As the team observed the Peterson family through the one-way mirror, they saw George staring fixedly at the floor while Sally sobbed quietly. George made no attempt to reach out to his wife. Henry, however, gazed at the young woman with obvious concern. Molly reached out and touched Sally's arm. Sally looked up and tried to smile through her tears.

The message from the team read as follows: "Sally and George, we congratulate you for having the courage to come together tonight to work on your relationship with each other and with Molly and Henry. We share your pain as you enter a time of separation. Remember, we will be glad to work with you individually at any time, or with the two of you as a couple when there are no active affairs to interfere.

"Henry and Molly, we have discussed many circumstances in your families of origin that may have caused you pain in the past and that may still bring you pain in the present. This week, however, we urge you to look for conditions in your families of origin that have helped you in some way, or of which you are proud, or for which you are especially grateful."

CHAPTER 25

More Consultation for JoEllen

JoEllen Madsen found herself struggling with a problem of her own. In the months between her final session with the Petersons as a family and the commencement of individual work with Molly, she had developed a significant personal relationship with an attractive middle-aged gentleman, recently divorced. This man flattered JoEllen with his enthusiastic, undivided attention for several delightful weeks. Then, beginning at about the time JoEllen started conjoint sessions with Molly and Henry, he began to withdraw. He cancelled dates at the last minute. He made tentative dates, cautioning JoEllen that he might have to cancel at the last minute. He alluded to outings with other women and talked about not being ready to settle down.

JoEllen was hurt; there were no two ways about it. She had been hesitant about becoming emotionally involved with this man in the first place, because of the timing. She knew that recently divorced people are often in emotional turmoil, too upset to make important new decisions. But affection and hope overturned caution. Now JoEllen was paying the price.

As the trainee joined her discussion group the Monday after her most recent session with the Petersons, she couldn't help comparing herself with George's wife, Sally. JoEllen recognized that in a very similar situation years earlier in her life with Chip, she had opted to stay in her marriage a good deal longer, only to have it fail anyway. Given this personal experience, along with her theoretical training at the institute, JoEllen believed that Sally was making the right decision in leaving sooner rather than later. A spouse absorbed in an affair makes a halfhearted partner at best.

But still there was the terrible problem of dealing with the loss of one's most cherished relationship, one's marital partner—or one's significant other, for that matter. JoEllen couldn't ignore the similarities between her own situation and Sally's in the present moment. After all, JoEllen's own boyfriend was sending unmistakable danger signals. Should she, like Sally, choose to end her relationship? What about the loneliness, the emptiness that would surely follow? Why was life so difficult, anyhow?

In a somewhat grim mood, JoEllen asked Madeleine Sweet for half an hour of consultation with her discussion group.

"The Peterson case?" Madeleine asked.

"The Peterson case."

When JoEllen's turn came, she described Molly's telephone request for an intergenerational session and Kurt's reasons for accepting that request. Then she fast-forwarded the videotape of the session to show George's initial defense of his extramarital affair. The group watched as George explained how his father was able to have multiple affairs and his mother at least one, so he felt he had the right. Then JoEllen stopped the machine.

"Well, now, there's certainly a major intergenerational theme!" Rose remarked.

"JoEllen, didn't you mention at our group meeting last week that Henry's father also had an affair?" asked Harry, the clergyman.

"Yes, he did, Harry. In fact, Henry's father actually left his mother and married the other woman."

"Wasn't Henry rather bitter about that?"

"Yes, he was," said JoEllen. "However, Henry seems to believe he has avoided the mistakes of his father by remaining within his marriage, thereby not deserting his mother, from his own point of view."

"Interesting," said Harry thoughtfully. "How does Henry justify the hurt he is causing?"

"Henry blames it on Molly. He says she just shouldn't be so insecure. He says he has assured Molly he won't leave her, and he seems to feel that that should take care of the matter."

"What about the other women, JoEllen? How does he justify hurting them?" continued Harry.

"Well, I think Henry feels the other women don't have a right to get hurt. He says he warns them from the very beginning that he isn't going to leave his wife."

"How about Henry's mother, then?" Harry persisted. "Does Henry think insecurity was the major problem in his mother's case as well?"

"No. Henry sees his mother's situation in a different light because his father left her to marry someone else. Henry believes his father was wrong to leave his mother. He doesn't criticize the affair itself."

"I see."

Gretchen spoke up. "It amazes me how sexist Henry's analysis is. It's OK to run around on your wife, no matter that she's miserable about it; and its OK to disappoint one female lover after another too. Just so you get high and stay high on your hormones."

Madeleine entered the discussion for the first time. "Gretchen," she said, "a therapist with an addictions perspective might believe that Henry has a sexual addiction—he certainly seems to want to get high! But given the length of time between his affairs, I think his actions are basically voluntary. However," Madeleine continued, "you are also introducing a feminist analytical perspective here, whether you know it or not. Some feminists have criticized systems-based family therapy, particularly the structural school, because the model aimed at remedying family disruption by creating an executive subsystem to make decisions. The executive subsystem was to be the marital pair, if such a pair existed."

"What's wrong with that?" Harry interjected.

"For early family therapists," Madeleine continued, "this meant working to create a well-bonded marital pair who could function effectively as head of the family. With parents firmly established at the top of the family hierarchy, children could be relieved of inappropriate triangulation and enmeshment."

"That sounds pretty good to me," Harry remarked again. "So what's the problem?"

"Early family therapists often achieved their goals," Madeleine continued, "and helped create effective executive subsystems to head the family. But as feminists later perceived, all too often these therapists unquestioningly supported male dominance within the executive subsystem, to the great disadvantage of the female."

"Here we go again," groaned Harry. "*Someone* has to head the family. Why *not* the male? I don't mean to sound patriarchal or sexist, but there has to be a way of determining who gets his way when there's a disagreement between spouses."

"Harry!" gasped Rose. "What are you saying?"

"Well," Harry muttered and then reiterated, "somebody has to make the major decisions."

Bob, the nurse, spoke then. "Power corrupts," he said. "That's another widely believed maxim that I think has a lot of truth to it. I think males today develop a sense of special entitlement from messages provided by the wider culture. That sense of entitlement can lead to situations like we're discussing in the Peterson family. George, for example, has seen affairs come and go that benefit his father at the expense of his mother. So he believes he's entitled to the same privilege."

"Exactly," said Madeleine. "In this culture males do have considerably more power than females. And feminists have pointed out that while systems theory may be correct—changes in parts of wholes do seem to affect all other parts—still, some parts seem to have more effect, or more power, than others. That seems especially true for human systems."

"What do you think about that, Harry?" asked Rose.

"Well . . . I suppose men do have more power in this society, but perhaps they should," growled Harry.

"But Harry, I believe unequal power can lead to abuse!" exclaimed Rose. "What do you think, Madeleine?"

"Family therapists supported the difference in power between men and women for years without even recognizing they were doing it," Madeleine responded thoughtfully, not quite answering the question.

Now Gretchen asked the question: "Yes, but do you think the difference in power contributes to abuse of women, Madeleine?"

"In many cases, there is evidence that it does," the supervisor said thoughtfully. "Physical abuse, for example, while occasionally perpetrated by the female, is overwhelmingly committed by the male. So now systems therapists are at least paying attention to the power differential. Families need cohesive marital and parental subsystems to model affection, nurturance, and decision making for children, but those subsystems don't need to put the man above the woman."

"You know, though," mused Rose, taking the role of devil's advocate, "Harry's right in a way. *Somebody* has to make decisions in a family. What if a husband and wife disagree? If the male isn't given power automatically, won't that lead to a lot more fighting?"

"Herein lies the mystery and grace of human relationships!" laughed Madeleine. "I said we had identified a problem of power imbalance between the sexes. I didn't say we had the answers as to what to do about it yet! But perhaps, with awareness, spouses can learn to develop creative means of decision making that don't require coercion of the woman."

"Women sure are willing to give up a lot of their potential power to keep their mates," sighed JoEllen. "Here's Molly Peterson, a college-educated woman able to support herself financially. Yet she has spent most of her adult life trying to preserve her marriage to a husband who lets her earn most of the family income, take on the bulk of responsibility for child-rearing, do most of the household chores, and play hostess to his current infatuations."

"That partly reflects the strength of the societal value for marriage," said Madeleine. "I know it well, as I haven't been able to find a partner myself. So I personally know the social slights a single woman can experience."

There was silence in the room for a few moments. Everyone thought about his or her own personal situation.

Then JoEllen burst out: "But it's not just that, Madeleine—marriage isn't just a matter of achieving social status! For a lot of women, especially, it's a matter of financial survival. Even more important, marriage provides companionship, a sense of purpose, and a shared life. Children, perhaps."

"Of course, JoEllen," Madeleine responded. "Marriage is all of those things too."

"And then there's the matter of affection and love," the trainee continued in an impassioned tone. "I believe Molly Peterson has loved Henry throughout most of their years together, despite her anger at him. Molly's enjoyed living with this man for the most part. She's said so herself, and I believe her."

"That's hopeful information," Madeleine replied. "When a therapist identifies major strengths in a relationship, often a failing marriage can be rebuilt. That's what the work of a therapist is about in many ways—identifying strengths that can help a family overcome its problems."

"That's true!" the trainee responded with enthusiasm. Then, suddenly, her facial expression changed. "But . . . ," she continued, letting her voice drift.

"But what?" Madeleine prompted.

"Madeleine," JoEllen blurted then, "how do you decide when you are staying in an unsatisfactory relationship too long, only hoping to get those things you want, someday, sometime?" Her fervent question caught everyone's attention immediately.

"Just what are you asking, JoEllen?" Madeleine inquired. "Tell us more."

"It seems that I keep dealing with issues like the Petersons' right in my own life," the trainee responded. "To make a long story short, I'm having trouble with my boyfriend. I'm wondering if I should leave him, like Sally's leaving George."

"How have your personal difficulties with relationships been affecting your work with clients, JoEllen?" Madeleine inquired sternly.

The trainee sighed. "Not too much, to the best of my knowledge, Madeleine. At least not so much as before. I think I'm learning to separate my personal life from my professional life. But I must admit I'm scared for Sally Peterson, as I'm scared for myself. If Sally leaves George, she'll be all alone, and probably for some time."

"And you're worried about being all alone again yourself," reflected Bob in a sympathetic tone.

"I sure am," replied JoEllen.

"I'm really sorry, JoEllen," said Rose. "I'm sorry to hear you're having a hard time again in your personal life."

"But let me give you a compliment!" Madeleine Sweet interjected in a different tone. "JoEllen, despite my previous question, I saw no signs of personal complications affecting your work with the Petersons in the segment of tape you showed today."

"Thanks, Madeleine!" said the trainee. "I'm glad to hear that."

"And do you think that was true for the rest of your session?" asked Madeleine.

"To the best of my knowledge, I kept my own issues separate, Madeleine."

"Excellent," responded the psychologist. "I wish we had more time to discuss your personal situation today, JoEllen, but we don't. We have Rose's tape to review yet. But I think it would be a good idea if you considered counseling for yourself and your boyfriend. What do you think?"

"That makes sense to me, Madeleine."

"Do you think your boyfriend would agree?"

"I'm not sure. But if not, maybe I'll go myself for help in deciding what to do."

"Very good," said Madeleine. "Do you want ideas for referrals, or do you have a therapist in mind?"

"I'd like to go to the same person I counseled with after my divorce," the trainee replied. "But I doubt if my boyfriend would agree. I'm afraid he'd think the therapist was on my side from the beginning."

"Your boyfriend might be right, too!" joked Madeleine. "Let me know if you need a referral, JoEllen. I have two or three people in mind that I believe would work well with you."

"Thanks, Madeleine."

"You're welcome. And now, Rose, it's time for you."

After Rose's case review, the discussion group adjourned for the week. JoEllen went home and called her boyfriend. She asked him to go into counseling with her as a couple.

CHAPTER 26

❀

Molly and Henry Come to Terms with the Past

On the following Wednesday evening, Molly and Henry arrived for their session early. They came together. They filed into the office and sat down next to each other. JoEllen noticed a different body language between the two: they seemed almost to lean toward one another. Their faces radiated.

"You two look different to me this evening," the trainee began the session. "What's happened for you this week?"

Molly spoke first, her voice tone warm and filled with pleasure. "Henry and I are getting back together again, JoEllen," she said. "My husband told me a couple of days after our joint session with George and Sally that he'll give up his affairs."

"Give up his affair with Marlene, or give up his affairs altogether?" Although Molly's words seemed clear enough, JoEllen wanted to make sure.

Henry spoke then. "It's time, JoEllen. I've decided. I want Molly back, and if I have to give up my affairs to do it, well, I guess that's what I have to do."

As JoEllen listened to the man, she realized she wasn't totally surprised to hear these words, but she wasn't expecting them, either. She wondered what had changed Henry's mind.

"What's changed for you, Henry?" the trainee inquired with genuine curiosity. "Molly's been insisting that you give up your affairs for years. What's different for you now?"

Henry's expression sobered. "When I watched what happened with Sally and George in here last week, JoEllen, I couldn't help feeling really bad. For Sally, especially. I think George is making a mistake. Sally's a fine girl. It's a shame my son is going to lose her."

"Is Sally really leaving George?" asked JoEllen.

"Yes," Henry replied sadly. "Sally went to stay with her friends right after last week's session, and George is being stubborn as a mule about it. He won't ask Sally to come back; he says it's her decision. Meantime, he's stepped up his affair with Nancy, almost to make a point."

"To make a point?"

"Yes. To let Sally know she can't run his life."

"How do you feel about that, Henry?"

"I feel pretty bad, to tell you the truth. Sally's hurting, and I hate to see that. She's a decent person. And George will have a hard time finding another woman with qualities like hers."

"Does that remind you of you and Molly, perhaps?"

"Well, I'm not so dumb I can't see I treated Molly just like George is treating Sally. But I guess I believed Molly would stay with me, no matter what she said."

"But she hasn't stayed with you, Henry, and still you've been choosing to continue your affair with Marlene." The trainee pushed a little.

"That's true, JoEllen. But I expected Molly'd break down and come back to me eventually. After all, she and I have been together for a number of years. But I'm not so sure about Sally. Sally's young; she'll have plenty of chances besides George."

"Do you think George is making the wrong decision then, Henry?"

"Well, I sure think that boy should reconsider. But George says he wants his freedom."

"How about you, Henry?" asked JoEllen. "You've always said you want your freedom too."

"Sure I want my freedom," Henry replied. "But it's suddenly struck me that it isn't just Sally who has choices. Molly may be an older gal, but she has this other guy waiting for her right in the wings."

"So now you're willing to do what you need to do to bring Molly back."

Henry sighed. "In my ideal world, I'd have a wife who didn't mind me having occasional flings. But Molly does mind, and I don't want our marriage to break up, like George and Sally's. So I'll do what I have to do."

"Henry," Molly interjected in a disturbed tone, "I don't think in an ideal world husbands would run around having affairs with other women. Would you want me to run around having affairs with other men? You don't seem very happy about Herbert."

A bit of the old Henry flashed then. "Molly, of course I don't want you running around with other men like Herbert. You still don't get it. You don't do it the right way. You get too emotionally involved."

"Henry," JoEllen reminded the man gently. "Remember the session with your mother, Elsbeth, when we learned that a major reason you have affairs is to protect yourself emotionally, so that no one woman can hurt you too much by ignoring you? Is that so much better than having affairs because you love someone emotionally?"

Henry scowled. For a few moments it looked as if the session were about to go back into a fray in which Molly would be blamed and Henry rejected. But suddenly a smile lit up the struggling man's face.

"You know," Henry said candidly, "I have to say I like my wife a whole lot emotionally. I suppose you could say I love her, and I want to keep my emotional involvement with her. That's why we're here."

Molly's face lit up. "Listen to that, JoEllen!" she exclaimed. "Listen to what Henry is saying! Finally, after all these years, it sounds like I come first!"

"You sure as hell do come first," Henry said, in a growl that was strong and clear. A long moment of silence punctuated these words. Molly and Henry smiled broadly at each other.

"Am I right in determining that you two want to put your marriage back together now and are willing to do what it takes?" asked JoEllen after taking in the long smile.

"You sure are," said Henry.

"That's right, I guess," said Molly.

"There's one more thing we need to talk about, then," continued JoEllen. "This may be difficult, but it's too important to overlook. Molly, what about your relationship with Herbert?"

Molly's face fell for a moment. "You know, I haven't talked with Herbert lately. Herbert's a fine man and I don't want to hurt him."

"But you will break up with him, won't you, Molly?" This from Henry, who actually allowed a humble, pleading tone to enter his voice.

"Henry, I want to, but it's hard."

"Sure it's hard, but will you do it?"

"Henry," said Molly, "Tell me again that you want me more than anybody else."

"I do," said Henry.

"Do you really mean that you will give up not only Marlene but any future affairs with other women?"

"I do," said Henry, "and I mean it."

"Then I will give up Herbert and come back to live as your wife, Henry." Molly's voice was solemn. The atmosphere in the office was somber, almost tender.

JoEllen allowed a long moment of silence to underscore the couple's vows. She smiled. "Hey, you two," she said then, "this feels almost like a marriage ceremony in here!"

Both Molly and Henry nodded, gazing into each other's eyes. After a few respectful moments, the telephone rang. It was Kurt, of course.

"The team feels that discussing the results of this week's homework assignment may help these two strengthen their decision to get back together. Be sure to ask Molly and Henry what they came up with."

"OK, Kurt," replied JoEllen.

She turned to the couple. "The team is interested in the results of your latest homework assignment," she said in a straightforward manner. "What did you two learn about your families of origin that made you proud or grateful? What skills did you learn that might help you rebuild your marriage?"

Molly smiled. She was still gazing at her husband. "Did you do your assignment, Henry?" she asked fondly.

"I sure did," he said. "I enjoyed this one."

"Me too," said Molly. "It made me remember some of the good times."

"I remembered some good times too," responded Henry.

"For example?" prompted JoEllen.

"Well," Henry replied, "I remembered how proud I was of my father when I was a boy. He was always reading the biggest books! Because of his plans to become a priest, Dad was highly educated. During my childhood, when he still came home in the evenings, I remember him quoting long sections of books and poems. That helped me when I met you, Molly! You've always been such a nut when it comes to reading."

Molly laughed. "Yes Henry," she responded, "and my interest in books came from my own family—both my mother and my father.

Dad was abusive, but only when he was drinking. At other times, he was a real gentleman and he loved to read. He encouraged me to go to college. So did my mother. I'm very grateful to both my parents for that, because my education gave me a key to another life."

"So you share a family background that valued education," said JoEllen.

"That's right," said Molly.

"What other gifts did your families provide for you?"

"My mother was very loyal to us children and very loving," said Molly. "She did her best to protect us from our father when he got drunk. My brother was also loyal to my mother and me. He did his best to protect us from my father whenever he could."

"My mother was loyal and loving toward us boys and toward her own sister too," said Henry. "Mother's sister was ill a good deal of the time, as I remember. It wasn't just that the sister babysat for us kids sometimes, like she was doing that night my mother wouldn't let me in. Mother took care of her sister many times too. She had a severe kind of asthma."

"So there was a lot of love and loyalty shared in each of your families," JoEllen reflected. "What else do you remember that was helpful and good?"

"Well, there was no physical abuse in my family," Henry replied. "Dad wouldn't allow it."

"That was one of the things that attracted me to Henry," Molly said. "He was never physically violent."

"That is a Peterson family strength," JoEllen reflected.

"Yes, and while there was physical abuse in my family," continued Molly, "Dad still did his best to be a good father. He worked very hard to provide for us. Times were tough and he never gave up."

"These qualities of love, loyalty, and hard work are very important," reflected JoEllen. "They are virtues that allow families to survive. Both of you have been fortunate to experience them. Now, how can you draw on these good qualities to help build a better marriage for yourselves?"

Molly and Henry sat silent, thinking. Molly was the first to speak.

"Well," she said, "I think I've incorporated my family's loyalty. It's part of what's kept me with Henry so long and it has a lot to do with why I'm going back to him."

"That's true for me too," said Henry. "I've been with Molly so long, she's my family now."

"Good," said JoEllen. "And how about the love you experienced in your families of origin? Can you draw on that to help rebuild your marriage?"

"You bet," said Henry. "I knew my mother loved me all these years, even though I was mad at her about that time she locked me out. I understand what happened better now. It helped to talk with my mother here in the office. I guess I can trust Mom more than I knew, and that makes me love her more. I think I can let myself get closer to Molly now."

"That's very important, Henry," said JoEllen.

"And it makes me feel more hopeful about our future," said Molly. "Henry, if you think you can risk getting closer to me now, I would love to be closer to you. I was lucky in that I almost always felt loved as a child, at least by my mother."

The telephone rang again.

"You know," said Kurt, "this conversation is reminding the team back here of Boszormenyi-Nagy's concept of the family ledger[43]—that families keep an unconscious tally of credits and debits that must be settled over time. Henry may have unconsciously felt 'owed' because of what he experienced as disloyalty on the part of his mother. To some degree, he took that unpaid debt out on Molly, by having affairs. But now Elsbeth has explained and apologized. That should balance the ledger pretty well for Henry, but not for Molly. Check it out."

JoEllen put the telephone down, pursed her lips, and let out a small whistling sound.

"What's that?" Henry asked.

JoEllen plunged into the task. "Henry," she said, "do you remember how you explained that you had a hard time getting close to any woman after your mother let you down? After that night when Elsbeth wouldn't let you into the house?"

"Hell, yes, I sure do."

"Did you feel as if your mother owed you something for that disloyalty?"

"I guess I did."

"How did you feel when your mother explained what happened that night from her point of view, here in the office, and apologized for hurting you?"

"I felt one whole lot better, like I said before the phone rang."

"Good. Now, there may be some repair work to do for Molly, too."

"Some repair work for Molly?"

"Yes. There still may be a problem for Molly."

"What kind of problem?"

"Henry, remember how we speculated that what happened with your mother may have led to your having affairs, as a way of protecting yourself?"

"Yes . . . and I suppose there could be some truth to it."

"Molly was the one who was most hurt by those affairs."

"Hm. Well . . . I suppose she was."

"Your wife may feel as if you owe her an apology, just as your mother apologized to you.

"Hm."

"How about asking Molly?"

"Well—all right, then." Henry turned to his wife. "Molly," he said in a low voice, "how about what JoEllen just said? Do you think I owe you an apology?"

"Oh, Henry," Molly replied, "I don't know. I feel so much better just understanding what was happening."

"Was it so bad, Molly?" Henry persisted in a small voice.

"I guess it was," his wife replied simply.

"Well, then, Molly," Henry spoke softly. He grimaced, and then continued: "I'm sorry. I want our marriage to work. I won't do it again."

Molly's face relaxed into a glowing smile that grew and grew, and tears flowed unnoticed down her cheeks.

JoEllen felt a strong urge to reach out and give Molly a hug as the woman gazed long at her husband. But she didn't. She knew she wasn't the one that Molly needed. To her own surprise, the words burst right out of the trainee's mouth: "Come on, Henry! How about giving your wife a hug!"

And suddenly Molly and Henry Peterson were engaged in a powerful embrace, and they both were crying. JoEllen felt tears come to her own eyes too. She took a tissue before placing the box in reach of her clients, who were paying her absolutely no attention by that time.

Several moments passed in moving words and promises, and then the telephone rang.

"Come on back, JoEllen. It's time for the team's message," said Kurt.

JoEllen took advantage of the brief interruption brought by the telephone to ask the couple if they wanted to return the next week. Henry hesitated. Molly nodded in the affirmative.

"Henry, she said, I still haven't told Herbert that I'm going back with you. I think I need one more session after I talk with him. I may need some support!"

"OK," said Henry.

"We'll make another appointment, then," said JoEllen. "Same time next week?" Both Petersons nodded, and JoEllen left the office to join the team.

From behind the mirror, Kurt, John, Sandra, Kevin, and JoEllen watched Molly and Henry Peterson as they held each other's hands, hugged each other, and told each other how, this time, they were going to do things right. Many members of the team felt the couple's experience right through the mirror, and their own eyes grew suspiciously misty.

The team's message for the evening read as follows: "Molly and Henry Peterson, we commend you for your commitment to each other this evening. The team believes that due to the courage each of you has displayed, you have every chance of rebuilding your marriage into a more fulfilling relationship than you have ever experienced before.

"Moreover, we are sure that you have already resolved many problems together successfully in the past. Your homework for this week is to discuss what has worked for you successfully before. How have you made decisions that worked? How have you resolved disputes? Think of specific examples from your own experience as husband and wife.

"We wish you well."

CHAPTER 27

Terminating Therapy

Molly and Henry strolled into the training office the next Wednesday evening, side by side. The two looked more relaxed than JoEllen remembered ever having seen them before. They seated themselves together in the office, pulling their chairs close. Molly reached out and took Henry's hand.

"It looks to me as if you folks are getting along rather well this week," JoEllen began the session, teasing her clients gently.

"Yes, we are," replied Molly. "This is almost better than when our marriage began, JoEllen."

"I haven't let myself feel this close to Molly in years," said Henry. Grinning, he held up his big hand enclosing Molly's smaller one for JoEllen to admire. "Molly and the kids moved back in with me this week."

"How did it go?" JoEllen asked.

"Actually, the moving was a bit of a melee," Molly replied. "The kids and I had collected more junk in that apartment than I realized. And without George to help this time . . ."

"George and Sally are still separated?" asked JoEllen.

"They sure are," said Henry. "Sally has hired a lawyer. She's planning to file for divorce as soon as the attorney can get the papers drawn up."

"I'm sorry to hear about that, although I'm not surprised," said JoEllen.

"George is too damned stubborn to ask Sally back," said his father. "He always has been stubborn as a mule."

"Not unlike his father," Molly said gently.

"Well . . . ," Henry growled. Then he smiled sheepishly and continued, "Maybe the kid will come to his senses before it's too late. After all, if the old man did, there's hope!"

"Yes," said JoEllen seriously. "You're providing George with a very different role model now, Henry. The boy may be pretty confused. A heart-to-heart talk might be in order. Have you tried one yet?"

"Well, no," said Henry. "I've changed too fast to understand myself, much less try to explain anything to my son. But I do feel bad about George and Sally."

"Henry," said Molly. "I'd be so happy if you tried to talk with our son. I have, and George just said I didn't understand."

"Well," said Henry, "maybe I'll give it a go one of these days."

"It probably couldn't hurt, Henry," said JoEllen, "as long as you're careful to tell him you love him no matter what he decides. George may need you later to pick up the pieces."

"Yeah. The kid's an adult now, and he'll make his own decisions no matter what I say."

"That's right," said JoEllen.

Molly broke in then, "I'm so glad you suggested that Sally stay somewhere besides my apartment, JoEllen. It would have been terribly hard for her to be caught in the middle of my reconciliation with Henry, when her marriage is on the rocks."

"Yes," said JoEllen. "Hopefully, Sally's friends are providing her with the emotional support she needs."

"I hope so," said Molly. "We certainly haven't seen much of her."

"Now tell me," continued JoEllen, "how are Josh and Charlotte doing with all this?"

"They're both very happy, even though Josh liked Herbert a lot. Josh told me yesterday that Henry and I had better stay together this time or he'll never forgive us!" said Molly.

"Charlotte really hated that apartment," said Henry. "I should have asked my family to come home a long time ago."

"Henry, you did your best, considering what you believed all these years," Molly said kindly. "You said right along that we were all welcome back, remember?"

Henry gave his wife a grateful glance, and nodded.

"By the way, Molly, have you talked with Herbert yet?" asked JoEllen.

"I have," the woman responded in a sad tone. "I told him I was going back to Henry. He was very upset."

"Do you think Herbert believed you?"

"Oh yes, because I had to return some things of his that he had left at my apartment."

"You actually saw Herbert this week, then?"

"Yes I did," said Molly. "It was very hard. We both cried. But Herbert was wonderful, really. He said he understood and wished me well."

"Herbert sounds like a fine person," said JoEllen.

"He is. I'll miss him."

"How about you, Henry? Have you talked with Marlene this week?"

"Yes I have," the man responded. "She got pretty mad at me, and called me a thing or two. That relationship is over."

"Truly over?"

"Over," said Henry with finality.

"So here both of you are tonight," responded JoEllen, "as husband and wife, reunited in your own home, cleared of other entanglements."

"What a relief," said Molly.

"Amen," said Henry.

"Well, it looks as if we've achieved our goal," said JoEllen. "What shall we do now?"

Molly and Henry looked at each other. Henry spoke. "JoEllen, this is nothing against you, but we feel we don't need to come back here after tonight."

JoEllen grinned. "That's all right, Henry! These sessions are for your benefit, not mine. You two make me work pretty darned hard!"

"You bet we do," said Henry with a grin. "But you don't exactly let us off the hook easy, you know, JoEllen."

"I should hope not!" the trainee exclaimed. "Let's see now. If you two aren't planning to return, let's review exactly what brought you here and what you've accomplished. Does that seem like a good idea?"

"Sure," said Henry.

Molly nodded.

"So what brought you here, and what have you accomplished?"

"We came back to counseling to work on our marriage," said Molly.

"And what have you achieved?"

"We've done that," said Henry. "We've put our marriage back together."

"So you've accomplished your goal," said JoEllen.

"Yes we have." This time it was Molly who spoke, her tone strong and confident. "We've done what we came here to do."

"That about says it all," said JoEllen. "You've achieved your goal, so there's no need to come back next week. Let's face it—counseling is *work!*"

"You're darned right it's work," huffed Henry. "Of course, if our family has more problems in the future, would it be OK for us to come back?"

"Of course," said JoEllen.

"That's good," said Henry. "You know, I never expected much from this counseling business, but it's turned out to work pretty well for us."

"From you, Henry, I consider that a major compliment!" JoEllen smiled. "Now, how shall we use the rest of this hour? How about discussing your homework assignment?"

"Sounds fine," said Molly.

"No problem," said Henry.

"OK," said JoEllen. "Let's start with you, Molly. "The homework, as I remember, was about decision-making processes that have worked for you and Henry in the past."

"I found the assignment pretty difficult, to tell the truth," said Molly. "Most of the time it seems Henry and I just disagreed in the past. We didn't seem to resolve very much."

"That may seem true, but allow yourself to remember times when you *did* make decisions that worked, or *did* resolve disputes successfully."

"Well . . . ," said Molly, wrinkling her forehead.

"Come on, Molly," Henry interjected impatiently. "You know we didn't *always* just fight. We made decisions that worked."

"I'm sure that's true, Henry," encouraged JoEllen, turning to the man. "Give us an example."

"Well," Henry began, "when Molly and I began looking for land to build our house, I wanted to live out in the country but she wanted to be in the city. But Molly also wanted to be near water and I didn't particularly like the idea—I was worried about the bugs. We decided together to look for country property on a lake. And that's exactly what we did."

"Henry," Molly spoke up with enthusiasm, "that's true!"

"So how would you describe the process you used?" asked JoEllen.

"We compromised, of course," said Henry.

"Yes," responded JoEllen. "Each of you listened to what was important to the other as well as to yourself, and then made sure you each got something you really wanted."

"That's true," said Molly again.

"Can you think of another example?" asked JoEllen.

"Hm," Molly said, looking puzzled again. Then she brightened. "Yes, I do have another example. When Dr. Lang, Josh's psychologist, called to warn us that Josh might be suicidal, Henry and I worked together very closely. He stayed home to help me keep an eye on Josh, and I was careful to make Henry's favorite meals so he wouldn't be too upset about staying home. We agreed to build fires in the fireplace at night to make the time more fun. And I remember we had some wonderful evenings. At least I did."

"I enjoyed those evenings very much too," Henry said thoughtfully. "I felt as if I got to know my son better, and I liked all the things Molly did to make the time more pleasant."

"How did you actually decide what you were going to eat in the evening, or when you were going to build a fire?"

"Why, we asked each other what we wanted," said Henry.

"Was that an unusual thing for the two of you to do—ask each other what you wanted?" asked JoEllen.

"I guess it was," Henry responded.

"Can the two of you agree to talk with each other regularly now about what you would like to do in the evening?"

"We sure can," said Henry.

"I'd like that," said Molly.

"Good, these are exactly the kinds of tools I hoped you could identify," continued JoEllen. "You can make life much happier for each other if you consciously talk about what you want, and are open to compromise. What are some other examples of decision-making processes that have worked for you?"

"Well," said Henry, "we've planned some great vacations together."

"Is it easy for you to agree where to go, what to do, and that sort of thing?"

"For the most part, I guess it's been easy," said Molly. "Henry usually decides where we'll go, and I plan the meals. We frequently take canoe trips, which we both enjoy."

"So canoe trips are a good example of how you two can cooperate well together."

"Yes, they are," said Molly.

"What about other trips?"

"Oh, we take lots of trips," Henry replied. "Canoeing, biking, skiing, that sort of thing."

"Do you enjoy taking such strenuous vacations, Molly?" asked JoEllen. "They sound like a lot of work to me, to tell the truth!"

"Oh yes, I really do," Molly replied. "That's not a problem for me. But there *is* one major problem with trips. Henry and I haven't talked about it yet. I'm almost afraid to bring it up with him."

"What's that, Molly?" asked Henry, looking uneasy.

Molly made a face, and sat silent.

"What is it, Molly?" This time it was JoEllen who prompted.

The woman took a deep breath, and then forged ahead. "Henry's friends!" she blurted. "Sometimes Henry invites them along on our trips!"

"Molly, my friends are important to me!" Henry exclaimed in a pained voice. "I'm willing to quit having affairs, but I can't just cut my friends completely out of my life!"

"How often do you invite friends along on your trips, Henry?" asked the trainee.

"Too often!" Molly answered for him.

Henry and Molly stared at each other then. There were obviously issues to be resolved that the two hadn't thought through yet.

"Talk to Molly about your need for friendships, Henry, and what kind of friendships you want to have," guided JoEllen.

"All I want, Molly," Henry said to his wife, "is for you to agree that I can bring friends along on *some* of our trips. After all, you enjoy hiking and biking with a group of good people as much as I do."

"That's true, Henry," Molly said, "sometimes." The word *sometimes* sounded loud and strong.

"Sometimes?" repeated JoEllen.

"Only sometimes," Molly replied emphatically. "I hate it when you bring women along and carry on with them, Henry!"

"Oh!" said Henry, relieved. "That's no problem, then, Molly. I've already promised not to have any more affairs!"

Molly looked doubtful. Henry saw his wife's expression and his own face became worried.

"Come on, Molly," the man said in a petulant tone, "won't you let me keep my friendships if I promise that's all they are, just friendships?"

Molly still looked uncomfortable, but she responded in a low voice: "I suppose so, Henry."

The telephone rang.

"Ask Molly if she'd be willing to let Henry continue to go out dancing by himself every evening." Kurt hung up without saying anything further.

When JoEllen presented the team's question, Molly's facial expression became even more uncomfortable. "Oh," was all she said.

"Well, what's wrong with that?" asked Henry testily.

"Take a look at Molly," JoEllen said.

"I am looking at Molly! So what the hell's the matter?" Henry asked impatiently. "So what more does she want from me?"

Molly's features rotated into a hopeless pattern.

"What are you feeling right now, Molly? Tell Henry," prompted JoEllen.

Molly responded in a voice that sounded as hopeless as she looked. "I feel so left out when you're with other people, Henry." She let out a long sigh. "It isn't just a matter of affairs. You don't pay me any attention when you're with other people even when I'm there too, and I feel like a has-been. I try to pretend it doesn't bother me, but everybody knows it does."

JoEllen spoke quietly then. "Henry, it isn't just the sexual boundaries that need to be protected to keep a marriage special."

"Well," said Henry, "a man's got to have *some* freedom! What else does she want from me?"

"And Henry would *never* give up his evenings out dancing alone," said Molly, looking even more hopeless.

JoEllen had a sudden sense of panic that everything that had been accomplished so far might go down the drain. Molly and Henry might decide after all that their marriage couldn't work.

The telephone rang.

"Ask these two to use the tools for problem solving that they identified earlier, the ones that have been successful for them in the past."

"OK. Thanks!" the trainee responded.

JoEllen repeated the team's instructions, and then reviewed the skills Molly and Henry had identified: talking things through, finding out what was most important for the other, taking care that each received at least a part of what was wanted.

"How can you each get what you need, while respecting your partner's needs?" the trainee finished.

Molly and Henry looked at each other. Molly spoke first.

"Henry," she said, "it isn't that I don't want you to have friends. I just need to know I come first."

"You do come first! I tell you that all the time!" her husband replied, clearly annoyed.

"You need to show me, so I can believe you," Molly responded simply.

"How can I show you? You're so insecure!" Henry retorted.

JoEllen interrupted the man immediately. "Henry," she said sternly, "in marriage, the idea is to build each other up, not tear each other down. If Molly's feeling insecure, it's partly because you have given her every reason to feel that way in the past."

Molly's facial expression became animated then. "You're right, JoEllen!" she cried loudly. "That's *it!* Most of the time I don't feel insecure at all! But I sure do when Henry treats me like I don't exist!"

"Molly," JoEllen turned to the wife with an equally stern expression, "it's important for you to tell Henry exactly what kind of behavior you need from him so that you can feel secure in your marriage. Henry needs to know, so that he can decide if the marriage is worth it to him."

Molly's expression sobered. "Henry," she said slowly, taking a deep breath, "I need to know that I matter to you, not just in words in this office but in real life."

"Of course you matter to me, Molly," Henry responded defensively. "I've told you that over and over, at least a thousand times. What else can I say?"

"Telling me isn't enough. I need you to *act* like I matter. That means not having affairs *and* not leaving me alone all the time *and* not flirting openly with other women right in front of me."

Henry scowled.

JoEllen spoke then. "Henry," she said, "remember the team's instructions? What is it you really need to feel good about yourself, that you can do without hurting Molly?"

"Well, I sure need my friends," the man replied. "I love Molly, but she really *can't* meet all my needs."

"Of course she can't, Henry, nor can you meet all of hers."

"So where does that leave us?" the man responded.

"Ask your wife again if it's OK with her if you have friends, Henry, and listen carefully to what she says."

Henry grimaced. "What about it, Molly?" he growled. "Are you trying to cut me off from all my friends?"

"No, Henry," his wife replied. "Please listen to me. I want you to have friends. But I need to know that I come first."

"How can I possibly let you know that, when you won't believe me when I tell you?"

Molly frowned, and looked helplessly at JoEllen.

"Can't you find a solution here, you two?" asked the trainee. "You both enjoy doing many of the same things. That's important! Many couples struggle over just finding something in common!"

"What are you getting at, JoEllen?" asked Henry.

"I want you two to decide for yourselves how you can resolve this impasse. What do you really want, Henry? What is your 'bottom line' in negotiating with Molly?"

"I want to stay married to Molly, but I have to have friends too."

"And your bottom line, Molly?"

"I want to stay married to Henry, but I have to feel like I count in the marriage."

"How can you two have a relationship in which you, Henry, can have other friends, and you, Molly can feel as if you count in the marriage?"

The question hung in the air. The silence grew long and became very uncomfortable. Molly looked over at Henry with a question in her eyes. Henry looked back, his expression glum. JoEllen had to fight an urge to jump in and rescue. But the solution had to belong to the couple.

At last Henry spoke. "You really don't mind my having friends, Molly?"

"No, I don't, Henry, as long as I know I come first."

"Would it be OK with you if I went out dancing if I took you, say, more than half the time? And flirted just with you those evenings?"

"That would be *wonderful,* Henry!" responded his wife.

"Of course," Henry's features broke into a rakish grin, "there will be those evenings when I'll want to be out by myself, and then I'll want to flirt with other women like crazy!"

"That's OK, Henry, as long as I don't have to watch! And especially if I know that you aren't out seducing somebody."

"Fair enough," said Henry. "I'll go dancing with you more than half the time, Molly, as long as I can still have some of my own nights on the town."

"And those evenings you take me with you, you'll dance with me most of the time?"

"Yeah, I can do that."

Molly and Henry looked at each other, and then broke into simultaneous grins. Molly suddenly stood up and gave her husband a graceful little curtsey, as if already out with him on the dance floor.

"Did we do it?" said JoEllen then, thinking at that point that therapy itself was very much like stepping to the dance. The therapist has to follow each client closely, as the dancer has to move in close step with the partner.

"Yes, we took care of that problem, I think," said Molly, taking her seat again. "But—we need to talk about the vacation trips again, JoEllen."

"Oh yes," responded the trainee. "The vacation trips. Talk to Henry about them now, Molly."

"Henry," Molly turned to her husband, "if I agree to welcome our friends on some of our vacation trips, will you promise to take me all by myself at least half the time?"

"Sure," said Henry. "That would be fine."

"And on the trips when friends are along, would you promise to flirt with me at least 80% of the time?"

"Eighty per cent of the time in whose opinion, yours or mine?" Henry tried to joke.

"Oh, Henry!" Molly cried out, exasperated.

"OK, OK, my love," the man replied with a sigh. "You sure drive a hard bargain, though."

"Henry, Molly, I think you two have made real progress tonight!" JoEllen exclaimed, taking on a cheerleading role now. "This is hard work, but you can do it!"

"Of course we can!" Henry grinned, a rakish flash in his handsome blue eyes reminding JoEllen suddenly of the smooth, debonair gentleman who had first entered the training office months before. She was glad Henry's strong spirit was alive and well, if struggling to redefine its role.

"We're getting close to the end of the hour now," the trainee said. "It's nearly time for me to go behind the mirror to talk with the team. But there's one other task I want to accomplish before we quit. May I tell you what it is?"

"Sure," said Henry, looking surprised.

"Of course," said Molly.

"Well," continued JoEllen, "a few sessions back, Henry came up with an intriguing story. It seemed to be about skiing, but it was really about relationships. Do you remember?"

Both Petersons nodded.

"The story about how you can get a rush by taking a fast run down a ski slope?" asked Henry. "You know you'll hit bottom, but you also know you can get another rush if you take another run?"

"That's the one," said JoEllen.

"It's a great story about life, isn't it?" said Henry warmly, his tone eager and compelling.

"Well, yes and no," replied JoEllen slowly.

"What do you mean, yes and no?"

"It seems to imply that when you've finished with the rush of one relationship, it's no matter—you can always get a new rush by starting another one."

"That's exactly what it does mean," the man replied, looking perplexed at JoEllen's apparent disapproval.

"What does this story do for your relationship with Molly, Henry?" asked JoEllen.

"Well, ah . . . ," began the man, retreating into silence.

"Can't you see that a story like this can help create problems between you and your wife?" the trainee continued. "Your 'rush' with Molly, that 'first flushes' stage, was over years ago. You're in a different phase of your relationship now. But this story guides you to seek a new rush with somebody else, over and over."

Henry looked glum. "Hm," the man said. "That's a problem for me, for sure."

"Is it a problem because you continue to crave that rush?"

"Sure," said Henry. "Doesn't everybody?"

"I don't think so, Henry," JoEllen replied. "There are other joys in human relationships to cherish even more than short-term thrills."

"Like what?" the man asked.

"You can answer that question yourself, Henry! What was the reason you asked your wife to come back to you?"

"Why, I missed Molly, of course. She's my best friend."

"Isn't there a lot to cherish in that feeling of friendship, and the memory of good companionship—all those long, caring years together?"

"Sure," said Henry. "But that's not the same as the rush other women provide. I've promised to give that up, but I'll sure miss it."

"Of course. But I'm worried that giving up the thrills may be especially difficult for you if you have a story like that ski-slope tale constantly on your mind."

"Well," Henry said, "I hope not. I'll do the best I can."

"The most important choices in life, like choosing to live faithfully with a spouse, may necessarily shut the door on other choices," JoEllen waxed philosophical.

"That excitement was awfully important to me," Henry reflected sadly.

"Maybe it was," said JoEllen. "But how about developing a new story now, to replace the ski-slope tale? You and Molly can develop a different story together, one that honors loyalty and love over the long haul."

"I suppose," said Henry. "But that kind of story would make an entirely different point."

"That's exactly the idea!" exclaimed JoEllen.

"Well, how would you do it?" Henry asked.

"I'm not sure," the trainee responded. "But you and Molly enjoy many sports besides skiing. Maybe you can work out a story that involves a different sport that honors your caring times, your long-term loyalty times."

Molly responded then. "What a funny idea, JoEllen," she mused. "It seems that Henry's always told that story about the ski slope. It certainly does tell me pretty clearly that I can't give him what he needs any more. I would very much like something different influencing our lives."

"Then take time to develop another story, Molly," prodded JoEllen. "A new story could teach a different truth."

"Well . . . ," the woman responded, thinking. "I've always enjoyed canoeing more than skiing, come to think of it. With skiing, you get to the bottom of the slope so darned quickly, and then you have to go all the way back up the hill again."

"Can you tell a story about canoeing, Molly? A different kind of story?"

"Hm," said Molly.

"Give it a go," said JoEllen in an encouraging tone.

"Hm. Well. A couple can have a real adventure in a canoe," Molly complied hesitantly. "Two people can paddle together for hours at a time. You can paddle like crazy and get plenty of thrills in the rapids, but you can enjoy the quiet places as well. The river can carry you slowly and gently, and you can listen to the wind, and the birds calling . . ."

"That's true!" Henry jumped in. "In fact, in the quiet places on a river you can come across some great surprises—herons, kingfishers, fish lurking behind logs, that sort of thing."

"And behind the bends in the river banks, you can float in the still pools and watch the trees reflecting in the water and the changing cloud patterns—it's very beautiful," Molly continued, her voice far away now.

Henry broke the spell. "Yes, but sometimes those darned pools can get pretty boring," he declared. "Especially on cloudy days."

Molly's face fell, and a familiar waxen smile began to mold her features.

"But then," Henry continued with a grin, making it clear he was teasing, "beyond the quiet pools the rapids may start again, and you can have as many thrills as you want."

Molly looked over at her husband and made a face at him. "You creep," she said crossly.

Henry continued, smiling broadly at his wife, "And a man can enjoy all that with the same woman in his boat the whole length of the river!"

The trainee, the husband, and the wife all sat for a moment with satisfied smiles shaping their faces.

"What do you think?" asked JoEllen. "Can this be your new story? Henry and Molly together in their own canoe, maybe in the rapids, maybe in the quieter water, maybe in the still pools, maybe back in the rapids, but always in the same boat, enjoying the ride?"

"Yes, I think it's a lovely story," said Molly.

"Hm. Might do," said Henry.

The telephone rang.

"It's time to come behind the mirror, JoEllen," said Kurt.

Kurt and the team members complimented the trainee on her work that evening. JoEllen smiled her acknowledgement.

"I was worried for a while that I was working harder than my clients," the trainee said, "and I know that's a 'no-no' in counseling. But I was wrong. Molly and Henry worked harder than I did tonight. It really is the clients who determine whether therapy is successful or not, isn't it? And for a couple, you sure need both people pulling in the same direction."

The other team members nodded thoughtfully, thinking of some of their own clients.

The team sent the following message to Molly and Henry that evening: "The team will miss working with you, Molly and Henry, but we are certainly proud of your accomplishments here at the clinic. Not everyone we work with has the passion and persistence to put their marriage back together, as you two have done. We encourage you to pay attention to the new and more hopeful story you have created for yourselves this evening. A new story can help guide your way as you continue to build a better life for yourselves and your children.

"While we don't expect that you will need to return here, remember that the doors are always open. Even the best canoes may need maintenance from time to time. Best of luck to you in your new adventure."

CHAPTER 28

❀

JoEllen's Challenge

"How are you feeling about terminating marital therapy with the Petersons, JoEllen?" It was Dr. Madeleine Sweet, leader of JoEllen's Monday noon discussion group.

"Both happy and sad, I guess," the trainee responded. "I'm happy that Molly and Henry have been able to make the decision to get back together again, but I'll miss them."

"You know," said Rose, "that's the trouble with being a therapist. You lose your success cases too darned quickly, and the failures seem to stick around a lot longer than you want!"

"No one said this was an easy business," Madeleine responded seriously. Then she turned back to JoEllen. "Do you think the Petersons are likely to return to the clinic in the future?"

"I don't know," the trainee replied honestly. "This will be a very different lifestyle for Henry, and while I think he's going to be able to swing it, I certainly couldn't say for sure."

"Yes, it will be quite a change for the man," Madeleine responded. "That makes it pretty hard to predict how things will go."

"And then," JoEllen continued, "the two younger children, Josh and Charlotte, will have to adjust to their father's presence again. That could be awkward for them at first. Though Henry's decision to become more involved with his family is an admirable change, the children may find that they resent his intervening more actively in their lives, at least at first. They aren't used to it."

"That may be true," said Madeleine.

"Also, we don't know yet what will happen with George and Sally. If Henry does have a fatherly talk with his son, maybe George will decide to ask Sally back. If Sally should agree to return, I wouldn't be surprised if she asked for marriage counseling."

"JoEllen, if the younger Peterson couple should ask to come to the institute for counseling, would you want to take them on?"

"Yes, I would. Working with George and Sally wouldn't be easy, of course, but with the support of the team and the discussion group, I believe I could handle it."

"That's good, JoEllen. Now, briefly, what's going on in your own life? Is your own romantic relationship in better shape than it was last week?"

"Perhaps," said JoEllen with a sigh. "By that I mean that my significant other has agreed to go into counseling with me. At least he cares *that* much. I have no idea what the results will be, though. Will you give me some ideas for referrals, Madeleine? My boyfriend wants to see a therapist who doesn't know either one of us, and I can certainly respect that request."

"I have some good possibilities for you, JoEllen," said Madeleine. "Why don't you talk with me about it after group today?"

"Thanks, I'll do that, Madeleine."

At that, the discussion group went on to work with other trainees, other cases.

JoEllen Madsen knew that she now faced the challenge of achieving in her own life that which she had helped Molly and Henry Peterson accomplish in theirs: a fulfilling relationship with a significant other.

JoEllen was aware that this was not a goal toward which everyone would, or even should, strive. Some people prefer the independence of the single life. Some people simply do better when they are single—financially, emotionally, or both. But JoEllen's happiest years had been the ones she shared with Chip, before the affairs shattered their marriage. Now she felt ready to find another partner, one who would stay the course this time. To help achieve that goal, the trainee was willing to step into the therapeutic dance once more, this time in the role of client.

❀

Epilogue

What do you believe will happen next? Do you think Molly and Henry Peterson's marriage will succeed this time? Will the children, Charlotte and Josh, adjust successfully to living with their father once again? Will Henry Peterson invest sufficient time as husband and father to perform these important roles reliably and successfully at last? And will Molly find she truly wants to stay with her husband, after her exposure to other possibilities out in the real world?

What do you think will happen now with George and Sally Peterson? Will they remain apart, ending their marriage in legal divorce? Or might the example of Molly and Henry Peterson's changing help inspire the younger couple to try living together in marriage again? And what about Molly's hopeful beau Herbert, and Henry's feisty friend Marlene? What will happen next in their lives?

What about JoEllen Madsen, our hard-working trainee? Will she succeed in developing a committed relationship of her own? If not, why not? If so, do you think it will be with her current significant other, or with someone new? Will JoEllen's finding a committed relationship make a difference in how well she can carry out her chosen profession? Why or why not?

These questions, and perhaps many others you have asked yourself, have been purposely left unresolved in this book so that you can make your own decisions. Marriage and family therapists routinely face many unknowns, many uncertainties. That is the nature of the profession. Still, they must carry on their chosen work with skill and dedication. It is up to you to decide if you want to join them.

❀

Appendix

This appendix is prepared especially for students and teachers of family therapy, although all readers are encouraged to utilize it. The various questions prepared for each chapter are intended to stimulate further thinking and discussion.

CHAPTER 1
The Therapist Trainee

1. The author states that JoEllen Madsen was willing to make sacrifices for her marriage to Chip. What were these sacrifices, and what were her reasons? Have you known friends or family who have made similar choices? Can you imagine yourself making choices like these? Why or why not?

2. Have you ever made an agreement in which you consciously asked not to be told something you didn't want to know, as JoEllen asked Chip not to tell her if he were to have an affair? What were JoEllen's reasons for making such an agreement? What hazards were involved for her? Do you think JoEllen was aware of these hazards? Why or why not?

3. Do you think an unpleasant emotion like jealousy is always a sign of weakness or immaturity? Why or why not? What kinds of messages can an emotion like jealousy convey?

4. Chip Madsen obviously hurt his wife, JoEllen, with his extramarital relationships. Do you think this husband intended to hurt his wife? Why or why not?

5. How carefully did JoEllen plan her initial departure from her marriage? Do you think she did something wrong in leaving her marriage? Why or why not?

6. What were the major reasons that two different marriage counselors were unable to "save" JoEllen and Chip Madsen's marriage? Do you think the counseling "failed," since the marriage came apart? Why or why not?

7. What factors led JoEllen Madsen to engage in individual counseling after her divorce? In what ways was this counseling helpful for her?

8. What personal issues do you imagine JoEllen will need to deal with if she is to become a successful marriage and family therapist? Do you think the Family Therapy Training Institute made the right decision in accepting JoEllen, given her divorce? Why or why not?

9. What professional backgrounds are usually required for admission to training programs accredited by the American Association for Marriage and Family Therapy?

CHAPTER 2
The Peterson Family

1. Why did Molly Peterson refuse to consider family counseling when it was first recommended by Martin Meyers, the school psychologist who worked with her older son, George Peterson, and who was instrumental in helping George complete high school?

2. What were the reasons the younger Peterson boy, Josh, was referred twice to special education for evaluation?

3. What parenting behaviors of both Molly and Henry Peterson do you think might relate to the poor school performance of their sons, George and Josh? Why do you think Charlotte, by contrast, was able to do so well in school?

4. For what reasons was Molly Peterson distressed to learn that Josh was referred to special education for suspected behavioral disturbances?

CHAPTER 3

An Interview with the Parents

1. What self-care practices were adopted by the school social worker, Roger Steinberg? What were his reasons? How might his self-care practices affect his clients? What do you think about Roger's decision to make self-care a priority?

2. What were Henry Peterson's views on physical punishment for children? Where did they come from? Did Henry practice what he preached? Do you think Roger Steinberg agreed with Henry on this issue? How do you know?

3. What were the reasons for Roger's detailed questions concerning Josh's early developmental history?

4. Henry and Molly Peterson disagreed on whether Josh's behavior at home was disturbed, and they disagreed on whether enrollment in special education would be a good idea or not. Describe the differences in these parents' points of view. From what you know so far, do you believe Josh is a good candidate for special education? Why or why not?

5. In what way did Henry Peterson's unexpected interest in the photograph of his son seem significant to Roger Steinberg?

CHAPTER 4

JoEllen's First Case

1. Achieving "clinical membership" in the American Association for Marriage and Family Therapy requires substantial classroom training, supervised clinical practice, and ongoing group supervision and consultation. About how many years of postgraduate training does achievement of this status usually require?

2. What were the professional backgrounds of the members of JoEllen's Wednesday evening training team? What was the professional background of Dr. Kurt Knaak, supervisor of the team?

3. What kind of equipment was installed in the family therapy training office and the observation room for the therapy team? What procedure was legally required to use this equipment? How might clients feel about the special equipment and the observation process?

How might the trainees feel? Why do you think the equipment was used in the training process?

4. What mistakes do you think JoEllen made even before she began her interview with the Callan family? How do you think she should have begun her work differently? Be specific.

5. After the Callan family was actually seated together in the little office, JoEllen immediately began her interview. When do you think the trainee made her first mistake in the interview process? Why? What do you think she might have done differently to steer the interview in a more helpful direction?

6. What were JoEllen's major feelings toward each of her clients: John, Warren, and Lucy Callan? How do you know? How do you think JoEllen's feelings toward her clients may have interfered with the interview process?

7. Why do you think John Callan ran out of the therapy office? Be specific. What do you think JoEllen should have done at that point, if anything?

CHAPTER 5

Consultation with the Team and the Discussion Group

1. What did JoEllen learn from the referral sheet for the Callan family, filled out by the agency secretary, that might have made a significant difference in the way the trainee conducted her interview? In what ways might knowing the referral information in advance have made a difference?

2. Why are case notes routinely kept in agency files describing ongoing work with every client?

3. What is a "process recording"? Why do you think Dr. Kurt Knaak required that JoEllen make a process recording before reviewing the Callan case with her Monday noon discussion group?

4. What was the purpose of the noon discussion groups at the institute? What was the professional background of Dr. Madeleine Sweet, leader of JoEllen's Monday noon group? What were the professional backgrounds of each of the other members of the Monday noon discussion group?

5. How did the group members help make JoEllen feel safe enough, despite her failure with the Callan family, to consult with them openly?

6. What ideas to improve her work did JoEllen discover on her own, through writing out her process recording?

7. How did the group assist JoEllen to better understand the Callan case? What suggestions did the various members offer as to more effective ways to work with a troubled family such as this?

8. Describe the concept of joining. In what ways is successful joining important to the outcome of the therapy process?

9. According to Madeleine Sweet, what tasks must all parents accomplish themselves in order to parent successfully? How did this information help JoEllen better understand why her interview with the Callans ended so abruptly?

10. Dr. Sweet told JoEllen that John Callan's misbehavior was probably a symptom of Lucy and Warren Callan's unhappiness in their marriage. What were her reasons for believing this might be the case?

11. Dr. Sweet states that "to a youngster, impending separation of the parents is often experienced as a direct threat to personal survival. The whole world feels like it's falling apart." Do you agree with this statement? Why or why not? Can you think of examples in your own life experience with family or friends that might support or refute this point of view?

CHAPTER 6
Another Referral for Family Therapy

1. What specific behaviors did Josh Peterson exhibit in the classroom that led his seventh grade English teacher, Mrs. Anderson, to refer him to special education for evaluation?

2. For what reasons did the school social worker, Roger Steinberg, believe that Josh did not qualify for special education as "behaviorally disturbed"? Why did the special education teacher, Mrs. Henke, believe that Josh *did* qualify for special education?

3. For what reasons did Henry Peterson want his son in special education? Why was Molly Peterson opposed?

4. How did George Peterson affect members of the M-team meeting, although he was not present?

5. Describe the concepts of least restrictive environment and mainstreaming. Why do you think educators and social workers keep these concepts in mind when developing educational plans for children?

6. Why do you think the school social worker, Roger Steinberg, and the school psychologist, Martin Meyers, recommended family counseling for the Petersons, not just individual counseling for Josh?

7. Why do you think Henry and Molly Peterson opposed family counseling but were willing to seek individual counseling for their son?

8. Think of your own family and friends. Have you ever encountered a situation in which the parents of a troubled child were willing to seek counseling for that child but not for the family as a whole? If so, what were the reasons?

CHAPTER 7
Precipitating Events

1. Do you think Molly had reason to be upset about Henry's teaching dancing classes? Why or why not? Do you think the discussion between Henry and Molly about the classes was constructive? Why or why not? What else do you think Molly could have done if she wanted to change her husband's behavior? What would you have done, if anything, in circumstances like these?

2. Why did Dr. Lang, Josh Peterson's psychologist, breach client confidentiality by informing Molly that Josh had recurrent suicidal thoughts?

3. How did Dr. Lang's information change the dynamics in the Peterson household?

4. How did Josh Peterson change after he began counseling with Dr. Lang? Why do you think these changes occurred? Was it the counseling itself, the changed Peterson household dynamics, both, or something else?

5. What happened to the relationship between Molly and Henry Peterson after Josh grew beyond his suicidal impulses and began to do exemplary work at school?

6. After Charlotte's shoplifting incident, the girl insisted she "didn't know" why she stole the earrings. Do you think Charlotte was lying? Why or why not?

7. Charlotte, normally an excellent student, failed her junior year subsequent to the shoplifting incident. What do you think could be possible reasons?

8. What led Molly Peterson to consult with the school social worker, Roger Steinberg, again after Charlotte's school failure? Why do you think it took so long for Molly to talk with Roger?

9. How did Roger help meet Molly's needs, both emotional and informational?

CHAPTER 8

Beginning the Therapy Process

1. In an initial interview at the institute, why was a trainee's first task to obtain permission in writing from the client to use the special equipment in the training office?

2. What techniques did JoEllen use to begin to establish rapport with the Peterson family that she did not use with the Callans?

3. How did the Peterson family respond to the equipment in the training office? How did JoEllen deal with their response?

4. How did JoEllen work to "join" with the Peterson family in a constructive therapeutic relationship? Was her task easy or difficult? How do you know?

5. How did Henry respond to JoEllen's initial efforts to engage him in therapy? How did JoEllen cope with Henry's behavior? Would you have done anything differently? Why or why not?

6. How did Molly respond to JoEllen's initial efforts to engage her in therapy? How did JoEllen cope with Molly's behavior? Would you have done anything differently? Why or why not?

7. Henry apparently felt threatened by the idea that family counseling might be required to deal with Charlotte's shoplifting and school failure. What is the evidence for this? What do you think Henry was afraid of?

8. How was the consultation team helpful in assisting JoEllen to keep this reluctant family in the therapy office? What approach did the team suggest? How well was JoEllen able to carry out the team's suggestion? Can you think of anything else she might have done?

9. What was the contract for counseling agreed on by JoEllen Madsen and Molly and Henry Peterson? Why do you think establishing a contract is important? Why do you think JoEllen determined this contract with the Peterson parents, not with the children?

10. Describe the concept of a presenting problem. What was the Peterson family's presenting problem?

11. Describe the concept of a precipitating event. What was the precipitating event that caused Molly to make an appointment at the Family Therapy Training Institute?

12. Why did JoEllen suspect there might have been a recent change in the Peterson family situation? What change was she later able to identify? Do you think it is reasonable that a change such as this could influence Charlotte's behavior? Why or why not?

13. George, the Peterson's older son, also once had a problem in school. JoEllen believed this fact supported her working hypothesis that the family as a whole was the appropriate client for therapy. Do you agree? Why or why not?

14. What do you think was the purpose of the message from the consultation team?

CHAPTER 9
The Systems Perspective

1. For what reasons are family therapists reluctant to assign diagnoses to individual family members who are experiencing problems? What practical considerations often force the assignment of diagnoses, however?

2. Define the term *identified client.* Who was the identified client the Peterson family brought to therapy? Who would have been the identified client several months before? Several years before?

3. Do family therapists believe that problem behaviors of an identified client always relate to troubles within the client's family as a

whole? Why or why not? In the case of a client whose troubled behaviors seem unrelated to family problems, why might the therapist still prefer to work with the family as a whole?

4. For what reasons are troubled families often reluctant to enter therapy? Why are even those families who enter therapy often reluctant to change?

5. Develop your own definition of *system,* using those offered in this book or those you may have encountered elsewhere.

6. What are several important characteristics of systems? Are these characteristics the same or different for subsystems and suprasystems?

7. Do systems theorists view cause and effect as a linear process? Why or why not? What do systems theorists mean when they talk of circular causation?

8. Can systems theory help with predictions for exactly how change will occur? Why or why not?

9. Describe the concept of boundary in systems theory. What kind of boundary does a system require to remain healthy? Why?

10. Compare and contrast "open" systems and "closed" systems. Can a completely closed system survive, according to systems theory? Why or why not? Can a totally open system survive? Why or why not?

11. What is the fundamental goal of every system, according to systems theory? Does this goal make sense to you, given your own understanding of how the world works?

12. Describe the concept of tension in systems theory. Is this similar to, or different from, the concept of tension in the Freudian theoretical approach?

13. Define *feedback.* What information does positive feedback convey? Negative feedback? Which type of feedback is most likely to lead to behavioral change? Why?

14. What is a feedback loop? In what ways may feedback loops be interrupted? What can occur if feedback loops are interrupted?

15. Describe the systems concept of the steady state. How is this concept somewhat different from that of homeostasis? Why is the concept of steady state extremely important in systems theory?

16. When a child misbehaves, what working hypothesis will a systems therapist want to check out? Do you think this working hypothesis will always be confirmed? Why or why not?

17. What information from the Peterson family tended to confirm for JoEllen Madsen her initial working hypothesis that Charlotte Peterson's troubled behavior could indicate trouble in the Peterson family as a whole?

18. In which major subsystem of the Peterson family did JoEllen suspect the family's main problem lay? What were her reasons? Do you agree with JoEllen's interpretation of the evidence so far? Why or why not?

CHAPTER 10
Marital Distress

1. When Molly Peterson told JoEllen that the family had had a good week and probably didn't need further therapy, JoEllen considered Molly's "resistance" to therapy normal. She began to explore Molly's reasons for resistance openly. How did the systems perspective guide JoEllen to take this approach?

2. How did the consultation team assist JoEllen to focus the early part of her interview? Why do you think Dr. Knaak called JoEllen exactly when he did?

3. What personal issues does Henry raise for JoEllen early in this session? How does the trainee respond? If you were in JoEllen's place, do you think you would have responded as she did? Why or why not?

4. Why does the NASW code of ethics guide social workers to avoid dual relationships with clients?

5. Why does the team instruct JoEllen to pay attention to the feelings she experiences as Henry talks with her?

6. When Molly cannot acknowledge that she is upset when Henry flirts, JoEllen turns to Charlotte. In family therapy, different family members are often encouraged to interpret what is happening for other members from their own point of view. How well does this tactic work for JoEllen in this session?

7. How did Molly's experiences with her father, as described in this session, affect her relationship with Henry?

8. Describe the role that Josh assumed in this session when he got up and nearly left the office. Why do you think Josh adopted these behaviors? Do you think he was aware of what he was doing? Why or why not?

9. How did JoEllen use posture to enhance her authority in this session? What other new skills and abilities from her training do you recognize in JoEllen's successful work in keeping the family together in the therapy office?

10. Why did the team call JoEllen behind the mirror for an early consultation?

11. Describe what was troubling the trainee, causing her to lose touch with the present and abdicate leadership of the therapy session.

12. How did the issue of "right and wrong" with respect to extramarital sexual affairs confuse and immobilize JoEllen? What alternative perspective was provided by systems theory that enabled the trainee to transcend her confusion?

13. Describe Murray Bowen's concept of triangulation. How might this concept apply to the Peterson case?

14. What do you think JoEllen meant when she told Molly Peterson that jealousy and insecurity could be viewed as "good friends"? Can you remember an episode in your own life in which jealousy and insecurity might be viewed as "friends"?

15. What do you think was the purpose of the consultation team's message for the week? Why do you suppose the team instructed the family not to try to make any changes, but only to observe and gather information?

CHAPTER 11

Consultation and an Analysis of Family Structure

1. JoEllen reports to her discussion group that the application of systems theory to her own life was a revelation to her. Describe that revelation in your own words.

2. How did the actions of the members of JoEllen's Monday noon discussion group help her take on the risk of personal therapy in a group setting?

3. How did experiences of criticism in JoEllen's early life apparently affect her response to constructive criticism in adulthood?

4. Describe how "reparenting" techniques can help correct emotional problems from the past.

5. Who comprised the spousal subsystem in the Peterson family? The parental subsystem? In what ways are spousal and parental subsystems the same? In what ways are they different? Do you think these subsystems are weak or strong in the Peterson family? Why?

6. Who comprised the sibling subsystem in the Peterson family? Do you think this subsystem is weak or strong? Why?

7. What is an "enmeshed" family? In what ways does the Peterson family show evidence of enmeshment?

8. Do you agree that Henry and Charlotte form an enmeshed subsystem in the Peterson family? Why or why not? Do you agree that Molly and Josh form an enmeshed subsystem? Why or why not?

CHAPTER 12

Family Therapy in Systems Perspective

1. When did family therapy begin to develop in the United States? Why does the author believe there are so many different schools of systems-based family therapy today?

2. Compare and contrast the concepts of intrapsychic vs. interpersonal behavioral causation. Which is emphasized by the followers of Dr. Sigmund Freud? By systems-based family therapists?

3. What was Dr. Donald Jackson's concept of "identified patient"?

4. How could Jackson's concept of "homeostasis" be used to help explain puzzling behaviors, such as bed-wetting in an older child?

5. How did Jackson use systems theory to predict that improvement of an "identified patient" in a troubled family might result in the commencement of undesirable behavior by another person in the same family?

6. The social work profession recognized the importance of work with families as wholes long before the dramatic rise of family therapy in the 1950s. What factors might help account for the overshadowing

of the earlier wholistic social work perspective by Freudian psychological theory?

7. Did Virginia Satir believe that individuals' thoughts and feelings were important in working with families as wholes? Did Satir think individuals' perceptions were more or less important than did Don Jackson?

8. What four rigid communication styles did Satir identify in troubled families? Which, if any, of these communication styles have been exhibited so far by the various members of the Peterson family?

9. Think about your own life. Can you remember an example of a "double bind" that you, another family member, or a close friend may have experienced? How were you or the other person affected? Was the situation resolved? If so, how?

10. What was Satir's perspective on the importance of self-esteem? For what reasons did she provide large quantities of nurturance in her therapeutic work? How might gender have affected Satir's perceptions and style?

11. Describe Murray Bowen's concept of triangulation. Is triangulation normal under certain circumstances, or always problematic? Do you remember a situation in your own life in which triangulation became a problem? If so, please describe.

12. Describe Bowen's concepts of differentiation of self and the multigenerational transmission process. How are these concepts related? How does differentiation of self differ from Bowen's concept of emotional cutoff?

13. Which family subsystems did Salvador Minuchin believe were of primary importance to maintaining healthy family functioning? What were the primary functions of these subsystems from his theoretical perspective? Why did Minuchin believe that strong, clear boundaries between subsystems were important? From what you know so far, are clear boundaries between subsystems present in the Peterson family?

14. Describe Minuchin's concepts of enmeshment and disengagement. Provide examples for each one either from the Peterson case or from your own life experience.

15. Define Minuchin's concept of joining. Why is it important for the therapeutic process?

16. Describe Minuchin's concept of unbalancing the system. Why might a family therapist want to unbalance a family system, or otherwise interfere with a family's steady state?

17. What is "circular questioning" and how did the Milan school of family therapy use this technique? Think of an example in which JoEllen Madsen used circular questioning in her work with the Petersons.

18. How did the Milan school use a one-way mirror and a consulting team of therapists? From what you can tell so far, did JoEllen's training program utilize the one-way mirror and consultation team in somewhat the same way?

19. What evidence, if any, of a constructivist approach to family therapy have you observed in JoEllen Madsen's training or therapeutic work so far?

20. How may sexism in the wider society have promoted some of the troubles in the Peterson family? Has JoEllen's work so far demonstrated a recognition of the insights of the feminist critique of systems-based therapy? If so, how? If not, why do you think this might be so?

21. Which of the therapeutic schools or approaches described in this chapter have you recognized in JoEllen's work so far? In your opinion, can a family therapist today do his or her work using the perspective of one school only? Why or why not?

CHAPTER 13

An Exercise in Reframing

1. What evidence of an enmeshed subsystem comprising Charlotte and Henry can you identify at the beginning of this chapter?

2. What examples of triangulation can you identify at the beginning of this chapter?

3. For what reasons did JoEllen ask Charlotte to change seats with her mother, Molly, early in this session?

4. Define the concept of reframing. How did JoEllen reframe Charlotte's protection of Henry's secret affair for Molly? Does this reframe make sense to you? To Molly?

5. Why do therapists sometimes teach their clients to use "I feel" statements, rather than statements that specifically point blame at someone else?

6. Why do you suppose the team coached JoEllen to stand during part of this session?

7. Notice that every end-of-session message to the family from the team begins with a compliment, even though a compliment may be difficult to come by. For what reasons do you suppose the team's messages begin in this way?

8. What is the good work that the consultation team encourages Charlotte and Josh to continue at the end of this session? Why do you suppose the team makes this particular suggestion?

CHAPTER 14

Reframing as a Therapeutic Tool

1. Who originated the term *reframing?* Describe this concept in your own words. What are some examples of reframing that have been described in JoEllen's work so far?

2. Why do family therapists sometimes reframe fighting behavior between members of a couple as a sign of intense commitment to one another?

3. In what way do LaClave and Brack consider reframing to be a "second order" change?

4. How can shifting a client's perception from "problem" to "process" in reframing sometimes help facilitate behavioral change?

5. Describe the concept of paradoxical intervention. Can the reframing process be a type of paradoxical intervention? If so, give an example of such a reframe. Is the reframing process always a type of paradoxical intervention? If not, give an example of a reframe that is not also a paradoxical intervention. Give an example of a paradoxical intervention that is not also a reframe.

6. With what types of families can paradoxical interventions be especially effective? For what reasons?

7. With what types of clients should paradoxical interventions *never* be attempted? Why?

8. What are some basic ethical concerns to consider in the use of paradoxical interventions? Why are these concerns important to all therapists?

9. Do you agree that most reframes—even those that are also paradoxical interventions—simply reveal a different part of the truth to clients, so that they are unquestionably ethical? Why or why not?

10. Why is it usually important for a therapist to understand clients fairly well, especially their unique perceptions of the world, or their worldview, before attempting reframing?

11. How do pacing and joining help therapists better use therapeutic techniques like reframing? Describe these techniques and give examples.

12. In the previous chapter, the consultation team reframed Charlotte and Josh's misbehavior as "good work" and encouraged the children to do more of it. Given the analysis of reframing presented in this chapter, in what ways do you think the team probably expected such a reframe to affect the Peterson family, and why? For example, how might such a reframe shift the family's perception of the children's misbehavior from "problem" to "process"? Specifically, how might such a perceptual change be likely to affect Molly and Henry? Charlotte and Josh?

CHAPTER 15
An Early Termination

1. Why do you suppose Henry brings a tape recorder to this session?

2. What do you think Henry means when he says "My wife's trying to control me again"?

3. What do you suppose made it difficult for the children, Charlotte and Josh, to discuss the results of their "homework" in front of their parents?

4. How does JoEllen Madsen make it possible for the children to discuss their homework in this session?

5. Describe the specific behaviors that Charlotte and Josh believed helped keep Molly and Henry from fighting with each other. From the children's perspective, how did their misbehavior help keep their parents from fighting with each other? How well did these strategies work?

6. As a result of consciously recognizing how their rescuing efforts worked and the personal cost, the children decided to change their behavior. Describe the thinking processes of each child in as much detail as possible. Do their decisions seem realistic to you?

7. Think back on your own life. Can you remember a situation in which you or a sibling may have misbehaved in order to induce your parents to communicate with each other? Or a situation in which your misbehavior *did* cause your parents to communicate with each other more constructively than usual, even though you had no conscious intention of creating such a result?

8. What do you suppose is the reason the team telephoned JoEllen just when they did, to have her ask Molly if a change in the children's behavior would be "enough" for her?

9. Why do you suppose the team called just when they did to urge the trainee to develop a new contract with Henry and Molly, this time for marital counseling?

10. Explain in your own words how triangulation may interfere with problem solving by a marital couple. What early family therapist coined the term *triangulation?*

11. If you were JoEllen, would you have wanted to proceed with marital counseling despite Henry's refusal to give up his affair? Why or why not?

12. Explain why Kurt Knaak wants to unbalance the steady state in the Peterson family. Do you agree or disagree? Why? What are the risks?

13. If you were Molly Peterson, would you want the team to proceed with marital counseling despite Henry's refusal to give up his affair? Why or why not? How do you think she felt when the team refused?

14. Why do you suppose Molly and Henry both refused individual counseling when that option was offered without condition?

15. What do you think of the part of the team's message for the week that states that Molly and Henry demonstrate the passion and desire "necessary, but not sufficient, to make a good marriage"?

CHAPTER 16

A Conference among Institute Supervisors

1. What were the educational backgrounds of the five supervisors at the Family Therapy Training Institute? What were their credentials with respect to the American Association for Marriage and Family Therapy?

2. Why did the supervisors "staff" students at the institute on a regular basis?

3. How did the concept of confidentiality pertain to the staffing of students at the institute? Why do you think confidentiality is important for trainees and clients alike?

4. What did Don Miller mean when he said that JoEllen was "overidentifying" with her clients? What does it mean to overidentify with another person?

5. What did Maria Sanchez mean when she said she thought JoEllen was "projecting" her own feelings onto her clients? What does it mean to project one's feelings?

6. What issues of transference and countertransference does Sara Weiner identify? Does it seem reasonable to you that JoEllen was experiencing countertransference? Why or why not?

7. Describe the issues of sexism examined in this conference of supervisors. How do these issues relate to the feminist critique of systems-based family therapy introduced in Chapter 12?

8. What factors besides sexism and societal norms may keep people in troubled marriages? Discuss considerations that are mentioned in this chapter and identify any others of which you may be aware.

9. What reasons do Sara Weiner and Madeleine Sweet provide to explain why they have worked with couples involved in an active

affair? What do you think of their reasons? Why do you suppose that Kurt Knaak insists on taking a "purist" position with his trainees?

10. Madeleine Sweet is described as "overprotective" of her trainees in this session. Do you agree? Why or why not?

CHAPTER 17

Consultation and Ethical Considerations

1. Why do you think JoEllen was reluctant to discuss her previous session with the Petersons in her discussion group? How do you think the trainee was feeling? What do you think she was afraid of?

2. How did JoEllen use systems theory to support her desire to provide marriage counseling even in the circumstance of an active affair? What do you think of her argument?

3. Describe what you think happened within JoEllen when Madeleine Sweet criticized her approach to persuading Henry to give up his affair. Why do you think she reacted the way she did? How did Madeleine deal with JoEllen's behavior?

4. Describe the ethical considerations involved in precipitating a crisis for a troubled family. What do you think of JoEllen's concern? Of Bob's response?

5. According to perspectives provided in this chapter, how might a good counselor do a disservice for a client by helping to stabilize a troubled marriage? What do you think of this argument? Why?

6. List several reasons why marital counseling is more likely to succeed when neither spouse is actively engaged in an extramarital relationship. Are these reasons convincing to you? Why or why not?

CHAPTER 18

A Family Crisis

1. At the beginning of this chapter, what strategy do the Peterson children demonstrate that allows them to avoid triangulation between their parents in times of conflict?

2. Why do you think Molly Peterson wrote her rival Marlene a personal note? Why do you think she wrote the note just when she

did? Can you imagine why Molly did not just pick up the telephone and call Marlene?

3. What do you suppose led Molly to ask her daughter, Charlotte, to read the letter that she wrote to Marlene? In what position did her request place Charlotte? How did Charlotte respond to her mother's request?

4. Describe the role Josh took after Molly asked him to read her letter to Marlene. How do you think Virginia Satir would categorize the boy's behavior?

5. How useful was the meeting between Molly and Marlene? Can you imagine enduring such a meeting yourself? How do you think you would have behaved in this meeting if you were Molly? If you were Marlene? If you had to choose to be in either woman's position, which would you choose? Why?

6. What do you think about Molly's decision to leave her marriage after the meeting with Marlene? Do you agree with this decision? Why or why not?

7. Why do you suppose Molly decided to leave the family home, taking the children with her, rather than ask her husband to find a new place for himself? Do you think she made the right decision? Why or why not?

CHAPTER 19
Further Complications

1. What were Molly's initial hopes upon leaving her husband? Do you know of another circumstance in which one spouse has left a marriage, apparently in a last-ditch effort to save it? If so, what were the results?

2. While conditions for doing homework were anything but desirable in the little apartment, Charlotte and Josh did excellent schoolwork while living alone with their mother. What do you think might account for this fact?

3. Put yourself in Charlotte's position. How do you imagine the young girl felt when it began to look as if her mother might divorce her father and marry Herbert? Why do you think Charlotte called Henry

to tell him about the possibility? Do you think the girl was being disloyal to Molly? Why or why not?

4. What do you think made Henry telephone Molly and tell her to come home, after he learned about her relationship with Herbert? After all, Henry had an ongoing relationship of his own, with Marlene. Describe what you think Henry's conscious reasons were for calling Molly, and then explore other reasons you think may have been important and of which Henry was probably less aware.

5. What do you think Henry means when he tells Molly that she is his "primary relationship"? Why do you suppose this assertion has worked in the past to keep this marriage intact? Why do you suppose it no longer works so well?

6. Henry and Molly have different views on the appropriateness of extramarital affairs, and also on the relationship of affection to affairs. How might sex-role socialization and sexism in the wider society influence their differing views?

7. Why do you suppose Molly called for an appointment at the Family Therapy Training Institute when she did?

CHAPTER 20

Molly Returns for Counseling

1. Why do you suppose JoEllen made a practice of calling ahead to learn about her appointment schedule in advance?

2. How does JoEllen help focus this session when Molly introduces several topics in the very beginning?

3. Using a systems perspective, explain why the consultation team believed that Charlotte's actions, which seemed to Molly to be a "betrayal," were intended instead to save Molly and Henry's marriage. In what way was this purpose different from "betrayal," although Molly might not understand the difference without counseling?

4. JoEllen acted on a "hunch" and asked Molly about her childhood. What were some of the clues that triggered her hunch? Were JoEllen's questions about Molly's childhood ones that might likely have been asked by systems theorist Don Jackson, as described in Chapter 12? By Salvador Minuchin? By Virginia Satir? Why or why not?

5. How did JoEllen use empathy to help Molly get beyond anger at her daughter?

6. Describe the "messages" about marriage and the woman's role in marriage that Molly learned as a child. Specifically, how were these messages transmitted to Molly? What do you personally think about the content of these messages?

7. Describe how Molly's childhood experiences with her abusive father may have enabled her to stay in a marriage full of pain.

8. How is it that Molly may have blamed herself for the failure of her marriage? Do you think she was to blame? Why or why not? How might self-blame have influenced Molly's actions and choice of lifestyle once she left her marriage?

9. JoEllen labored mightily to assist Molly to see the parallels between herself and her mother. Why do you think Molly was unable to make the connection for so long?

10. The team warned JoEllen that she was working harder on her client's behalf than the client. What do you think might be problematic about a therapist working harder than the client?

11. Why do you suppose Molly was finally able to take a new point of view regarding her responsibility toward taking care of Henry's needs, as opposed to her own and her children's needs?

12. For what reasons do you think the consultation team urged Molly in the end-of-session message to "go slow"?

CHAPTER 21
Henry Receives a Summons

1. Why do you suppose Molly sent her divorce summons via a mutual friend and not the county sheriff?

2. For what reasons do you think Henry was surprised to receive the summons, given that his wife had already left him?

3. Why do you think Henry did not want a divorce?

4. Why do you think Molly asked for custody of the children, occupancy of the family home, and child support, when shortly before she had said she wouldn't do any of those things?

5. What influenced Henry to make an appointment for individual counseling? How successful was this counseling and why?

6. For what professional reason did JoEllen refuse to discuss Molly and Herbert's relationship with Henry? How easy or difficult do you suppose it was for her to refuse? Do you think the trainee did the right thing? Why or why not?

7. Upon whom does final responsibility (and credit) for saving a marriage rest, the therapist or the couple engaging in therapy? Why?

8. How would you feel in this situation if you were Marlene? If you were Herbert? What practical considerations should everyone remember when entering into a relationship with a newly separated or divorced person?

CHAPTER 22
Resuming Family Therapy

1. Why do you suppose JoEllen was grateful for the presence of the consultation team behind the mirror when she resumed therapy with Molly and Henry Peterson as a couple? How was her attitude toward working in front of the team different from what it was at the beginning of training at the institute?

2. If you were Molly, do you think you would have agreed to attempt marriage counseling with Henry after such a long separation? Why or why not?

3. For what reason do you think JoEllen asked each member of the couple to state their personal goals at the very beginning of the therapy session?

4. What pioneer in family therapy identified roles like placating, blaming, and super-reasonable, which Kurt Knaak used in analyzing the enactment between Henry and Molly in this session?

5. The consultation team suggested that JoEllen ask Henry which was more important to him, to be "right" or to "have a fulfilling relationship." If you personally were asked such a question, how would you answer it? Why? How did Henry avoid the serious thinking this question is designed to provoke?

6. Explain in your own words how Henry's recollection of being locked out by his mother as a child has affected his relationship with Molly and with other women.

7. Describe how Henry uses logic to protect his own feelings, yet denies the importance feelings in general, especially Molly's. Describe how Molly defers to Henry in order to meet his emotional needs, yet believes her own feelings may not be important. How do you explain these paradoxes? What messages from the wider society may support them?

8. How important do you view feelings in your own life? Logic? Do you make efforts to balance their influence and, if so, how?

9. Take a look at the consultation team's message for the week. If Molly and Henry do their homework, what do you think they will discover about themselves?

CHAPTER 23

Intergenerational Family Therapy

1. Why do you suppose JoEllen was worried that the grandmother would not attend this session?

2. What information did the seating arrangement selected by Henry, Molly, and Elsbeth Peterson begin to convey to JoEllen?

3. Describe the fears that may have prevented JoEllen from discussing, as early as possible in the session, the night Henry felt "left in the cold." Do you think her fears were realistic? Why or why not?

4. How did Elsbeth help take care of the trainee's fears?

5. Describe the event in which Henry felt betrayed by his mother. In your opinion, was Henry actually betrayed? Why or why not? What else might Henry's mother, Elsbeth, have done to try to meet Henry's needs as well as her own? How do you imagine this event was experienced by Henry's father, Douglas? What might Douglas have done to help meet Henry's needs as well as his own?

6. Describe the Oedipus complex. If you are a male, can you remember consciously experiencing anything like this in your own life? If you are a female, can you remember ever wanting to "do away with"

your mother and marry your father (a comparable psychological tendency known as the Electra complex)?

7. What do you think JoEllen meant specifically when she said "I think we've gotten somewhere"? Why do you think the team decided to end the session at this point?

8. What do you think was the intent of the team's end-of-session message for the week?

CHAPTER 24

Intergenerational Marital Therapy

1. Why do you suppose Sally asked Molly if she could attend a counseling session with the older couple? Why do you think she didn't just make an appointment on her own?

2. Sally had been warned by George that he might want to pursue extramarital affairs, as his father had. Why do you suppose she chose not to believe him?

3. How does George redefine the concept of faithfulness in marriage? Do you think he believes what he says? Why or why not?

4. Molly tells Henry that he may have had a good marriage but that she herself has not. Do you believe it is possible that the same marriage can be experienced as good by one spouse and bad by the other? Why or why not?

5. Describe the intergenerational marital issues the Peterson family experienced.

6. As Henry complains that Molly is too insecure, the team instructs JoEllen to ask Molly how she has managed to be strong enough to stay with Henry for so many years. How is this an example of reframing? Can you find other examples of reframing in this chapter?

7. Why do you think JoEllen pointed out to Molly that Henry had probably helped her hone her survival skills? Do you agree that this may have been a reason she stayed in her marriage? Why or why not?

8. Do you agree with JoEllen that George may still be trying to gain Henry's approval as an adult? Why or why not?

9. What do you suppose led JoEllen to ask Henry how Sally should compete with Nancy?

10. How has Henry apparently reconciled his own affairs with the fact that he believed his father was wrong for having one? What do you think of Henry's rationale? Does it have the affect on his marriage that he wants?

11. Does JoEllen seem more or less persuasive in trying to sell George on the requirement of putting aside his affair for counseling than she was with his father before him? Why do you suppose this request fails as well?

12. What do you suppose leads Sally to make George choose between her and Nancy right in the therapy office?

13. What do you think is the intent of the team's message for the week?

CHAPTER 25

More Consultation for JoEllen

1. What parallels with Sally Peterson was JoEllen experiencing in her own personal life? How might these similarities affect her work as a therapist? How common do you think it is that a therapist must deal with personal issues similar to those of clients?

2. Why did Gretchen view Henry's behavior as "sexist"?

3. Describe the feminist's criticism of early systems-based family therapy, especially the structural school. What do you think of this critique?

4. What societal conditions do you believe support marriage? What societal conditions may undermine it? Do you think the experience of men and women in marriage is similar? Why or why not? Which gender do you believe benefits most from marriage? Why?

5. From your own point of view in life so far, what are some important positive aspects of marriage? Some important negatives? How might a therapist's personal perception of the value of marriage affect his or her work as a marriage counselor?

6. What is your perception of male dominance or "entitlement"? Have you observed anything like this in your own life? Do you think

male dominance can lead to misuse of power, to the disadvantage of females?

7. What do you think about JoEllen Madsen's decision to ask her boyfriend to go into counseling with her?

CHAPTER 26

Molly and Henry Come to Terms with the Past

1. What "body language" signalled JoEllen that things had changed between Molly and Henry? How did she check this out?

2. Why do you suppose JoEllen kept repeating her questions to Henry as to exactly what he meant by giving up his affairs and exactly what had changed for him?

3. In your own words, explain what made Henry change his mind and decide to give up his extramarital affairs.

4. How did JoEllen compare Henry's emotional needs for affairs with Molly's? Did Henry understand why JoEllen made such a connection? How do you know?

5. Had the session degenerated again into a "fray in which Molly would be blamed and Henry rejected," who do you think would have blamed Molly and for what? Why? Who would have rejected Henry and for what? Why?

6. How easy do you think it will be for Henry to give up Marlene in order to make his marriage work? How easy do you think it will be for Molly to give up Herbert?

7. Why do you think the team instructed JoEllen to have Henry and Molly review the strengths of their respective families of origin?

8. What was the purpose of the teams introduction of Boszormenyi-Nagy's "family ledger"? Do you think JoEllen's application of this concept was fair to both Molly and Henry? Why or why not?

9. What do you think about JoEllen's suggestion to Henry that he give Molly a hug at the end of the session?

10. What do you think is the purpose of the team's message for the week?

CHAPTER 27
Terminating Therapy

1. Do you agree with JoEllen that, if Henry talks with George, he should let the young man know he will love him regardless of what he decides? Why or why not? In what important ways is the relationship between father and son different from that of therapist and client?

2. What risks do third parties incur in extramarital relationships, even when conducted with partners separated from their spouses?

3. Why did Henry and Molly decide it was time to terminate counseling? Why did JoEllen agree?

4. For what reasons do you think JoEllen continued the session after the decision to terminate counseling? Why do you think she chose to review the team's homework for the week?

5. What decision-making processes did Molly and Henry identify that worked for them in the past?

6. Why do you suppose JoEllen interrupted Henry when he called his wife "insecure"? What does the trainee mean when she tells Henry he has given Molly every reason to feel insecure in the past? Be specific.

7. Why do you suppose JoEllen fought the urge to jump in and "rescue" when Henry and Molly seemed unable to resolve their relationship problems on their own? Why didn't the therapist just propose various solutions herself?

8. Do you agree that a tale like the "ski slope" could actually influence Henry toward having multiple affairs? Why or why not?

9. How do you think having a new "story" in their lives might help Molly and Henry rebuild their marital relationship? What therapeutic school frequently uses stories to assist in the therapy process?

CHAPTER 28
JoEllen's Challenge

1. How likely do you think it is that Henry and Molly Peterson will return for marital therapy in the future? Why?

2. How well do you think the Peterson children will adjust to living with their father again? How likely do you think it is that the Peterson family as a whole will return for therapy? Why?

3. How likely do you think it is that George and Sally Peterson will request marital therapy? Why?

4. Why do you suppose JoEllen's boyfriend is willing to see a counselor, but only someone that neither person knows?

5. How likely do you think it is that JoEllen's relationship with her significant other will succeed? Why?

6. Do you personally think a marital relationship provides the best life situation for every mature adult? Why or why not?

❀

Notes

1. American Psychiatric Association. *Diagnostic and Statistical Manual of Mental Disorders* (4th ed.). Washington, DC: American Psychiatric Association, 1994, pp. 623–627.

2. Davidson, M. *Uncommon Sense: The Life and Thought of Ludwig von Bertalanffy.* Los Angeles: J.P. Archer. quoted in Michael Nichols and Richard Schwartz, *Family Therapy* (3rd ed.). Boston: Allyn & Bacon, 1995, p. 88.

3. *Webster's New World Dictionary,* Second College Edition. David B. Guralnik, Editor in Chief. New York: Simon & Schuster, 1984, p. 1445.

4. *Webster's,* p. 468.

5. Gitterman, Alex, and Germain, Carel B. Social Work Practice, A Life Model. In Beulah Compton and Burt Galaway, *Social Work Processes* (4th ed.). Belmont, CA: Wadsworth, 1989, p. 117.

6. Wheatley, Margaret J. *Leadership and the New Science, Learning about Organization from an Orderly Universe.* San Francisco: Berrett-Koehler Publishers, 1992, p. 126.

7. Wheatley, *Leadership and the New Science,* p. 126.

8. Compton, Beulah, and Galaway, Burt. *Social Work Processes* (5th ed.). Pacific Grove, CA: Brooks/Cole, 1994, pp. 121–124.

9. Satir, Virginia. *Conjoint Family Therapy* (rev. ed.). Palo Alto, CA: Science and Behavior Books, 1967.

10. *Webster's,* p. 513.

11. Compton and Galaway, *Social Work Processes,* p. 122.

12. Compton and Galaway, *Social Work Processes,* pp. 123–124.

13. Aylmer, Robert C. Bowen Family Systems Marital Therapy. In Neil S. Jacobson and Alan S. Gurman (Eds.), *Clinical Handbook of Marital Therapy.* New York: Guilford Press, 1986, pp. 107–146.

14. Nichols, Michael P., and Schwartz, Richard C. *Family Therapy, Concepts and Methods* (3rd ed.). Boston: Allyn & Bacon, 1995, p. 88.

15. Nichols and Schwartz, *Family Therapy* (3rd ed.), pp. 20–22.

16. Nichols and Schwartz, *Family Therapy* (3rd ed.), p. 38.

17. Horne, Arthur M., and Passmore, J. Laurence. *Family Counseling and Therapy* (2nd ed.). Itasca, IL: F. E. Peacock, 1991, pp. 15–17.

18. Horne and Passmore, p. 25.

19. Satir, Virginia. *Peoplemaking.* Palo Alto, CA: Science and Behavior Books, 1972, p. 116.

20. Bandler, Richard, and Grinder, John. *Frogs into Princes, Neuro Linguistic Programming.* Moah, UT: Real People Press, 1970.

21. Nichols and Schwartz, pp. 371–376.

22. Horne and Passmore, pp. 78–79.

23. Minuchin, Salvador, and Fishman, H. Charles. *Family Therapy Techniques.* Cambridge, MA: Harvard University Press, 1981, p. 247.

24. Wells, Carolyn, and Zastrow, Charles. Social Work with Families. In Charles Zastrow, *The Practice of Social Work* (5th ed.). Pacific Grove, CA: Brooks/Cole, 1995, pp. 240–241.

25. Minuchin and Fishman, p. 67.

26. Horne and Passmore, pp. 90–97.

27. Nichols and Schwartz, pp. 122–123.

28. Nichols and Schwartz, p. 128.

29. White, Michael, and Epstein, David. *Narrative Means to Therapeutic Ends.* New York: Norton, 1990, pp. 42–48.

30. Nichols and Schwartz, p. 134.

31. Coyne, James C. Toward a Theory of Frames and Reframing: The Social Nature of Frames. *Journal of Marital and Family Therapy,* 2(4), 1985, p. 338.

32. Watzlawick, P., Weakland, J., and Fisch, R. *Change: Principles of Problem Resolution.* New York: Norton, 1974, p. 95.

33. Jones, Wayne C. Frame Cultivation: Helping New Meanings Take Root in Families. *The American Journal of Family Therapy,* 14(1), 1986, p. 57.

34. Kersey, Barbara, and Protinsky, Bud. Reframing and Embedded Directives: A Complementary Intervention Strategy. *Journal of Strategic and Systemic Therapies,* 3(2), 1984, p. 18.

35. Jones, Wayne C. Frame Cultivation: Helping New Meanings Take Root in Families. *The American Journal of Family Therapy,* 14(1), 1986.

36. LaClave, Linda J., and Brack, Gregory. Reframing to Deal with Patient Resistance: Practical Application. *American Journal of Psychotherapy, 43*(1), January, 1989, p. 69.

37. Hare-Mustin, Rachel. Treatment of Temper Tantrums by a Paradoxical Intervention. Presented as part of a paper at the meetings of the Division of Psychotherapy, American Psychological Association, Marco Island, FL, February, 1975.

38. Coyne, James C., p. 339.

39. Gale, Jerry E., and Brown-Standridge, Marsha D. Ratification and Utilization: Hypnotic Techniques to Facilitate Reframing During Early Marital Therapy. *Journal of Marital and Family Therapy, 14*(4), 1988, p. 371.

40. Jones, p. 60.

41. Kersey and Protinsky, p. 17.

42. Gale, Jerry E., and Brown-Standridge, Marsha D. Ratification and Utilization: Hypnotic Techniques to Facilitate Reframing During Early Marital Therapy. *Journal of Marital and Family Therapy, 14*(4), 1988, p. 373.

43. Boszormenyi-Nagy, I., and Spark, G. *Invisible Loyalties.* New York: Harper, 1973.

TO THE OWNER OF THIS BOOK:

We hope that you have found *Stepping to the Dance: The Training of a Family Therapist* useful. So that this book can be improved in a future edition, would you take the time to complete this sheet and return it? I'd really like to hear from you. Thank you.

School and address: ______________________________

Department: ______________________________

Instructor's name: ______________________________

1. What I like most about this book is: ______________________________

____

____

2. What I like least about this book is: ______________________________

____

____

3. My general reaction to this book is: ______________________________

____

4. The name of the course in which I used this book is: ______________________________

____

5. Were all of the chapters of the book assigned for you to read? ______________

If not, which ones weren't? ______________________________

6. In the space below, or on a separate sheet of paper, please write specific suggestions for improving this book and anything else you'd care to share about your experience in using the book.

____

____

____

____

____

Optional:

Your name: ______________________ Date: ______________________

May Brooks/Cole quote you, either in promotion for *Stepping to the Dance: The Training of a Family Therapist* or in future publishing ventures?

Yes: _________ No: _________

Sincerely,

Carolyn Cressy Wells

FOLD HERE

NO POSTAGE NECESSARY IF MAILED IN THE UNITED STATES

BUSINESS REPLY MAIL

FIRST CLASS PERMIT NO. 358 PACIFIC GROVE, CA

POSTAGE WILL BE PAID BY ADDRESSEE

ATT: *Carolyn Cressy Wells*

Brooks/Cole Publishing Company
511 Forest Lodge Road
Pacific Grove, California 93950-9968

FOLD HERE